Anthony Thwaite

Collected Poems

ENITHARMON PRESS

First published in 2007
by Enitharmon Press
26B Caversham Road
London NW5 2DU

www.enitharmon.co.uk

Distributed in the UK by
Central Books
99 Wallis Road
London E9 5LN

Distributed in the USA and Canada
by Dufour Editions Inc.
PO Box 7, Chester Springs
PA 19425, USA

ISBN: 978-1-904634-39-3 (hardback)
ISBN: 978-1-904634-56-0 (de luxe slipcased
edition of signed and numbered copies, each one
containing a handwritten poem from the collection)

Enitharmon Press gratefully acknowledges the financial support of
Arts Council England, London.

Some of the new poems (Poems 365–379) have appeared in the
following journals: *Antiquity*, *London Magazine*, *Poetry Review*,
Spectator, and the *Times Literary Supplement*.

British Library Cataloguing-in-Publication Data.
A catalogue record for this book is available
from the British Library.

Typeset in Caslon by Servis Filmsetting Ltd
and printed in England by
Cromwell Press

for Ann

Contents

from THE STONES OF EMPTINESS (1967)

from INSCRIPTIONS (1973)

NEW CONFESSIONS (1974)

from **POEMS 1953–1983** (1984)

from SELECTED POEMS 1956–1996 (1997)

from A MOVE IN THE WEATHER (2003)

NEW POEMS

from *Home Truths* (1957)

1 *Oedipus*

If she who first embodied me
From swollen foetus crouched beneath
Hot sallow blood and milk, if she
Speaks through your eyes, tastes of your breath,
Then hide me where I cannot see.

For when you spoke, it was her face
Which looked through mists of flesh and age
And saw a child. In your embrace
I trudged a lifetime's pilgrimage
From prince's birth to king's disgrace.

I snuggle in your belly: you
Who banish all love's doubts but this
Can never see what sickness grew
Under the sweet drug of your kiss,
Who buckled on a cripple's shoe.

Held fast against your breast, I find
A shapeless memory takes shape
Upon the pillow. Heart and mind
Blunt both my eyes in blind escape
And when I waken, I am blind.

2 *The Silent Woman*

Take whatever just reward
Is yours to take and yours to keep,
Drag your bench to the full board;
Eat; drink; and after, sleep.
My house is yours, bread, milk and bed.
You have what flesh has coveted.

21

Do not ask me why I give
Shelter to no one else but you.
Hooded in silence, let us live
Without a thought of lodgers who
Shared the cup where now your lip
Sours the drink at which you sip.

And do not ask me what I see
When, waking from a frowning dream,
Your heavy eyes uncover me
Knotting the sheets until they seem
Horned like a dragon, in whose lair
You've woken, drowsy with despair.

For if you asked, what answer could
Square truth with fable, love with lies?
History like this can do no good
To you, who have no memories,
No raven heart which hoards away
Sour milk, soiled sheets, of yesterday.

3   *Death of a Rat*

Nothing the critic said of tragedy,
Groomed for the stage and mastered into art,
Was relevant to this; yet I could see
Pity and terror mixed in equal part.
Dramatically, a farce right from the start,
Armed with a stick, a hairbrush and a broom,
Two frightened maladroits shut in one room.

Convenient symbol for a modern hell,
The long lean devil and the short squat man
No doubt in this were psychological,
Parable for the times, Hyperion
And Satyr, opposites in union . . .
Or Lawrence's *Snake*, to turn the picture round –
Man's pettiness by petty instinct bound.

But, to be honest, it was neither, and
That ninety minutes skirring in a duel
Was nothing if not honest. The demand
Moved him towards death, and me to play the fool,
Yet each in earnest. I went back to school
To con the hero's part, who, clung with sweat,
Learned where the hero, fool and coward met.

Curtain to bed and bed to corner, he
Nosed at each barrier, chattered, crouched, and then
Eluded me, till art and fear and pity
Offered him to me at the moment when
I broke his back, and smashed again, again,
Primitive, yes, exultant, yes, and knowing
His eyes were bright with some instinctive thing.

If every violent death is tragedy
And the wild animal is tragic most
When man adopts death's ingenuity,
Then this was tragic. But what each had lost
Was less and more than this, which was the ghost
Of some primeval joke, now in bad taste,
Which saw no less than war, no more than waste.

4 *Not So Simple*

Haiku, says the translator, is yes and no at once,
Something and nothing, this and this-not made one.
Well, '*we* are the barbarians' perhaps,
Minds trained on nothing but mind's insolence,
Vulgarians who expect
Poems – if not flowers – to be circumspect.

The single flower is more perfect than
The herbaceous border. Yet here a word can sprout
Opposites in itself, be rank and lush
As the careless garden of a careless man.
Three lines can simply mean
Something is being (will be) in the mind (or scene).

But that is not the heart of it by half:
Language is difficult, flowers can be seen
Simply. The heart of it is everywhere
Where things are, under the nervous masking laugh,
Not permanent at all.
An earthquake, or your elbow, cracks the wall.

Too many people wanting to eat too much,
The gentle gesture is more hustled now:
Children and gardens coddled, held too tight,
Cramp your great clumsiness, brittle at a touch.
One word is 'food'; it means
Simply whether your belly has rice and beans.

Houses are also less like poems and flowers,
Though easy to destroy; one spark can be
Quite unequivocal with a city of them.
To make an Act of God uniquely yours
Live in a paper house,
Set match to paper, make an emptiness.

Haiku, says the translator, is yes and no at once,
Something and nothing, this and this-not made one.
'Bogus,' I quickly say, 'Nothing so simple,'
Envying that bogus elegance, though neither
Haiku nor I explain
The simple brutes – fire: hunger: earthquake: pain.

5   *The Poet at Lake Nojiri*

He escaped the ninety million
To find a lonelier place
And each day found him sitting
Admiring nature's face
In the lake where, fifty feet below,
Great carp he never saw
Could watch the casual suicide
Clutching at a straw.

At first reflecting water
Straightened the city's stance.
The headlines' daily tragedies
Drowned in that bland expanse:
A boat moored in a sandy bay
And a hill on either hand
Were kinder to his blunted eyes,
Easier to understand.

And yet the gentle pastoral
Was soured at last, for he
Found in each grain of nature
Pathetic fallacy:
The yammering cicadas,
The moths smashed on the pane
Became his symbols. And the lake
Choked with atomic rain.

These second-hand impressions,
Each image half-aware
Of some illustrious ancestor
Who looked on nature bare,
Made him no happier; but then
(He thought) 'Nothing can pass
Between the sight and seer without
Distortion in the glass.

The narrow islands fester,
Steeped in their own dung,
Yet words in this backwater are
Too easy on the tongue.
The lake's isolation
Leads me too much astray,
Smothers the suicide's gesture with
What I don't want to say.'

Back to the ninety million
He soberly returned;
Resumed vicarious misery;
Sat restlessly; then burned
Some manuscripts; and pondered
On grief and happiness
And the smooth, lonely abstractions
He could not now express.

6   *Aesthetic Point*

Flower, yellow against green:
A jot of mist between
It and the autumn tree.
Well, this is what you see
In fact, a painted screen
Somebody's artistry.

But it is *real*, you say,
No one made it that way.
Not paint but its own pigment,
Not silk but fabric sent
Through natural roots: display
No artist ever meant.

You say these people hold
The secret, lost of old,
Which life and art should share.
These patterns do not stare
Me in the face, too bold
For here or anywhere

Still, there is always this
Side to such mysteries –
Small boys, all about six,
Beating with stones and sticks
A butterfly which is
Beyond these aesthetics.

Being not quite dead, it stirs
Feebly. The eye prefers
Death patterned on a screen.
Its yellow and its green
Lie smashed. The artist blurs
The too deliberate scene.

So this is life and that
Is art, the duplicate
Which stares life in the face,
And this uncanny race,
So cruel, so delicate,
Shows each its separate place.

7 *To My Unborn Child*

Nothing is known but that you are
And move under her hand and mine,
Feeding and sleeping, clandestine
Agent and close conspirator.
You mould your own unique design
And grow frail roots nine months in her.

Collision of erratic spores
Moved eyes to bud, fingers to swell
Out of the light, and now he walks
On water, and is miracle.

What you will be the uncertain world
Waits for and watches, nor can make
Provision for each loose mistake
You drop when, far beyond the fold,
The days you pass, the routes you take
Teach you to be shy or bold.

The tent of flesh, the hut of bone
Shelter him on pilgrimage
And blood and water build for him
A flooded road, a shifting bridge.

Not yet real, we make for you
A toy that is reality.
The secret country where you lie
Is far from it, but no less true,
And both are dangerous to the eye
That fears what flesh and fate may do.

Tent, hut and bridge are weak as he
And yet unnumbered travellers
Have spent dark nights encamped in such
Retreats, and trod such paths as hers.

You who will soon step down through blood
To where earth, sky and air combine
To make you neither hers nor mine,
Think: you now stand where many stood
Who, each in his own unique design,
Was weak and strong and bad and good.

And yet these murmurs cannot break
The doors which you alone unbar,
And we who know all this must know
Nothing is known but that you are.

8 *Child Crying*

My daughter cries, and I
Lift her from where she lies,
Carry her here and there,
Talk nonsense endlessly.
And still she cries and cries
In rage, mindlessly.

A trivial anguish, found
In every baby-book.
But, at a fortnight old,
A pink and frantic mound
Of appetites, each look
Scans unfamiliar ground.

A name without a face
Becomes a creature, takes
A creature's energies.
Raging in my embrace,
She takes the world and shakes
Each firm appointed place.

No language blocks her way,
Oblique, loaded with tact.
Hunger and pain are real,
And in her blindness they
Are all she sees: the fact
Is what you cannot say.

Our difference is that
We gauge what each cry says,
Supply what need demands.
Or try to. All falls flat
If cure is wrong or guess
Leaves her still obdurate.

So through uncertainties
I carry her here and there,
And feel her human heart,
Her human miseries,
And in her language share
Her blind and trivial cries.

from *The Owl in the Tree* (1963)

9 Things

Some lie in a specimen-case
In a jumble of randomness,
Things I have picked up
From the ground or a junk-shop tray:
A terracotta lamp,
An ammonite, a toad
Carved from an old root,
Worked flints, a handful of sherds,
A bamboo whistle, stones
Rubbed and shaped by the sea,
And a snuff-box with a loose lid.
Others pile high on shelves
Or get stacked up on the floor:
Magazines, albums, jugs.
Walled up, I sit among things.

Elsewhere, in the attic or drawers,
Are letters, programmes, notes
On backs of envelopes, guides
To castles, postcards, stamps.
One of these days, we say,
We'll sort the whole lot out,
Tie things in bundles, throw
Most of the clobber away.
But we never shall, of course.
My pockets bulge with stuff
After walking through a ploughed field.
Things stick to me like burrs,
Or muck to a caddis worm.
Freud has explained it all
But not, somehow, to me.

Hoarding a load of crap
May be hoarding a load of crap
To the analyst; but I think
What I really want is things
To tell me what I have been.
I cosset my memory
Like some people their cat.
And that, I suppose, is a way
Of saying that I'm ashamed
To go on collecting stuff.
True: somewhere in my mind
Is an ideal picture of life
In a bare unfurnished room
With a notebook and pen. But then
What would I have to say?

10   *The Boys*

Six of them climbed aboard,
None of them twenty yet,
At a station up the line:
Flannel shirts rimmed with sweat,
Boots bulled to outrageous shine,
Box-pleats stiff as a board.

Pinkly, smelling of Bass,
They lounged on the blue moquette
And rubbed their blanco off.
One told of where to get
The best crumpet. A cough
From the corner. One wrote on the glass

A word in common use.
The others stirred and jeered.
Reveille was idled through
Till the next station appeared,
And the six of them all threw
Their Weights on the floor. Excuse

For a laugh on the platform. Then
We rattled and moved away,
The boys only just through the door.
It was near the end of the day.
Two slept. One farted and swore,
And went on about his women.

Three hours we had watched this lot,
All of us family men,
Responsible, set in our ways.
I looked at my paper again:
Another H-test. There are days
You wonder whether you're not

Out of touch, old hat, gone stale.
I remembered my twenty-first
In the NAAFI, laid out cold.
Then one of them blew and burst
A bag; and one of the old
Told them to stow it. The pale

Lights of the city came near.
We drew in and stopped. The six
Bundled their kit and ran.
'A good belting would sort out their tricks,'
Said my neighbour, a well-spoken man.
'Yes, but . . .' But he didn't hear.

11   *Mr Cooper*

Two nights in Manchester: nothing much to do,
One of them I spent partly in a pub,
Alone, quiet, listening to people who
Didn't know me. *So I told the bloody sub-*
Manager what he could do with it. . . . Mr Payne
Covers this district – you'll have met before?
Caught short, I looked for the necessary door
And moved towards it; could hear, outside, the rain.

The usual place, with every surface smooth
To stop, I suppose, the aspirations of
The man with pencil stub and dreams of YOUTH
AGED 17. And then I saw, above
The stall, a card, a local jeweller's card
Engraved with name, JEWELLER AND WATCHMENDER
FOR FIFTY YEARS, address, telephone number.
I heard the thin rain falling in the yard.

The card was on a sort of shelf, just close
Enough to let me read this on the front.
Not, I'd have said, the sort of words to engross
Even the keenest reader, nothing to affront
The public decency of Manchester.
And yet I turned it over. On the back
Were just three words in rather smudgy black
Soft pencil: MR COOPER – DEAD. The year

Grew weakly green outside, in blackened trees,
Wet grass by statues. It was ten to ten
In March in Manchester. Now, ill at ease
And made unsure of sense and judgement when
Three words could throw me, I walked back into
The bar, where nothing much had happened since
I'd left. A man was trying to convince
Another man that somehow someone knew

Something that someone else had somehow done.
Two women sat and drank the lagers they
Were drinking when I'd gone. If anyone
Knew I was there, or had been, or might stay,
They didn't show it. *Good night*, I almost said,
Went out to find the rain had stopped, walked back
To my hotel, and felt the night, tall, black,
Above tall roofs. And Mr Cooper dead.

12   *An Enquiry*

'Hello. Mrs Newton? You won't know me but
I'm making an enquiry, some research
Into the marital problems of our time.
My name. . .? Dr Fell. Now I wonder if
You'd mind answering a few questions for me.
In confidence, of course.' Five floors above
The Ring Road, in a block of flats, alone
She sits and hears his decent level voice.
No terrified suspicion squats beside
The telephone she holds: for nowadays
People are asking questions everywhere
Of perfect strangers. Television-men
Brandish their little pencil-microphones
At anybody, and you have to speak.
'Now first, how long have you been married? Yes.
Number of children? Mm. Your husband's job?
There's quite a lot of detail to this work –
Enquiries need to have a mass of facts . . .'
Bored, with James up on business in Carlisle,
Nothing to watch, the children tucked in bed,
She warms a little to such confidence,
Telling the Doctor what time James gets home,
Who washes up at night, and how they spend
An average evening. 'And now, if you'll please
Answer a few more intimate questions, I . . .'

Quite suddenly, the brisk enquiring voice
Takes on the low drone of a shut-in fly
Circling the glowing magnet of the light.
'In bed . . . he tears your clothes off . . . then he ties . . .
Hands . . . breasts . . . puts his . . . are you listening. . .?
Tell me what it feels like . . . every bit . . .
You let him . . . please say something . . . does he make. . .?'
She holds the black and swollen instrument
Away, and lets a scream gush out of her
Which, magnified and twisted through its coils,
Reaches him, 'Dr Fell', panting, alone,
His white face staring from a call-box where
He's satisfied and spent. The line goes dead.
He pushes at the door, and feels the cold.

13   *Sunday Afternoons*

On Sunday afternoons
In winter, snow in the air,
People sit thick as birds
In the station buffet-bar.
They know one another.
Some exchange a few words
But mostly they sit and stare
At the urns and the rock buns.

Not many trains today.
Not many are waiting for trains
Or waiting for anything
Except for the time to pass.
The fug is thick on the glass
Beyond which, through honks and puffing,
An express shrugs and strains
To sidings not far away.

Here no one is saying goodbye:
Tears, promises to write,
Journeys, are not for them.
Here there are other things
To mull over, till the dark brings
Its usual burdensome
Thoughts of a place for the night,
A bit of warm and dry.

On Sunday afternoons
The loudspeaker has little to say
Of wherever the few trains go.
Not many are travellers.
But few are as still as these
Who sit here out of the snow,
Passing the time away
Till the night begins.

14   *County Hotel, Edinburgh*

'Miss Minnes spends each winter with us here:
October through to May.' In the lounge
Miss Minnes sits and knots her hair
Through two bony fingers, and seems to cringe

When anyone walks by her. 'Yes, she comes
Of a very good family, up Inverness way.'
Miss Minnes sits doing complicated sums,
Dressed in a leather jerkin, day after day.

'She never speaks to anyone.' Long white face
Where eyes lie sunk in dreams, or maybe not.
In the television parlour she takes her place
For a minute or two, and then stalks out to sit

In the lounge and knot her hair and stare, stare
At the two electric bars which warm the room
From October through to May. If people cared
For Miss Minnes's seventy years, would she assume

They only meddled? 'Money's no object there.'
Among the debris of *The Field, The Sphere*
And last week's *Scotsman*, she, with lank grey hair,
Sits silent, twitching, winter by wintry year.

15   *The Fly*

The fly's sick whining buzz
Appals me as I sit
Alone and quietly,
Reading and hearing it
Banging against the pane,
Bruised, falling, then again
Starting his lariat tour
Round and round my head
Ceiling to wall to floor.

But I equip myself
To send him on his way,
Newspaper clutched in hand
Vigilant, since he may
Settle, shut off his shriek
And lie there mild and weak
Who thirty seconds ago
Drove air and ears mad
With shunting to and fro.

And I shall not pretend
To any well of pity
Flowing at such a death.
The blow is quick. Maybe
The Hindu's moved to tears
But not a hundred years
Of brooding could convince
My reason that this fly
Has rights which might prevent
My choosing that he die.

And yet I know the weight
Of small deaths weighs me down,
That life (whatever that is)
Is holy: that I drown
In air which stinks of death
And that each unthought breath
Takes life from some brief life,
And every step treads under
Some fragments still alive.
The fly screams to the thunder.

Death troubles me more rarely
Than when, at seventeen,
I looked at Chatterton
And thought what it might mean.
I know my children sleep
Sound in the peace they keep.
And then, suddenly calm,
The fly rests on the wall
Where he lies still, and I
Strike once. And that is all.

16 *Hedgehog*

Twitching the leaves just where the drainpipe clogs
In ivy leaves and mud, a purposeful
Creature about its business. Dogs
Fear his stiff seriousness. He chews away

At beetles, worms, slugs, frogs. Can kill a hen
With one snap of his jaws, can taunt a snake
To death on muscled spines. Old countrymen
Tell tales of hedgehogs sucking a cow dry.

But this one, cramped by houses, fences, walls,
Must have slept here all winter in that heap
Of compost, or have inched by intervals
Through tidy gardens to this ivy bed.

And here, dim-eyed, but ears so sensitive
A voice within the house can make him freeze,
He scuffs the edge of danger: yet can live
Happily in our nights and absences.

A country creature, wary, quiet and shrewd,
He takes the milk we give him, when we're gone.
At night, our slamming voices must seem crude
To one who sits and waits for silences.

17 *The Cry*

I woke to hear a cry that might have been
One of the children, ours or a neighbour's: a cat,
It could have been, or a bird, or a dream
Woken out of so quickly it took itself into day.

Through the whole day the cry was in my head,
Clear, but not high or low or known. And so
Because it lacked a name, it nagged at me.
It hung like a dry leaf on the edge of my mind.

The wind of a whole day tugged at it, seemed
Sometimes to shift it while I talked or listened or ate:
But it stayed, stayed the whole day till in bed again
I moved into sleep, the cry going with me to sleep.

And now I wake again and have things to do.
I think the leaf has fallen, the cry has gone.
It meant nothing, I know. Yet I write it down
And hear it again as I write, as I let it go.

18   *Disturbances*

After the darkness has come
And the distant 'planes catch fire
In the dusk, coming home,
And the tall church spire
No longer stands on the hill
And the streets are quiet except
For a car-door slamming – well,
You might say the houses slept.
An owl calls from a tree.

This is my house and home,
A place where for several years
I've settled, to which I've come
Happily, set my shears
To the hedge which fronts the place,
Had decorators in,
Altered a former face
To a shape I can call my own.
An owl calls from a tree.

43

Only, sometimes at night
Or running downhill for a train,
I suddenly catch sight
Of a world not named and plain
And without hedges or walls:
A jungle of noises, fears,
No lucid intervals,
No calm exteriors.
An owl calls from a tree.

The place I live in has
A name on the map, a date
For all that is or was.
I avoid hunger and hate:
I have a bed for the night:
The dishes are stacked in the rack:
I remember to switch off the light:
I turn and lie on my back.
An owl calls from a tree.

19   *Night Thoughts*

Darker than eyes shut in a darkened room,
Colder than coldest hours before the dawn,
My nightmare body leaves its bed to walk
Across the unseen lawn
Where apples nudge my feet. They force a shout
Inside my throat which, struggling, can't get out.

I am awake. The dream is over now.
No one is in the garden, nor has been.
You lie beside me while I count the things
Tomorrow will begin
In idleness, omission or false choice,
In lack of purpose or uncertain voice.

You sleep, and in the dark I hear you breathe
Through certainties, responsibilities.
Sometimes you tell me of your own strange dreams.
Mine are banalities,
Trudging down trodden paths to find a heap
Of fragments unromanticized by sleep.

Letters unwritten: papers on my desk:
Money: my age: things I would not have said
Given another minute to decide.
I stifle in my bed,
Searching for other names to call it by,
This blankness which comes down so finally.

But names are nothing, dreams are nothing, when
The day unrolls itself from second sleep.
Reluctantly, I wake: shave: choose a tie.
These daily things are cheap,
The small wage paid to keep my nightmares small:
Trivial, dull: not terrible at all.

20 *Difficult*

Not much is simple: you can never say
Straight out what ten more minutes will make worse.
The clean page, the new cheque-book, never stay
Like that, like the morning far too bright to last.
Reading a poem over, you can rehearse
Till the words are no longer there. The past
Silts up, stifles, practice ruins the trick.
My mind gropes at simple arithmetic.

Gropes, and misses its footing. All the time, you're sure
That the line is straight, the page turned, the thought
At the back of your mind needs only a nudge to cure
The uncertainty. Every three months or so
I clear my desk, discovering what I ought
To have thrown away at once three months ago.
And then it's simple: except to dither over
Trash, scraps I never wanted to discover.

Not much is simple: water, sleep, the pure
Labour of digging a patch of ground. But then
You can't live on these. What makes me feel secure
The times when I am, isn't simple at all –
The ordering of time, the punctual skills, the pen
Flowing without a blot: a miracle
That out of disorder even so much can be
Simple. I jib at the word *complexity*.

And I am right, I suppose. A home, a wife,
Children, are simple properties, whose care
And love and order frame a simple life.
Valuing this is easy, keeping it
Much harder: for, come pat and unaware,
And stealthily, a bland indefinite
Ghost blots the page, clutters the desk, and says
'Not much is simple, nevertheless.'

21   *Dead and Gone*

This blackbird stared at us six feet away,
Set in a hedge, its poise at once too pure,
Too sure and still to be a real bird:
We, in the room, through glass, watched it and still
Without fear, in the hedge, it stood and watched us too.

Caught in the moment of alighting, died.

Caught by no cat: I looked for blood, or mess
Of feathers disarrayed. And certainly no hawk.
Here – where the suburbs cheat a violent death
By natural tooth or claw – it gripped a twig
With each long plucking claw, fanned out its wings,
Threw back its head and beak.
                              Only its eyes,
Glazed to opaqueness, said that something died.

My daughter, three years old, whose practical eyes
See spiders, flies and ladybirds asleep,
Who lays out berries for them when they wake,
Asked me what I would do. 'I'll bury it –
Put it in a hole.' 'And will it hide like me?'

No need, though, for such ceremony as this.
We left the bird – memento, incident
Strange in the level course of things – all night.
In the morning, nothing. The leaves ruffled where
It took its stance, one of them crumpled by
The gripping claw. A hole where nothing was
Before or after. Buried in blank air.

This small death, vanishing from time and place,
Left this small gap, a childish question asked
And never answered: 'Why did the bird go?'
Well, common sense would answer with a cat
Prowling from neighbouring gardens. Maybe so.
And yet, dead of old age or whatever else,
Those wings, heraldic, that full throat thrust back,
Those blind white eyes, announced some hiding-place
Shared with the spider, ladybird and fly,
With child and man. And could not tell us why.

Come from a distant country,
Bundle of flesh, of blood,
Demanding painful entry,
Expecting little good:
There is no going back
Among those thickets where
Both night and day are black
And blood's the same as air.

Strangely you come to meet us,
Stained, mottled, as if dead:
You bridge the dark hiatus
Through which your body slid
Across a span of muscle,
A breadth my hand can span.
The gorged and brimming vessel
Flows over, and is man.

Dear daughter, as I watched you
Come crumpled from the womb,
And sweating hands had fetched you
Into this world, the room
Opened before your coming
Like water struck from rocks
And echoed with your crying
Your living paradox.

23   *A Sense of Property*

After the usual rounds at night
In the house and property called my own,
Front door, back door, bolted tight;
Fire raked down; stove stoked high –
I climbed the stairs and there, alone
On the landing by the nursery,
I saw my daughter watching me.

In fact, a baby in her cot
Asleep, beyond that firm closed door.
But twenty years from now, and not
Our sole sweet charge, our special grace,
She stood like someone glimpsed before
In book or crowd: and in her face
The future marked its time and place.

I knew she was not real, and gone
Within a moment. So I went
Through all the trivial jobs, and on
To bed. But, half asleep, I lay
And wondered how impermanent
The future is, yet day by day
My daughter walks it on its way.

That daughter will not be my own
As house and property are mine,
For in that moment I was shown
A stranger at my baby's door,
A stranger made by some design
Not ours, and hammered out before
She took the shape her mother bore.

But in a curious happiness
I faced that fact, and knew at once
That child and woman would express
Through every known and unknown thing
(Each of them her inheritance)
A permanence in everything,
While acquisitions clog and cling.

She sleeps so light that if I go
Into her room, she turns and stirs.
The house is quiet, its rooms all show
A locked and barred security.
And in my sleep, deeper than hers,
I watch her stand and look at me,
Stripped of possessions and made free.

24 *Looking On*

Hearing our voices raised –
Perhaps in anger,
Or in some trivial argument
That is not anger –
She screams until we stop,
And smile, and look at her,
Poised on the sheer drop
Which opens under her.

If these, her parents, show
How the gods can fail,
Squabbling on Olympus,
How can she fail
To see that anarchy
Is what one must expect,
That to be happy
One must be circumspect?

But the reverse is true
Also, when we kiss,
Seeing herself excluded
Even from that kiss.
The gods' too gross affairs
Made myths for innocent men,
So the innocent eye stares
At love in its den.

Like a strange motley beast
Out of an old myth,
Anger and love together
Make up her own myth
Of these two who cherish,
Protect, feed, deny,
In whose arms she will flourish
Or else will die.

25   *Sick Child*

Lit by the small night-light you lie
And look through swollen eyes at me:
Vulnerable, sleepless, try
To stare through a blank misery,
And now that boisterous creature I
Have known so often shrinks to this
Wan ghost unsweetened by a kiss.

Shaken with retching, bewildered by
The virus curdling milk and food,
You do not scream in fear, or cry.
Tears are another thing, a mood
Given an image, infancy
Making permitted show of force,
Boredom, or sudden pain. The source

Of this still vacancy's elsewhere.
Like my sick dog, ten years ago,
Who skulked away to some far lair
With poison in her blood: you know
Her gentleness, her clouded stare,
Pluck blankets as she scratched the ground.
She made, and you now make, no sound.

The rank smell shrouds you like a sheet.
Tomorrow we must let crisp air
Blow through the room and make it sweet,
Making all new. I touch your hair,
Damp where the forehead sweats, and meet –
Here by the door, as I leave you –
A cold, quiet wind, chilling me through.

26   *White Snow*

'White snow,' my daughter says, and sees
For the first time the lawn, the trees,
Loaded with this superfluous stuff.
Two words suffice to make facts sure
To her, whose mental furniture
Needs only words to say enough.

Perhaps by next year she'll forget
What she today saw delicate
On every blade of grass and stone;
Yet will she recognize those two
Syllables, and see them through
Eyes which remain when snow has gone?

Season by season, she will learn
The names when seeds sprout, leaves turn,
And every change is commonplace.
She will bear snowfalls in the mind,
Know wretchedness of rain and wind,
With the same eyes in a different face.

My wish for her, who held by me
Looks out now on this mystery
Which she has solved with words of mine,
Is that she may learn to know
That in her words for the white snow
Change and permanence combine –
The snow melted, the trees green,
Sure words for hurts not suffered yet, nor seen.

27   *House for Sale*

A house gone derelict where, splayed
Like metal branches, pipes jut out
Where once the Ascot hung: we tread,
Disturbing letters on the mat
Pushed through the door a year ago –
'The Owner, No. 6' – and blow
Dust from the mantelpiece. The soot
Slops in the grate and, underfoot,
Goes tracking everywhere we go.

Each twelve by ten of empty room
Marks out a musty cell, which bed,
Chair, table, hideous jug made seem
A kind of home inherited
By someone we have never known.
Yet nothing by itself has grown
To make it permanent, and now
Patches of wall alone show how
A man had made it look his own.

Tramping through vacant echoes, we
Sniff out the damp and scuff at floors,
Knock plaster from the ceiling, see
Mouseholes in cellars, wrench at doors
That will not open. Windows face
Into the yard where weeds embrace
The neighbourhood's old wheels and tins,
A sluggish commerce which begins
To mould it to a different place.

Living in this, could we begin
To set to rights what others left
In casual indiscipline,
Its grace or ugliness bereft?
Houses, indeed, are flimsy stuff,
For mortar is not strong enough
To keep an emptiness alive,
And chairs and tables can't revive
The rooms which they were tenants of.

Where people live – known rooms, or those
Windows through which we look and see
Families round tables, doors that close
On lived-in places – these are free
Of everything we pry through here:
The blank foundations where we peer
On unknown lives which, moving on,
Have told us only that they've gone
And what they've left we cannot share.

28 *Scars*

How, after thirty years of not
Much daring wildness or bad luck,
Do I have so many? No one shot
At me from rooftops, ran me down,
Used me for bayonet practice. Stuck
In small remembered moments, they
Mark even smaller wounds: yet have grown
As I have, to this very day.

The palm of my right hand, scraped raw
By ash and gravel, takes me to
Myself at seventeen: I saw
The athlete had some praise I lacked,
And so I ran for the House. I grew
Hearty and keen. And then one day
I slipped at relay-practice, cracked
My wrist and tore the flesh away.

A bit of travel, too: one thigh
Grazed by stony reefs at sea
Off Libya, swimming: and by
My left wrist, where a window fell
At thirteen in Vermont, I see
A quarter of an inch of white.
A doctor's room in Muswell Hill
Made one of them. A certain light

Shows up one eyebrow ruffled where
A beer glass hit it, up in Leeds –
My only brawl. The bristly hair
At the tip of my chin is sparse because
At nine I fell off a chair. It bleeds
Still, if I close my eyes. Yet not
One rates my passport; minor flaws,
So minor that they show me what

A whole half lifetime did not wound.
There is just one I can't explain:
A thin curved band which goes half round
My little finger, like a ring.
It must have hurt, and yet the pain
Means nothing to me: like the scars
I've never worn, like suffering
Not named in small particulars.

29 *Massacre*

The news of suffering, great spell of breath
Over these things I have not heard or seen:
Why do I make this photograph my own
View of a huddled-up but noisy death?
Some finger made the shutter close, which then
Opened the lens to what I have not done.

This newspaper open, that hides my face,
Shows me a body laid along a street
And nothing but its emptiness. The weight
Of guilt must feel less heavy when no trace
Of private guilt is there.
                              I stand and pull
The trigger which can do nothing else but kill.

Savage but bland, cased in a mesh of tweed,
My brief-case at my feet, my bottom firm
On a firm seat on a suburban line,
I speed away, face hidden. When I bleed
I blame the razor, secateurs, or thorn
And not the time or place where I was born.

But still the sharp light lies along that back
Sieved through with bullets and then left to lie.
Men write down words like *crime* and *tragedy*,
Men put down black on white and white on black.
And I see nothing as I travel home
But feel blunt heads lie heavy on each bone.

30   *At Enoshima*

Level and grey, the sea moves from the east
Carrying fish-heads, cartons, broken glass:
Here a rice barrel bursts out of its staves,
Chicken-bones crunch under as I pass.
The holy island does without a priest
But catches tourists after souvenirs,
So picnic litter sprawls in with the waves
To leave a scurf along this stretch of sand,
Cast-offs and shiftings of the shifting land.

And it is here, along that wavering path
Of plastic lemonade jars, bottles, straws,
I find this other souvenir of Japan,
Swept in by tides to join the common shore's
Museum of rejection: a thin lath,
A pointed stake, a spar of wood, a grave
Not made of lasting stuff, to mark a man
Whose name I cannot read, an age and date
I puzzle out like an illiterate.

He died two months ago, in March. It's just
Those characters I know. The flowing brush
Moves elegantly on, leaves me behind
To dumbly feel the holy island crush
That body, now anonymous, to dust.
Whatever else he was I do not know,
Except his dying left for me to find
His cheap memorial. Ignorant, foreign, I
See nothing but this wood, this mystery.

31 *The Barrow*

In this high field strewn with stones
I walk by a green mound,
Its edges sheared by the plough.
Crumbs of animal bone
Lie smashed and scattered round
Under the clover leaves
And slivers of flint seem to grow
Like white leaves among green.
In the wind, the chestnut heaves
Where a man's grave has been.

Whatever the barrow held
Once, has been taken away:
A hollow of nettles and dock
Lies at the centre, filled
With rain from a sky so grey
It reflects nothing at all.
I poke in the crumbled rock
For something they left behind
But after that funeral
There is nothing at all to find.

On the map in front of me
The gothic letters pick out
Dozens of tombs like this,
Breached, plundered, left empty,
No fragments littered about
Of a dead and buried race
In the margins of histories.
No fragments: these splintered bones
Construct no human face,
These stones are simply stones.

In museums their urns lie
Behind glass, and their shaped flints
Are labelled like butterflies.
All that they did was die,
And all that has happened since
Means nothing to this place.
Above long clouds, the skies
Turn to a brilliant red
And show in the water's face
One living, and not these dead.

At Manhood End the older dead lie thick
Together by the churchyard's eastern wall.
The sexton sweated out with spade and pick
And moved turf, clay, bones, gravestones, to make room
For later comers, those whose burial
Was still far off, but who would need a tomb.

Among the pebbles, in the molehills' loam,
Turned thighbone up, and skull: whatever frail
Relic was left was given a new home,
Close to the wood and farther from the sea.
Couch-grass grew stronger here and, with the pale
Toadstools and puffballs, masked that vacancy.

In April, on a day when rain and sun
Had stripped all distances to clarity,
I stood there by the chapel, and saw one
Lean heron rising on enormous wings
Across the silted harbour towards the sea.
Dead flowers at my feet: but no one brings

Flowers to those shifted bodies. The thin flies,
First flies of spring, stirred by the rain-butt. Names
Stared at me out of moss, the legacies
Of parents to their children: *Lucy, Ann*,
Names I have given, which a father claims
Because they mean something that he began.

Cool in the chapel of St Wilfred, I
Knelt by the Saxon wall and bowed my head,
Shutting my eyes: till, looking up to high
Above the pews, I saw a monument,
A sixteenth-century carving, with the dead
Husband and wife kneeling together, meant

For piety and remembrance. But on their right
I grasped with sudden shock a scene less pure –
A naked woman, arms bound back and tight,
And breasts thrust forward to be gnawed by great
Pincers two men held out. I left, unsure
Of what that emblem meant; and towards the gate

The small mounds of the overcrowded dead
Shrank in the sun. The eastern wall seemed built
Of darker stone. I lay: and by my head
A starling with its neck snapped; nestling there,
A thrush's egg with yolk and white half spilt,
And one chafed bone a molehill had laid bare.

Frail pictures of the world at Manhood End –
How we are shifted, smashed, how stones display
The names and passions that we cannot mend.
The lych-gate stood and showed me, and I felt
The pebbles teach my feet. I walked away,
My head full of the smell my nostrils smelt.

from *The Stones of Emptiness* (1967)

I

Emptying the teapot out
Into the drain, I catch sight
Suddenly of flies at work
On some rubbish by the back
Of the shed, and standing there
Smell the small corruption where
A fishbone makes its measured path
Into the leaves, into the earth.

II

Under the raspberry canes I prod to light
Two Roman sherds, a glint of Roman glass,
A bit of bellarmine, some stoneware scraps,
And searching on might find the rougher wares,
Friable, gritty, Saxon: porous stuff
That lets the rain leak through, the dew absorb,
Frost craze and crack. *Frango*, I break, becomes
Fragment, the broken pieces to be joined
To give a date to everything we own.

III

The little duchess, aged four hundred, stirs
To feel the instruments break through the lead.
Troy stands on the nine layers of its filth
And I tread out another cigarette.

IV

Compost of feasts and leavings, thick
Layer after layer of scourings, peelings, rinds,
Bone pressed on potsherd, fish-head sieved to dust,

And in the spoil-heaps goes the fly, the quick
Mouse with her pink brood, and the maggot, slow
To render down the fat. Trash, husk, and rust,
Grass sickled, scythed, and mown, hedge-clippings, leaves,
Wet infiltrations, skins and rags of skins,
Humus of twigs and insects, skeletons
Of petals.
         Stale loaves and fishes so divided out
They feed five thousand trees, five million roots.

V

Pipes void it to the sea,
The Thames chokes on its way.
We live on what we spend,
Are spent, are lived upon.
Nothing has an end.
The compost is my son,
My daughter breeds the dust,
We become ash, air,
Water, earth, the past
Our daughters' sons share.

34   *At Dunwich*

Fifteen churches lie here
Under the North Sea;
Forty-five years ago
The last went down the cliff.
You can see, at low tide,
A mound of masonry
Chewed like a damp bun.

In the village now (if you call
Dunwich a village now,
With a handful of houses, one street,
And a shack for Tizer and tea)
You can ask an old man
To show you the stuff they've found
On the beach when there's been a storm:

Knife-blades, buckles and rings,
Enough coins to fill an old sock,
Badges that men wore
When they'd been on pilgrimage,
Armfuls of broken pots.
People cut bread, paid cash,
Buttoned up against the cold.

Fifteen churches, and men
In thousands working at looms,
And wives brewing up stews
In great grey cooking pots.
I put out a hand and pull
A sherd from the cliff's jaws.
The sand trickles, then falls.

Nettles grow on the cliffs
In clumps as high as a house.
The houses have gone away.
Stand and look at the sea
Eating the land as it walks
Steadily treading the tops
Of fifteen churches' spires.

35   *Underneath*

From someone's transistor a quarter-mile away
The sound of someone's band lifts over gardens
And finds me here examining a weed
Trowelled up among hundreds in the patch of waste
At the end of this narrow bit of property
I own on the edge of London, where the clay
Starts one spade down, going as far below
As the roof of my house is high, and reaching water
Clear underneath, held in its caves and pockets,
Trapped, unevaporating, silent, cold,
But working back through roots and tall foundations
To mushroom up anywhere, now here
In the roots of the three-leafed weed I hold in my hand,
Disturbed for a moment by that distant band.

36   *The Pond*

With nets and kitchen sieves they raid the pond,
Chasing the minnows into bursts of mud,
Scooping and chopping, raking up frond after frond
Of swollen weed after a week of flood.

Thirty or forty minnows bob and flash
In every jam-jar hoarded on the edge,
While the shrill children with each ill-aimed splash
Haul out another dozen as they dredge.

Choked to its banks, the pond spills out its store
Of frantic life. Nothing can drain it dry
Of what it breeds: it breeds so effortlessly
Theft seems to leave it richer than before.

The nostrils snuff its rank bouquet – how warm,
How lavish, foul, and indiscriminate, fat
With insolent appetite and thirst, so that
The stomach almost heaves to see it swarm.

But trapped in glass the minnows flail and fall,
Sink, with upended bellies showing white.
After an hour I look and see that all
But four or five have died. The greenish light

Ripples to stillness, while the children bend
To spoon the corpses out, matter-of-fact,
Absorbed: as if creation's prodigal act
Shrank to this empty jam-jar in the end.

37 *Lesson*

In the big stockyards, where pigs, cows, and sheep
Stumble towards the steady punch that beats
All sense out of a body with one blow,
Certain old beasts are trained to lead the rest
And where they go the young ones meekly go.

Week after week these veterans show the way,
Then, turned back just in time, are led themselves
Back to the pens where their initiates wait.
The young must cram all knowledge in one day,
But the old who lead live on and educate.

38 *Habit*

Solemn administrator, cowled creature
Ruling your lines in a book devised for
Recording our customs and our nature,

You impel such movements as keep us alive,
Eating, sleeping, always on the move
To the place where we must never arrive –

For that would be to break your rhythm,
Allowing us too easily to become
Mere animals of irregular stab and spasm.

Yet you are animal too: all of us know
That Pavlov's dog salivated for you,
That you tell the log-rolling elephant what he must do.

Patron of babies and the very old,
Adversary of clerks dreaming of Gauguin, shield
Of sergeant-majors doing what they are told;

Keep you as we may, singly or bunched together,
You grow into one hard carapace whatever
Soft twigs and shoots underneath wanly stir.

Put in compartments, like a honeycomb
You spill from cell to cell, leaving no room,
Stifling with sweet indulgence all who come

Prying or bustling, scouring with mop and rake.
On holiday, you are the last thing we take
But take you we do, and when it's over bring you back.

If we break you, we may get fat, grow young, go mad,
Wondering why we listened to what you said
Or wondering in the end whether you're all we've had.

Resented, you weigh us down like Atlas his world:
Cherished, you allow us without pain to grow old:
When we die, our children inherit you before we are cold.

39 *Two Faces*

One gets inured to having the wrong face.
For years I thought it soft, too pink and young
To match that shrewd, mature, and self-possessed
Person behind it. In a forced grimace
I saw all that I *should* have been, the strong
Line linking nose to mouth, the net of care
Fixed by the concentration of the eyes.
Such marks upon the lineaments expressed
Things that I wanted most, but would not dare,
Prevented by the innocence I despised.

Yet now, this morning, as I change a blade,
Look up and clear the glass, I recognize
Some parody of that scored, experienced man.
But this one, as I take it, seems afraid
Of what he sees, is hesitant, with his eyes
Shifting away from something at my back.
No, this is not the one I recognized
Proleptically in mirrors; neither can
He any longer see what firm lines track
Back to that innocence he once despised.

40 *Street Scene: Benghazi*

Two ram's horns married with a bit of gut
Wail on the pavement near the Sport Café
As Mustafa and I walk by the shut
Emporia this blue December Friday.

Mustafa wears a trim Italian suit,
Reads Sartre in the Faculty of Arts,
Writes poems behind dark glasses, is acute
About 'some' and 'any' and the various parts

71

Of speech. He will go far – maybe in Oil.
Whereas this flautist, swathed in motley shawls,
Unshaved, one-eyed, from whom the dogs recoil,
Seems at a dead end. Poverty appals

More when it sweetly insinuates and smiles.
Mustafa notices. 'A marabout,' he says,
Explaining the presence: explanation reconciles.
I notice the moth-holes in the faded fez.

'That man is wise and holy,' Mustafa says,
And puts a piastre in the wizened hand.
I avoid his glance. To Allah let there be praise.
Round Barclay's DCO the armed guards stand.

41   *The Stones of Emptiness*

Isaiah 34: 11

Eroded slabs, collapsed and weathered tables,
Porous and pocked limestone, rubble of schist:
They are the real blocks where the real foot stumbles,
Boulders where lizards move like Medusa's prey
Freed from their stone trance. Here the stone-eyed exist
Among pebbles, fossil-bearing images
Glaring their life-in-death in the blinding day.
At the dark cave's mouth they stand like effigies.

They define the void. They assert
How vast the distances are, featureless, bare.
Their absence creates the extremest kind of desert,
A sea of sand. They are to the desolate earth
What a single hawk is to the desolate air.
And suddenly here, grouped in a circle
In the middle of nowhere, they form a hearth
Round a fire long since dead, built by an unknown people.

The soil profitless under their strewn acres,
Even so they harbour in their ungenerous shade
Flowers as delicate as they themselves are fierce.
Scorpions entrench under them, flat as dry leaves.
In parched wadi beds, coagulate in a blockade
Against all but a man on foot, who, waterless
And far from home, stumbles as he perceives
Only that line of confusion, the stones of emptiness.

42   Dust

Beautiful only when the light catches it
Arrested yet volatile in a shaft of sun,
Or under the microscope, like an ancient detritus
Of snowflakes: otherwise valueless debris.
The ash from my cigarette, the air from my lungs,
The soles of my shoes, the palms of my hands, breed it,
Absorb it, carry it, disperse it. The liquids of bodies
Dry to it in the end, and the sea's salt.

Created from the beginning, it carries its beginnings
Even to the end. Metals and minerals
Are crushed to its substance: in the desert
It is beyond the harshness of sand. Soft,
Disposable, it collects in corners, to be moved
Only to another place: it cannot be moved
Finally. Indestructible, even in fire
It shapes its own phoenix, and rises with the wind.

Each second shifts it, animates its grey
Weight, bearing down on pliant surfaces.
Analyse its origins, and you find the full range
Of everything living and dead. It obeys water,
Lying down to a drenching, but as the sun
Parches that adversary it re-forms and spreads
Further and further, to the eyes, the nostrils, the throat,
A thin dry rain, contemptible, persistent.

In a world of definable objects, each different from each,
It unites as denominator of all,
The common agent. I see the white page
Gathering its random calligraphy under my pen,
And see at the tip of the pen the fine motes swirl
Down to that point where a fragmented earth
Silently whirls in an air choked with nothing but dust:
The pulverization of planets, the universe dust.

43   *Cleaning a Coin*

The green encrusted lump
Stews in its vinegar.
I peck with a pocket knife
At accretions of shell and stone.
Sand flakes from the centre.

After three days of this
The alchemy takes over.
Through a mask of verdigris
A profile stares through,
Wild-haired and chapleted.

And there on the other side
A vestigial horse capers
Across an illegible
Inscription in Greek. I rinse
The tiny disc at the tap.

I keep it now on my desk
With the other beachcombings,
This rendering down of the last
Twenty-five centuries
To a scoured chip of bleached bronze.

44   *Buzzards Above Cyrene*

Alone or in wheeling squadrons of dozens, they move
High above the escarpment, drift to the plain below,
The sun with a certain light obscuring their wings
So that they vanish to narrowed points of darkness
Only to swing away a moment later
Becoming spread sails, gold, brown, distinct and huge
Over tombs, junipers, red stones, red dust
Caught in a still and windless stretch of blue.
But more than that, they impose a scale by which
You measure these golden ruins, these hanging gardens of fossils,
These clear imperial edicts and pieties
Cluttering the ledges with magnificence,
All narrowed to points of light in an unwinking eye
For which, fathoms down, a mouse freezes still, a lizard
Flashes, a dung beetle labours through dry thorns,
Regarded, moved over like a dowser's twig,
To twitch then, jerk down, pounce, finding nothing there
But these poor small spoils, these puny snacks and beakfuls
Littered among ruins, squalid among remains,
Ravaged, scavenged, picked clean among pink blooms.

45 *Arabic Script*

Like a spider through ink, someone says, mocking: see it
Blurred on the news-sheets or in neon lights
And it suggests an infinitely plastic, feminine
Syllabary, all the diacritical dots and dashes
Swimming together like a shoal of minnows,
Purposive yet wayward, a wavering measure
Danced over meaning, obscuring vowels and breath.
But at Sidi Kreibish, among the tombs,
Where skulls lodge in the cactus roots,
The pink claws breaking headstone, cornerstone,
Each fleshy tip thrusting to reach the light,
Each spine a hispid needle, you see the stern
Edge of the language, Kufic, like a scimitar
Curved in a lash, a flash of consonants
Such as swung out of Medina that day
On the long flog west, across ruins and flaccid colonials,
A swirl of black flags, white crescents, a language of swords.

46 *Silphium*

Thick-rooted and thick-stemmed,
Its tail embracing its stem,
Its flower-globes gathered in knots,
Now dead as the dodo,
The mastodon and the quagga,
Commemorated on coins
And in hideous Fascist fountains,
It stands as panacea
For whatever ill you choose,
Since no one living has seen it
Cure dropsy, warts, or gripe,
Flavoured a stew with it,
Or slipped it with a wink
As aphrodisiacal bait.

But there it all is in the books,
Theophrastus, Strabo, Pliny,
Fetching its weight in silver
In the market at Cyrene,
Kept in the state treasury,
Sold to equip the army
By Caesar, sent to Nero
As a rare imperial prize.
Where has it gone? The carious
Teeth of the camel, perhaps,
Have munched it away, or the goat
Scouring the dry pastures.
But I cannot credit the tough
Uncomplicated grasp
Of a plant loosening hold on life
Completely: I imagine a small
Hidden cleft in the worn rock,
Shaded by prickly pear,
Nervously footed by gecko,
Where, thick-rooted and thick-stemmed,
Its tail embracing its stem,
Those flower-globes gather in knots,
That solitary stance
Eluding the oil-prospectors,
The antiquaries, the shepherds,
Who are searching for something else
And need no panacea.

47   *Ali Ben Shufti*

You want coins? Roman? Greek? Nice vase? Head of god, goddess?
Look, shufti here, very cheap. Two piastres? You joke.

I poke among fallen stones, molehills, the spoil
Left by the archaeologists and carelessly sieved.
I am not above ferreting out a small piece
From the foreman's basket when his back is turned.
One or two of my choicer things were acquired
During what the museum labels call 'the disturbances
Of 1941'; you may call it loot,
But I keep no records of who my vendors were –
Goatherds, Johnnies in berets, Neapolitan conscripts
Hot foot out of trouble, dropping a keepsake or two.
I know a good thing, I keep a quiet ear open when
The college bodysnatchers arrive from Chicago,
Florence, Oxford, discussing periods
And measuring everything. I've even done business with them:
You will find my anonymous presence in the excavation reports
When you get to 'Finds Locally Purchased'. Without a B.A. –
And unable to read or write – I can date and price
Any of this rubbish. Here, from my droll pantaloons
That sag in the seat, amusing you no end,
I fetch out Tanagra heads, blue Roman beads,
A Greek lamp, bronze from Byzantium,
A silver stater faced with the head of Zeus.
I know three dozen words of English, enough French
To settle a purchase, and enough Italian
To convince the austere *dottore* he's made a bargain.
As for the past, it means nothing to me but this:
A time when things were made to keep me alive.
You are the ones who go on about it: I survive
By scratching it out with my fingers. I make you laugh
By being obsequious, roguish, battered, in fact
What you like to think of as a typical Arab.
Well, Amr Ibn el-As passed this way
Some thirteen hundred years ago, and we stayed.
I pick over what he didn't smash, and you
Pay for the leavings. That is enough for me.
You take them away and put them on your shelves
And for fifty piastres I give you a past to belong to.

48 *Butterflies in the Desert*

Thrown together like leaves, but in a land
Where no leaves fall and trees wither to scrub,
Raised like the dust but fleshed as no dust is,
They impale themselves like martyrs on the glass,
Leaving their yellow stigmata. A hundred miles
And they form a screen between us and the sparse world.
At the end of the journey we see the juggernaut
Triumphant under their flattened wings, crushed fluids.
Innocent power destroys innocent power.
But who wins, when their bloody acid eats through chrome?
In the competition for martyrs, Donatus won,
But the stout churches of his heresy now stand
Ruined, emptied of virtue, choked with innocent sand.

49 *At Asqefar*

At Asqefar the German helmet
Rests like a scarecrow's bonnet
On a bare branch.
The shreds of coarse grey duffel
Hang round the gap a rifle
Left in a shallow trench.

'Much blood,' said the shepherd,
Gesturing with his head
Towards the bald hillside.
A spent cartridge nestles
Among the dry thistles.
Blood long since dried.

Strange and remote, almost,
As these old figures traced
In Asqefar's cave:
There, pictured in red clay,
Odysseus comes back from Troy
Near the German's grave.

Twenty-five years since the battle
Plucked up the sand and let it settle
On the German soldier.
Far away now the living, the dead,
Disarmed, unhelmeted,
At Troy, at Asqefar.

50   *Qasida on the Track to Msus*

Towards sundown we came out of the valley
Along that track
Not knowing then where it led to, when we saw
The stone circles, the heaped cairns of stone, the stones
Arranged like coracles on the dry slopes.
The brown hills were empty. Only a buzzard
Stood in the sky, perceiving its territory.

Stopping, we knew the place for an encampment
Or what remained of one: the litter of pots,
The broken shafts of ploughs, battered tin bowls,
Sickles and shears rusting, the chattels of the living.
But there were the dead too, in those stone enclosures
Laid into sand below tattered banners, marked with a stone
At head and foot. For them the tents had moved on,
The blanketed camels, the donkeys heaped high
With panniers and vessels for water. And for us too:
We had passed beyond the wells and the fresh springs
Where the goats shuffled in black congregations,
Beyond even the last dry Roman cistern before Msus

At the end of a track we never intended to take.
Behind us, the barking of dogs and the wind from the sea,
Neither concerned with us nor the way south:
In front, the steppes of gazelles and scorpions
To be hunted or burned, for those who might venture
Further into that camouflage.

But, because it was sundown, we slept there and lay
Hearing the wind, watching the rising moon
Above stars falling like snow through constellations
We could not name. At dawn, we turned back
Into the accustomed valley, a settled place,
Going between tents and herds, yelped at by dogs,
Watched by threshers and gleaners, moving among men.
And still on that hillside the ragged flags fret
Over the abandoned implements and stones,
And now I shall never reach Msus,
Having turned back to the easy valley, while those
Who were not left behind rode, I suppose, south
To some name on the map I might just recognize
Or a day's ride beyond to a name I do not know.

The Letters of Synesius
(for Pablo Foster)

Synesius of Cyrene: born in Libya *c*. AD 370, died there *c*. AD 413. Greek
by ancestry, Roman by citizenship, he considered himself to be a
Libyan, a citizen of the Libyan Pentapolis, of which Cyrene, his birth-
place, was one city, and Ptolemais, of which he became bishop, was
another. He studied under Hypatia at Alexandria, visited Athens, went
as ambassador of the Pentapolis to Constantinople, and probably died
at the hands of a native Libyan tribe, the Austuriani.

*It seemed to me that I was some other person, and that I was one listening to
myself amongst others who were present . . .*

SYNESIUS to HYPATIA

You must know my way of speaking the truth bluntly has
followed me even to the bounds of Libya.

At Tocra
The ephebes set hammer and chisel to the wall
Each in his different way, with different skills.
Well-oiled conscripts, glistening and drunk,
Inscribe their achievements and their names and die.
The dragon inherits the Hesperidean gardens
And spawns small lizards, quicksilver on white rock.
Lethe has lights. The dark pools breed white fish
Nevertheless, and blind white crayfish.

Ask for the key
At the Military Academy where the Dean has just finished
Lecturing on the psychology of war.
The Jews have sacked Cyrene. In the tombs
Families sit round brewing tea.

Necropolis.
The Parliament building is locked. The wells are locked
At Gasr Lebia, where Justinian's queen
Is celebrated in mosaic: bull,
Fish, amphibious monster with a conch,
An eagle preying on a calf, crab's claws,
And perched on a curiously humped crocodile
A duck.

The wells are dry, the drillers cry for oil
And find dry holes. Concession 65
Spouts oil and blood. Great wonders come to pass.

The linguists say
The Berber cannot write but has an alphabet
No one can read. Tenders are asked
For a new road to Chad.

Somewhere between

Brega and Zelten, in a waste of sand,
A signpost on an oil-drum indicates
GIALO across the trackless distances.
The king is old. Undergraduates
Are taught philosophy by Egyptians now.
And at Tocra a boy indicates with gestures
How wide is Gamal Nasser's world. That face
Looks down as often as the king's, and smiles
Where the old man's is fatherly but stern.

Aristippus emigrated. There was visa trouble.
A cloud of dust in the east presages war
And the coming of the goat. Pink and yellow,
The posters proclaim in fancy Gothic script
'No word pease whill illeagal Isreil exists'
And 'Palesting was not Belfor's land to promise'
(Belfor the idolatrous, Baal the Ingilizi hound).

　　　　　　　　The ephebes have trouble
In mastering the Christian calendar,
The Latin alphabet. Teach us, they cry,
And go on strike. For the Franks, the wine is cheap
But when you walk the beach at the city's edge
The smashed Heineken bottles shine like grass:
Expensive mosaic. The earliest city lies here
Under this pile of donkeys' hooves. Dig here.
You find loom-weights from looms whose cloth has meshed
Into the sand, the salt, the lips of fossils.

I write between spells of guard between the watchtowers,
Or lecture on the English question-tag.

We have planted our fields for the fires lit by our enemies.

We have had wise men. Where are they now? we ask.
Aristippus, who taught that pleasure was highest good,
Callimachus, writing verses in his catalogue,
And, without false modesty, myself –
Synesius, mounting guard in my bishop's cope
And watching the setting sun run creases down
The great swathe of the Jebel.
                          I have seen
The Italian farmhouses house sheep and straw,
And vv IL DUCE flake from the pink walls,
Catching the last rays of the crumbling sun.
The fourth shore's harbours clog and choke with sand.

Severus the African, speaking slow Latin
With a Berberish accent, went on campaign.
Brute tribes were pacified, our cities flourished,
But the taxes rose, the coinage was debased
So that small coins are like water in the hand.
Our emperor died on the northern frontier
And so, in time, we turn to the east.
                         What stays
Is here, where some potter from Byzantium
Has pressed on the pot's foot his full-fleshed thumb.

The language with the unpronounceable sound
Made somewhere below the glottis inherits our tongue.
'Poets are followed by none save erring men,'
Said the Prophet, echoing Plato into the cave.

The ghaffir in his blanket under the stairs
Who prays five times a day to Allah the Good
Collects our garbage, has trachoma in one eye,
And shall assuredly inherit the Kingdom.

54   *LETTER III*

I would rather live a stranger among strangers.

The slopes below the cave are thick with flints.
Here they kept ammunition in the war,
And now tether a bullock to a post
Under the eaves of rock.
                       Places of the mind only,
Unvisited oases, tracks marked
On unreliable maps by engineers
Who saw the landscape from two thousand feet.

So it might be a god would wander
Over the landscape deserted by his people,
Looking for evidence that once they loved him.
Now they are gone. Delicate microliths
Like snowflakes litter the dry slopes, among thorns.

I am writing to you to talk about emptiness
Because this is empty country, 'where ruins flourish'.

At first you are frightened of dogs, their distant barks
Coming closer across the strewn, ungrateful rock,
And perhaps you pick up stones to shy them away.
You are right, you trespass. Take tea with them, learn the words
For 'please' and 'thank you', bark in Arabic,
Or whatever language is current at the time:
Try Berber, Greek, Latin, Turkish, Italian,
Compounds of these, gibbering dialects –
You will still sweat with fear, ducking down for stones
Which, it may be, are tools fashioned by men
Without a language.
                    To call a man a dog
Is an insult in many languages, but not to dogs.
They sniff the high octane at Benina as the planes take off,
Watching the passengers who have an hour

Between London and Nairobi, the pale transients.
Their yellow fur bristles, they yawn and snap.
At Hagfet er Rejma they patrol the tents,
Watching me glean the slopes for polished flakes.
My pockets are full, my hands are empty.
Look, dogs, how empty. This landscape is yours, not mine.

55   *LETTER IV*

Such are our celebrations, seasonable and of old tradition,
the good things of the poor.

Simon of Cyrene carried the cross. No Libyan
In collar and tie will carry anything.
'A proud people,' says the handout wearily,
Explaining nothing.
                        Lake Tritonis, place
Of Pallas Athene's birth, dries to a salt-pan
Where tin huts void their sewage. Erytheia,
Arethusa, Aegle, Hestia, are ghaffirs:
Their sweet songs are transistorized, relayed
From Radio Cairo across miles of sand.

A donkey and a microbus collide.
The donkey limps off, noisily urinates
By the side of the road, while the bus, crumpled like paper,
Waits for repairs and insurance policies.
The old survives by demanding nothing: the new
Frets in its expectations.
                        I am supposed
To lead my flock through darkness until such time
As the Kingdom descends, there is no more call for martyrs,
And the meek inherit the earth. In the new order
My people go hungry thus to cleanse themselves.

In the month of Ramadan the rain begins
This year. It is December, and the stars
Wane above grey clouds, are obscured by them.
The sea is coldly feverish. Lightning streaks
The yellow stucco and the shuttered rooms.
The honey-casks, the oil-jars and the wine
Lie at the wharf. No one puts out to sea.

What can cure the soul? What food nourish it?
Fasting by day, they feast by night and cram
Sin down their gullets. In the church beyond the wall
The heretics draw lots for martyrdom.
I have nothing more to say of the good life,
Except – having seen so much – that to suppose
Things better rather than different is a way
Of dying only, swivelled to the past.
It is easy for me to act the Jeremiah,
To juxtapose the anomalous, debased present
With the golden fragments of a golden age.
The indigenous survives: the donkey limps off unhurt.
The silphium plants wilt in the private gardens
Since men no more expect a panacea.

Those who are to come will call our Lord a prophet
Mistaken among prophets. Spiritual pride
Gives way to pride of status, money, dress.
Unearth a marble goddess and you find
Her groin defiled with soldiers' filthiness.
The Temple of Zeus is smashed, the figurines
Pulped into lime. Farzúgha's church protects
A tribe of bats and owls. At Tansollúk
The arch is crammed with masonry and sand.

In the garrison chapel we sing 'God Save the Queen':
A proud people, enjoined to pray each week
For her and Johnson too.
                                        Out of the sand
A scorpion heaves its fiery shoulders, smashed
By the spade, heavy with fire and venom. The old
Survives by demanding nothing: the new
Frets in its expectations. Simon bowed
Under the weight, the jeers. Something survives
As Ramadan and Christmas coincide
And we have little left to share but pride.

56   *LETTER V*

And who shall collect fruit from the desert?

The sea licks the shore with sly assurance
Where freestone masonry tumbles in pools.
Salt will never be worm-eaten, says the proverb:
It is the eater and preserver, fixed
Like mould on the surfaces of sherds, the fabric
Coins wrap themselves in, a sharp-tongued mineral,
The taste of thirst, the desert's brother, the sea's self.

I wait for something. The facile have a saying:
If life is hard on you, dwell in cities.
Watching the sea is a lifetime's occupation,
Empty of incident: looking inland
I see not emptiness but desolation.
The cities are fallen, Barca is forked with fire,
Ashes drift down on Tocra, Cyrene lies open
Like an enormous cave laid out for looting.
Here on the other side we have the sea
Rubbing and prying and investigating,
A faceless element, unharvested.

Cretans fish sponges: red mullet fills our plates
But we do not catch them. Red earth holds spilth of seeds
But we grow little, garner less. We have a mineral
More powerful than salt, liquid as sea,
Deep in its cave for looting, to sustain us.
Why should our old men sow, our young men reap?
The tall earth-delvers feed us royalties,
Our government takes tithes. Consider Esso:
It sows not, neither does it reap. Yet was ever
Woman arrayed like this one, in the Modern   ·
Grocery Store, trousered, in high heels? In the desert
Her man plucks golden fruit, Hesperidean
Apples whose juice flows richly to the sea
To be drunk by silver tankers.

                        Undergraduates, you
Who sit your final examinations, consider
Omar Mukhtar, old man on a horse,
Who died on the gallows tortured by his wounds.
'He would have been a ghaffir now,' said one
Keen student with a sneer.
                    Omar rests now,
Thirty-three years after his death, his tomb
Built like a pink carbuncle at the edge
Of Bereniké, Euhesperides,
Benghazi – cities beckoning the wise ones
Who once found life hard, who have claimed their inheritance
Out of the salt desert, the desert, the rock,
Preserver of fallen cities, of flesh, and of oil.

Shut up here in our houses, then, as in a prison, we were to our
regret condemned to keep this long silence.

This autumn I felt the cold in my bones when
In the fountain of Apollo the frogs were spawning.
Persephone was faceless. Above the Jebel
The thunder grumbled.

Fortune was elsewhere, ministering her mercies,
Dispensing luck to barbarians and atheists.
We on the coast repaired the aqueducts
But the water failed us.

Then winter came and the highways flooded,
Keeping us chained to our useless harbours,
Pent in by storms, letting our cattle
Wander uncared for.

Somewhere in the east the administrators filed us
Under a pile of disregarded papers.
We were forgotten, except by the hungry
Collector of taxes.

The Governor sends me a gilt-edged invitation
To celebrate the fourteenth year of independence.
There I shall see the outlandish consuls-general
Talking dog-Latin.

My cultivated friend, please try to send me
Whatever new books the sophists have published:
I have read the reviews in the six-month-old journals
And feel a provincial.

'We traded in shrouds: people stopped dying.'
Fortune frustrates even our death-wish.
The infant mortality figures were lost by
The census department.

Remember me now to my old friends and colleagues,
Discussing the Trinity and aureate diction:
Think of me here, awaiting the fires of
The Austuriani.

See where they squat behind the escarpment,
Ignorant of metre, of faction and schism,
Destined by favourless Fortune to be the true
Heirs of the Kingdom.

58   *LETTER VII*

I am breathing an air tainted by the decay of dead bodies.
I am waiting to undergo myself the same lot that has befallen so
many others.

Lethe, rock fissure, dark water, warm
Breath of white mist on drifting scum, not moving
Unless a white shape moves from rock to rock.
Nostrils drink steam, the air has shapes, can be touched,
Assumes phantoms. Drink here, drink, the brackish taste
On the roof of the mouth, closed with a green coin.
I am ready to descend, to enter the cave's mouth,
To put on the mist's habit, boarding the frail
Craft that has come to claim me.
                              In 1938
The Lido at Lethe was opened to the public
And a poem by d'Annunzio was unveiled
Limned on a carefully ruined stele. Balbo
Offered full citizenship to all who filled in
The necessary forms. Electric cables
Illuminated the forgetful waters and
Two wrought-iron gates guarded oblivion.
Bertolo Giannoni at about this time
Managed to reach the grotto's far wall
And scratched his name in letters a metre high.

Perhaps by some irony he was one of those
Crushed by the tank-tracks of Keith Douglas's troop
On the way through to Agheila and Tripoli.
Bertolo survives on the wall, having drunk the waters.

The filth of pigeons, two fig trees' silver leaves,
Roots splayed from rock channels. Persephone in fossils.
He threw the switch and the sixty-watt bulbs flashed on
Too feebly to desecrate the pre-electric dark.
I walked on duck-boards over the breathing lake.
The mist came walking towards me.
                                        Death is a mystery
Not needing these adventitious theatricals.
In the ancient darkness the eirenic shades sleep,
Forgetting Lethe, rock fissure, dark water, warm breath.

59   *LETTER VIII*

A camel with the mange, says the proverb, can shoulder the burden
of many asses.

When they came to ask me to serve
We were sitting over a dish of olives, drinking
Wine from Messa, the kind that tastes of stone.
We had been talking of Constantinople, the embassy
I relished so little, so far away from home.
And then they arrived, with their wallets of documents,
Their letters and seals stowed carefully away,
Their talk of Theophilus and the weather, nervously
Waiting their chance to snare me into God's acre
Before my due time. *Divine conspiracy*,
Somebody might have called it; but *duty*
Was the burden of their discourse, that
And those filial bonds they well knew bound me
To this Pentapolis, this Libya.
                                        In this land

92

No evangelist angled for souls, no missionaries
Humped bibles along the trade routes. The sick
Children are treated by the Adventists,
The Orthodox are visited by one priest
Whose tinny bell pierces the muezzin's cry,
The quiet white nuns herd schoolgirls here and there,
And over the dust and potholes of the town
The double-breasted cathedral sits like a presence:
Mae West or Bardot, depending on your age.
The Anglicans have 'Newmarket'
Among the officers', and their ladies', horses:
The National Anthem, punkahs from Poona, words
Hallowed in Gloucestershire and Ulster, and
Hymns of the rousing sort by Wesley and Lyte.
In this whole land there is not one Christian
With a Libyan passport.
                                    So I reluctantly
Accepted what they offered: Bishop, with power
Over five crumbling cities, fortress-farms,
Immitigable desert. And they accepted
My wife ('better to marry than to burn'),
My doubts, my flinching from the sweat and blood
Of trinitarian dogma. Thus I stand,
Flawed but chosen, bewildered by that choice,
Uncertain of creed, fouled in a Marian web,
Deafened by Alexandrian echoes, armed
With episcopal power in a parish of termites.
                                    Look,
At Birsis, among the rotten byres, a vaulted
Church in ruins, where a man hoes red
Soil fed with Roman water. In the rubble
A fragment shows, in frayed Greek letters, words
To the Lord, and something else I cannot read.
The servants of the Lord. Alone, he hoes and sings,
Singing to himself. Perhaps to someone else.

Brought up outside the pale of the Church, and having received an
alien training, I grasped at the altars of God.

The Dalmatians have landed their advance party
And the billeting-officer is hard at work.
I can now administer the Mass in Serbo-Croat
But the congregation is thin. I carry Christ
Like a burden on my tongue. Andronicus –
From tunny fisher's perch to governor's chariot –
Is excommunicated, but runs giddy still.
My bow sprouts mould in the yard, I have given away
My dogs, my saddle.
                              Once there was philosophy
But how can that clear stream run when I spend my days
Adjudicating ruridecanal tiffs at Hydrax or Darnis,
Squabbles about copes or the laying on of hands?
Hypatia, remember the hush in the lecture-room
When you entered serenely with your astrolabe
And began to enunciate truths?
                              Tonight at five
A conversation-lesson with the Praetor, whose Greek
Would not fill a sardine. Yes, I am peevish.
You may say it is the climate or the place or my time of life –
But I carry a burden that was given to me
Which I do not understand. Somewhere, God's plan
Is hidden in monoliths or a wafer of bread.
His purpose obscurely works through those Slavs on the hill
As I offer his flesh and blood. Neither Gentile nor Jew
In that Kingdom. So I puzzle it out, till I hear
A knock at my study door. Come in, Praetor, come.

61 *LETTER X*

*And yet this is nothing but what the ancient oracle announced as to
how the Pentapolis must end.*

What the oracle said was vapour swathing the rock,
And we could discern a finger writing in steam
As on a tiled wall the obscene words
Doing death to life in hints and half-promises.
'Libya shall perish by the wickedness of its leaders.'
Unequivocal, you think, for the oracle?
The ambiguities are all ours –
Rumours of referendum, of abdication:
Denials of rumours, official circumlocutions:
Whispers in cafés, public demonstrations,
Restoration of order, and if necessary
The 2 a.m. visits, the executions.
I hear the same story twice, and pass on
A third version, atomized by now
To fragments with different names and places,
But still – substantially, you say – but still
The truth holds, and the whisperers hold to it.
The oracle grins like a toad, and belches fumes.

Battus stammered and lisped. Coming to ask for a voice,
He was bidden instead to build an empire. Oracle,
You are the echo of ignorance, though I believe you.
For 'abounding in fleeces' read 'running over with oil'.

Conspicuous waste, money's confederate,
Marks the economy's frontiers. Tin cans,
Bottles, bones, blood, uncollected
In a city without dustbins, demonstrate
How well we are doing.
                              The cities of the plain

95

Flourished as we do, but a belly-dancer
At the Riviera or the Berenice
Will hardly call God down with his dust and ashes.
Dust and ashes are what is native here,
Unprophesied and sempiternal. Doom
Carries a drilling-rig in a Landrover,
A geologist from Yale, and a cloud of rumour
Stinking along the salt-pans whose flamingoes
Have flown away, over whose white plateaux
The ghibli blows from the south, bringing dust to the tongue.

Andronicus, imperialist British, wily
Egyptian agitator, Zionist, Polish agent
Disguised as an engineer – you have handed over
This traduced Kingdom. Equipped for Armageddon,
The alien cavalry rides off, but in the squares
Public loudspeakers broadcast messages
Of peace, stability, spontaneous joy,
Showing how once again etcetera
And how etcetera the future is
If only we hold firm. Etcetera.

The tomb of Battus, long located here,
In fact is there. No matter. He is dead.
The archaeologists can shift him as they please.
Fires, watchtowers, fires. The oracle, asleep,
Snores in her ancient dreams, and round her head
The angels, mingling with the harpies, weep.

War and famine have not yet annihilated it completely, as was foredoomed; but they are wearing it away and destroying it little by little.

Holes in the earth, places of snakes and fleas:
We shall creep in on our bellies, we shall find refuge
Among the ignorant, the outcast, those who merit
No conquest, being too low already.
There, I suppose, we shall die.
                              This 'resurrection'
I take as allegory, for when we die,
There, in a hole like a brood of field-mice, can you
Imagine our suffocated, wasted bodies
Assuming, in some flash of lightning, wings
To make us rise, harps to be struck for joy,
And crowns to inherit the Kingdom? The Kingdom is here.

Or here, where the woman near Sirte smiles,
Smiling with stained teeth, hands red with henna,
Holding a child whose nose is running and whose ears
Are pierced for ear-rings big as saucers.
So she smiles, accustomed, poor, expecting no change.

Long before dawn the cocks are crowing here:
Their catalogue of betrayal fills the night.
At six the sky is a dome of brilliant blue,
Only at the edges furred with a grey mist
Presaging another day of burning. Who will burn?
We are not martyrs yet, and if we are
We shall not burn but be trapped in our fastnesses,
Beyond the episcopal court, the Rood, the Grail.

Hesychius, I have seen your house, its dutiful mosaics
(Where you recorded your family and our God)
Erupting like waves from centuries of rain,
Seismic disturbance, tumult of war and anthill.
The long attrition begins, the mills of God
Grind us to dust the ghibli blusters north
Into the sea where no fleet aims to fan
With Dorian sails our northward passage home.
The woman near Sirte smiles, who is to come
After barbarians, pillage, drought; and we
Are dust in the holes of the earth and under the sea.

63 *LETTER XII*

*I am a minister of God, and perchance I must complete my service by
offering up my life. God will not in any case overlook the altar,
bloodless, though stained by the blood of a priest.*

I have reached the end. I shall write to you no more.
Dies irae is come. See the hole in heaven
The tribesmen of Cyrene showed to Battus.
I cling to the church's pillars. These are the Kingdom's last days.
Here are the stoups of holy water, here
The table of sacrifice. The victim is also here.

Set sail for Jedda or Jerusalem,
The miracles are due. Here is a splinter
They say is from the Rood, and here a flag
That has snuffed the air of Mecca. I leave myself
As an unholy relic, to be the dust
Neglected by the seller of souvenirs
Among his lamps, his bronzes, his rubbed coins.
Here by the shore God's altar is made whole,
Unvisited by celebrants, to be restored
By the Department of Antiquities.

Functional concrete (ruddled, grey, and brash)
Marks out what's lacking: marble, granite, wood,
The divine interstices.
                              I abdicate
Having survived locust, earthquake, death
Of children, failure of crops, murrain of hopes,
And am become that ambassador in bonds
Paul spoke of.
                    Now the muezzin calls his first
Exhortation, and the pillars fall.
Darkness is on the Jebel, tongues of flame
Bring ruin, not revelation. See how they lick
The rod of Aaron, Zelten's oily fires
Flaring against the night. The visions come.
The pilgrims have boarded, the pagans are at my throat.
The blood of a Greek is spilt for the blood of a Jew.
Altars are stained, a lamb is dragged by its legs
To bleed at the door of the house.
                                        Libya,
Image of desolation, the sun's province,
Compound of dust and wind, unmapped acres –
This is the place where Africa begins,
And thus the unknown, vaguer than my conjectures
Of transubstantiation, Trinity,
All those arcana for which, now, I die.

from *Inscriptions* (1973)

I have hidden something in the inner chamber
And sealed the lid of the sarcophagus
And levered a granite boulder against the door
And the debris has covered it so perfectly
That though you walk over it daily you never suspect.

Every day you sweat down that shaft, seeing on the walls
The paintings that convince you I am at home, living there.
But that is a blind alley, a false entrance
Flanked by a room with a few bits of junk
Nicely displayed, conventionally chosen.
The throne is quaint but commonplace, the jewels inferior,
The decorated panels not of the best period,
Though enough is there to satisfy curators.

But the inner chamber enshrines the true essence.
Do not be disappointed when I tell you
You will never find it: the authentic phoenix in gold,
The muslin soaked in herbs from recipes
No one remembers, the intricate ornaments,
And above all the copious literatures inscribed
On ivory and papyrus, the distilled wisdom
Of priests, physicians, poets and gods,
Ensuring my immortality. Though even if you found them
You would look in vain for the key, since all are in cipher
And the key is in my skull.

The key is in my skull. If you found your way
Into this chamber, you would find this last:
My skull. But first you would have to search the others,
My kinsfolk neatly parcelled, twenty-seven of them
Disintegrating in their various ways.
A woman from whose face the spices have pushed away
The delicate flaking skin: a man whose body
Seems dipped in clotted black tar, his head detached:

A hand broken through the cerements, protesting:
Mouths in rigid grins or soundless screams –
A catalogue of declensions.

How, then, do I survive? Gagged in my winding cloths,
The four brown roses withered on my chest
Leaving a purple stain, how am I different
In transcending these little circumstances?
Supposing that with uncustomary skill
You penetrated the chamber, granite, seals,
Dragged out the treasure gloatingly, distinguished
My twenty-seven sorry relatives,
Labelled them, swept and measured everything
Except this one sarcophagus, leaving that
Until the very end: supposing then
You lifted me out carefully under the arc-lamps,
Noting the gold fingernails, the unearthly smell
Of preservation – would you not tremble
At the thought of who this might be? So you would steady
Your hands a moment, like a man taking aim, and lift
The mask.
              But this hypothesis is absurd. I have told you already
You will never find it. Daily you walk about
Over the rubble, peer down the long shaft
That leads nowhere, make your notations, add
Another appendix to your laborious work.
When you die, decently cremated, made proper
By the Registrar of Births and Deaths, given by *The Times*
Your six-inch obituary, I shall perhaps
Have a chance to talk with you. Until then, I hear
Your footsteps over my head as I lie and think
Of what I have hidden here, perfect and safe.

To reconstruct an afternoon in an antique time
Out of a broken dish, some oyster shells
And an ashy discolouration of the otherwise ochreous soil –
This is an occupation for philosophers
With more than a taste for language-problems.
It has no value beyond itself. Not even
The scrupulous cataloguing of shape, disposition, provenance
Will alleviate the strong smell of futility rising
Like a cloud of midges: the site-notebook
Is, like what it records, a disjected and maybe random
Commentary without conclusions.
                              In a trial trench
On the excavation's southernmost flank, some young sprig
Teases a knucklebone out of a beautifully vertical
Wall, marks its cavity with a meat-skewer,
Ties to it something very like a miniature luggage-label
And drops it into a tray. Visitors observe
This performance with the set faces of persons determined
Not to be taken in; and in a sense
Their stance is a true one. Why, indeed,
Do I peer attentively at holes in roads
Or fossick about in the earth's disturbances
Or the mud of the foreshore? Imagining
Some lost groat or cup-handle will tell me
More about life than I know already,
Or simply a souvenir of luck and persistence?
I have stopped asking myself, accepting such furtive burrowings
As native to me, as mild and dim
As other people's secret traffickings.

No value, then, in these subterranean doings,
No moral to point, for once. Except I have
Some cold thought hovering here, which recognizes
The damp earthfall, the broken dish, the bone
Labelled and dropped in a tray and made to fit
In a pattern I have not guessed at yet, and may never,
But go on living with and through, no doubt.

66 *At Souillac*

Down the congested air, toothed beak and wing
Tear at each clinging couple stitched in stone:
Twisted within the whirlpool all go down
Where hooks and talons, fangs and pincers cling
Till the condemned are smothered, and they drown.

Outside, the air is warm, the light is clear,
The postcards concentrate on happier stuff
(A close-up of Isaiah is enough),
And nobody has anything to fear.
But something clings and will not let me off.

An allegory even saints condemn –
Ridiculous beasts and monsters, caricatures
Of evil doodled in the boring hours
When stonedust choked the throats of thirsty men –
Through that stone tunnel a dark torrent pours.

It breeds among the shadows, out of sight,
A chain of interlocking actions which,
As stone plaits over stone, and stitch with stitch,
Have nothing more to do with warmth and light
Than a crowned virgin stained as black as pitch.

Under the one step up into the hut
A toad broods by the sergeant's shabby boots.
A single light bulb, acid and unshaded,
Marks out, inside, a function of the state
As well as marking where one road has ended.

Slogans ('To be on guard is half the battle')
Assure the walls if not the occupants.
Only behind a door do I catch glimpses
Of cruder appetites: a brown thigh, supple
With bourgeois blandishments, coyly entices.

Ripped from some old *Paris Match* or *Playboy*,
This functionary's unofficial decor
Cheers me a little as I sit and wait
While name and date of birth and date of entry
Are slowly copied to a dossier sheet.

Outside, between the frontier posts, the hills
Are black, unpeopled. Hours of restlessness
Seep from the silence, silt across the road.
At last the sergeant puts away his files,
Hands me my papers. And I see the toad

Hop into darkness, neutral and unstopped,
Companion of the brown-thighed cover girl
Hidden behind the door, beyond the frontier,
Where appetite and nature are adept
At moving quietly, or at staying still.

68   Dead Wood

Worn down to stumps, shredded by the wind,
Crushed underfoot in brittle slaty husks,
The forest turned from wood to stone to dust.

The rind of bark peeled off in slivers, shed
Dry spores, mineral resins, scales of scrim,
Scattering huge-leaved branches under the sun.

These giants shrank to pygmies in the glare.
Basilisks flashed their petrifying eyes.
The whole plateau rattled with bones of trees.

Now oil-men bring the few gnarled timbers back
As souvenirs. A lopped stone branch lies there
To hold up books, or prop open a door.

69   At the Italian Cemetery, Benghazi

Meglio un giorno da leone che cent'anni da pecora.

MUSSOLINI

The old rhetoric inflated beyond rigour,
The Roman virtues in a cloud of sand
Blown to a mirage, detonate and roar
Like the lion, extinct since Balbo pressed the trigger
In 1936, far in the south. Here
A place of cypresses, a little Italy
Grazed by the desert wind, an enclave
For the dead, for a dead colony.
Among them all, not one unpolluted grave.
Mare Nostrum is someone else's sea.

The Mediterranean was to be a lake
Round which the imperium flourished. There came

Boatloads of dialects, music, priests,
A whole army: bushels of grain,
Cattle, tractors: archaeologists to make
The past justify the present. *Hang thirty a day
And resistance will stop. Subdue and civilize.*
The sun has flaked the neat stucco away.
Sepia fades from Cesare's, from Fabbro's eyes.
The sheep are slaughtered, the lion would not stay.

White villages were built, made ready, named
Heroically or nostalgically:
D'Annunzio, Savoia, Maddalena.
Rebels were strangled, nomads gaoled and tamed.
Dutiful bells rang across jebel and plain,
Ave Marias drowning the muezzin's cry.
Calabria, Naples, Sicily put out
Frail shoots into the hot breath of the ghibli.
Duce, Duce, the parched gullets shout,
Then the bombs fall, the echoes drift and die.

Vulgar memorials, stricken and deluded:
Marble sarcophagi, vain crucifix.
Walking here, why am I now reminded
Puzzlingly of what some cynic said:
Life is a preparation
For something that never happens? The Italian dead
Are gathered under their alien cypresses,
The path gives off its dusty exhalation,
The broken arm of an angel lifts and blesses
The lion-crazed, the shepherdless, one by one.

Down the mud road, between tall bending trees,
Men thickly move, then fan out one by one
Into the foreground. Far left, a soldier tries
Bashing a tame duck's head in with a stick,
While on a log his smeared companion
Sits idly by a heap of casual loot –
Jugs splashing over, snatched-up joints of meat.

Dead centre, a third man has spiked a fourth –
An evident civilian, with one boot
Half off, in flight, face white, lungs short of breath.
Out of a barn another soldier comes,
Gun at the ready, finding at his feet
One more old yokel, gone half mad with fear,
Tripped in his path, wild legs up in the air.

Roofs smashed, smoke rising, distant glow of fire,
A woman's thighs splayed open after rape
And lying there still: charred flecks caught in the air,
And caught for ever by a man from Antwerp
Whose style was 'crudely narrative', though 'robust',
According to this scholar, who never knew
What Pieter Snayers saw in 1632.

71   *Worm Within*

A souvenir from Sicily on the shelf:
A wooden doll carved out of some dark wood,
And crudely carved, for tourists. There it stood
Among the other stuff. Until one night,
Quietly reading to myself, I heard
It speak, or creak – a thin, persistent scratch,
Like the first scrape of a reluctant match,
Or unarticulated word
That made me look for it within myself

As if I talked to myself. But there it was,
Scratching and ticking, an erratic clock
Without a face, something as lifeless as rock
Until its own announcement that it shared
Our life with us. A woodworm, deep inside,
Drilled with its soft mouth through the pitch-stained wood
And like the owl presaging death of good,
Its beak closing as the dynasty died,
It held fear in those infinitesimal jaws.

So – to be practical – we must choose two ways:
Either to have some expert treat the thing
(Trivial, absurd, embarrassing)
Or throw it out, before the infection eats
The doors and floors away: this Trojan horse
In miniature could bring the whole house down,
I think to myself wildly, or a whole town . . .
Why do we do nothing, then, but let its course
Run, ticking, ticking, through our nights and days?

Day by day, day after day, we fed it
With straw, mown grass, shavings, shaken weeds,
The huge flat leaves of umbrella plants, old spoil
Left by the builders, combustible; yet it
Coughed fitfully at the touch of a match,
Flared briefly, spat flame through a few dry seeds
Like a chain of fireworks, then slumped back to the soil
Smouldering and smoky, leaving us to watch

Only a heavy grey mantle without fire.
This glum construction seemed choked at heart,
The coils of newspaper burrowed into its hulk
Led our small flames into the middle of nowhere,
Never touching its centre, sodden with rot.
Ritual petrol sprinklings wouldn't make it start
But swerved and vanished over its squat brown bulk,
Still heavily sullen, grimly determined not

To do away with itself. A whiff of smoke
Hung over it as over a volcano.
Until one night, late, when we heard outside
A crackling roar, and saw the far field look
Like a Gehenna claiming its due dead.
The beacon beckoned, fierily aglow
With days of waiting, hiding deep inside
Its bided time, ravenous to be fed.

Green bulwark of the chestnut heaves in air
Towards this window, cleaves and tosses spray
From leaf to leaf, its branched and clustered prow
Heavy under the clouds' insistent flow.
Its toppling weight flings higher than the house,
Falling and rising massively to where
A jet goes blundering, roaring on its way
Across a sky obscured with thickened boughs.

Rooted and restless, watching behind glass
Such fierce contenders harmlessly perform
Their rapt compulsions, now I turn away
And face books, papers, furniture, my day
Belittled by the sight, as if my own
Making was measured thus and could not pass
Tests so devised, or cast in such a form.
Each branch is shaken, every leaf is blown.

And so I look again, and find it now
As still and two-dimensional as some
Backcloth from *Hagoromo*, a green tree
In front of which masked men and spirits see
The pattern of their future, unperturbed
And not to be evaded. On one bough
A thrush has settled. Its clear measures come
Across clear lengths of distance, undisturbed.

And they will fall – bird, chestnut, house and all –
As surely as the rain, more quietly
Than the plane's swelling and withdrawing scream,
And gradually, like falling in a dream
Through boughs and clouds that scatter as we float
Downwards on air that holds us as we fall
Towards a landing place we never see,
Bare, treeless, soundless, cloudlessly remote.

74   *Entry*

Died, 1778; *Moses Ozier, son of a woman out of her mind,*
born in the ozier ground belonging to Mr Craft.

Christened with scripture, eponymously labelled,
You lie so small and shrunken in the verger's tall
Archaic writing. Born in the low water meadows
Down the end of lawns where you would be unlikely to walk
Supposing you'd ever got that far in life, no Pharaoh's daughter
Plucked you out of the bulrushes, for this was Yorkshire
And prophets had stopped being born. Your lunatic mother
Knelt in the rushes and squirmed in her brute pain,
Delivering you up to a damp punishing world
Where the ducks were better off, and the oziers wetly rustled
Sogged down in the marshland owned by Mr Craft.

It's sense to suppose you lasted a few days
And were buried, gratis, in an unmarked hole at the edge
Of the churchyard, the verger being scrupulous
And not wanting your skinny christened bundle of bones
To lie in unhallowed ground.

              Poor tiny Moses,
Your white face is a blank, anonymous
Like other people's babies. Almost two hundred years
Since you briefly lay by the cold and placid river,
And nothing but nineteen words as memorial.

I hear you cry in the night at the garden's dark edge.

75   *At Dunkeswell Abbey*

Below the ford, the stream in flood
Rises and laps the leaf-choked wood
And fallen branches trap thick mud.
Pebbles are swept like slingstones down
Runnels and channels sliced through stone
And in the hollows sink and drown.

On either side broad ramparts hold
The water back from copse and field,
Where a dry earthbank seems to fold
Protectively a hollow space
Of pasture edged with stunted trees
In its inert and curved embrace.

Six hundred years ago, great pike
Grown old in this man-fashioned lake
Swam through its lily clusters like
Dream-presences below the mind.
Dark waters stirred where now I stand
Hearing the distant stream unwind.

The stillness here was made to last.
Whatever shapes survive exist
In some faint diagram of the past,
A sketch-map tentative as those
Robbed walls whose simulacrum lies
In patches summer droughts expose.

One wall still overtops the trees
Beyond the ford, but bramble grows
Round rotten stone. What energies
Persist are harnessed to the stream,
Violent in flood, not curbed or tame,
And hurtling without plan or aim.

76   *Reformation*

The hazed meadows of England grow over chancels
Where cattle hooves kick up heraldic tiles
And molehills heap their spoils above slumped walls.
The cruck-beamed roofs of refectories nestle under
Sheds and barns, hay piled high where
Augustine and Aquinas chapter by chapter
Were read in these now lapsed pastoral acres.

Small streams wash the smashed crockery of Cistercians.
Stone-plaited carvings are wedged in gable ends
Of farmhouses, springs irrigate robbed chapels
Where all is marsh, reeds meshed among cracked altars.
A buzzard shrieks *yaa–i* in a tall tree.
Plainchant echoing along the valleys.
High hedges stand above spoiled finials.

And Sunday mornings see small meeting houses,
Reformed parishes and tabernacles,
Bethesdas and the whole wide countryside,
All split seven ways in sect and congregation,
Assembling to praise God from whom all blessings
Flow through his derelict priories, abbeys, cells
The afternoon sun will show, faint shadows among fields.

77   *Sea*

This sea has been going a long time,
Sluicing out gullies, chafing rocks,
Grinding boulders to pebbles, and scouring pebbles
Till the hard white veins stand out.

                                        It lifts its wet tons
Heavily from the low fathoms, it makes nonsense
Of timbers and lobster-pots, it polishes bottles
To frivolous bits of glitter, goes eating on
Through cliffs and headlands, thudding its steady fist
Into igneous layers gone cold after eruptions,
And the litter of low coasts is like confetti to it.

Tides don't tame it, the moon knows that,
Pulling and pushing with a slow, drugged rhythm:
They can't stop those pools and pockets swarming with its fry
When the great thing itself is almost out of sight
Flicking and flickering on the horizon –
It's coming back, it's gathering its windy breath
To stride back up its beaches, to knock again
Heavily hammering at its lost sea-bed
Now calling itself America or Europe,
Names to be carried awhile, till they tumble back
Into the boiling mess that started it all,
Hot seas without vessels, coasts, rocks, fish,
Unmapped, ungovernable, without tidy names.

78 *Elsewhere*

Elsewhere, the autumn wood fills with red leaves
Silently. Worm-casts spill across meadows.
Grass withers. The sun moves west, assigning cold.

Elsewhere, a magpie clacks into the trees.
A kestrel treads on air. The path is thick
With turfed-out snail-shells, and against a gate

A squirrel hangs as hostage. Elsewhere, too,
Smoke drifts across valleys, blossoms above towns
Invested by artillery. Along highways

117

Drivers hurry to suburbs where lawns lie
Heavy under rain, unmown. Elsewhere children
Are rawly born. And the moon inclines its light

On domes, torn posters, curfew guards. Elsewhere,
You sit on a bed while across the corridor
A scream spirals and jerks, again, again,

Then spins down fast and settles into sobs.

And no elsewhere is here, within your head
Where nothing else is born, or grows, or dies.
Nothing is like this, where the world turns in

And shapes its own alarms, noises, signs,
Its small aggressions and its longer wars,
Its withering, its death. Outside, begins

Whatever shape I choose to give it all
(Clouds ribbed with light, signals I recognize)
But you sit silent, narrowly, in a world

So light I feel it brush my cheek, and fall.

79   *Dead Metaphors*

A child refusing to be born, carried so long
It smothers the heart, dying as the mother dies.
A scar speaking in cold weather of the flesh it was.
A purlieu of levelled bricks where a house once stood.
A hand reaching out in the dark and closing on nothing.
A stain washed faint, neither wine nor blood.

And it is not a child, because we never met,
Nor is it a scar, because no wound was there,
Nor is it waste ground, because in the empty air
No house was ever built, and our hands were closed like fists
Keeping what we had, and whatever we spilt
Gathers like dry stuff a vague girl dusts.

80 *Switzerland*

In a valley in Switzerland a brass band marches.
The dapper chalets twinkle in the sun
Among the meadows and the well-drilled larches
And watercourses where streams briskly run.

Bravely the little drums pretend their thunder
To far-off crags whose melting snow brings down
A rattle of small pebbles buried under
Drifts deeper than the church spire in the town.

The soldier-citizens of the canton practise
Before an audience of sheep and cows.
As for the real thing, the simple fact is
Each keeps a well-oiled rifle in his house.

Duchies and principalities have fathered
These drums and cornets under angrier skies,
Bucolic bellicosities which gathered
The Ruritanian airs of paradise

Into a clockwork joke envious Europe
Could laugh at, play in, patronize, ignore,
As, poised between the saddle and the stirrup,
The Switzer was acknowledged as a bore.

The peaceable kingdom rests on marks and dollars
Beside the lake at Zurich, lined with banks,
Far from the towns draped with insurgent colours
Whose dawn breaks with the grinding tread of tanks.

The Alpine avalanche holds back this summer
Its fragile tons, and watches from the height
The nimble piper and the strutting drummer
Putting the valley's herbivores to flight.

81   *Now*

So many of them, and so many still to come:
They crowd the pavements, pour from the discreet chimneys
Of crematoria, advance with arms linked
Down avenues, protesting or celebrating,
Are spaded under sand and rock and clay,
And still come young and bloodily among us.
It will go on, nothing can stop it happening.

Given that first great sunburst, and the mindless time
Moving towards cell and union, coelacanth and midge,
What could prevent sparse tribes of hominids
Drifting like winged seeds over the land-masses
And ending up here, on the second floor
Of a house facing south, one Sunday in October,
Caught in the middle years and counting syllables?

82   *Generation Gap*

Outside, on the dark campus lawns,
An apoplectic howling goes
On and on, while inside dons
Sit glumly listening to the news
In nordic-brutalist maisonettes.

Outside, the grammar-school head boy
Now on a trip to God-knows-where
Shrieks for ten demons to destroy
The demons tearing his fuzzed hair.
The nuclear family goes to bed.

And quiet at last, as midnight comes,
The lowland mists creep through the grass
Towards the functional dark rooms
And leave a cloud upon the glass
That lasts till daylight, and beyond.

83 *Inscriptions*

Knickers Fisher has been at work again,
Using a compass point on the closet door,
But he's a miniaturist whose main concern
Is altogether different from the team
Exhibiting on the wall by the railway line:
SMASH THE STATE stands six feet high or more
In strong black paint where the track crosses the stream –
Opposites in the field of graphic design.

And in the middle scale are the stone slabs
Pecked out by masons dead these hundred years,
Gravestones along the passage to the town:
They make their claims too, with a different voice,
But still in hope and expectation. They
Exhort and yearn and stiffly mask the fears
Of men with large obsessions and small choice,
Burdened with flesh and law till judgement day.

Snow in January
Looking for ledges
To hide in unmelted.

February evening:
A cold puddle of petrol
Makes its own rainbow.

Wind in March:
No leaves left
For its stiff summons.

April sunlight:
Even the livid bricks
Muted a little.

Wasp in May
Storing his venom
For a long summer.

Morning in June:
On the sea's horizon
A white island, alone.

July evening:
Sour reek of beer
Warm by the river.

August morning:
A squirrel leaps and
Only one branch moves.

September chestnuts:
Falling too early,
Split white before birth.

October garden:
At the top of the tree
A thrush stabs an apple.

November morning:
A whiff of cordite
Caught in the leaf mould.

Sun in December:
In his box of straw
The tortoise wakes.

85　Points

This is the arrow which I, a warrior, shot,
Lifting up the bow-end:
Let it remind those who find it
To talk of me for ever.

KASA KANAMURA (fl. AD 715–33)

I

At the Yoshino Palace, in the fifth month,
Kasa Kanamura, laureate of Nara,
Anthology compiler, brocaded and pale,
Lifted the supple bow, drew breath,
Drew back the bowstring with the bamboo arrow
And smoothly let flow forth the tip of bright metal.

It lay where it fell, away from the target,
And lay as he left it.

He, struck (like no target)

With the thought of it lying
Where it had fallen
To stay there . . . And so
'I, a warrior' flowed smooth from his brush
On the scroll before him, as he fingered the syllables
And spoke without breath
And walked to his grave,
Who had seen the quick torrents
Shouldering the mountains
And the tumbling cascades
Race by the palace
(Stout-timbered, stone-walled) and
'In dread of their majesty'
Had sunk in his mind
To the rock-bed below,
And had stood, his mind floating
Like Mitsune after him . . .
Arrow, bright arrow
Fallen, there.

II

Fluted like this one, no longer than the first joint
Of my little finger, the bright bronze burnished
Under the weathers of twelve hundred years:
And not among grave goods, with cuirass and bracelet
Or gilded helmet or suppliant vessels,
But lodged in the thick grass of a humid summer
To lie under plaited leaves, under welts of mud,
Pressed down, trodden under, lost where it landed
In a curve out of air from bow, gut, pressure
Of fingers against arc of muscle, of air . . .

III

Today is the anniversary
Of Gamae, Nasamonian, one who ate locusts
And slept in the tombs of his ancestors
So as to dream prophecies:
Today such a man died
Somewhere in the desert north of the Psylli
Who were buried as they marched
To vanquish the South Wind.

And today, too, the anniversary
Of Arx, miner of obsidian,
Who lugged the black nuggets from a cliff on Lipari
To be fashioned by other men: and of Oyu,
Carver of bone amulets in Hokkaido:
Of Tacan, acolyte, of Chichen Itza – all
Inventions, you take it rightly, type-names of the nameless
Whose artefacts are numbered, labelled, filed
In corridors, in dustless libraries,
Mapped by distribution, plotted by computer,
Under whose alluvial tonnage the nostrils drew in air
And suffocated at the mortal touch.

Humbled among trophies, mementoes not only of death.

IV

At Karnak the lintels
At Thebes the pediments
At Antioch the walls
At Nineveh the pavements
At Konarak the platforms
At Sidon the bollards
At Troy the columns
At Angkor the terraces . . .
Yoshino fallen, the thousand ages
Drawn to the point of the tip of an arrow.

V

And at Augila the dates
The salt hills gushing water
And the crying of women
And Ghirza buried:
Acreage of stones
Above wells of water
And a flake of volcano
Flashing black fire,
Worked with the thumb
Shaped into sharpness
The tooth of the serpent
Hardened to stone
The flail of the scorpion
Petrified, polished

The armature perished
The poison crushed
To crystals of dust.

In the palm of my left hand
Among the unread lines
The arrowhead lies cupped:
Its point, still sharp, defines
Its purpose, its abrupt
Quiddity. To end
Function is not to kill,
Nor lack of it to die.
The thousand ages cram
Survival's narrow way
With fragments. What I am
Emerges from the rubble.

VII

A topography of debris – clay, stone, bronze –
Dry hills of Mamelukes, Ghadames slagheaps,
The tells of Troy, the tip of Aberfan,
The mounds and spills at boundaries, beyond limits,
Smoking like Golgotha
                    as the ash descends
Sealing the thrown waste, the scoured junk,
Burying the scourings, embalming the long lost.
                        No sudden blast of cobalt
In the revelations of August, the fleshprint
                        shadowed on stone
As ghost presence, instant eidolon, but
A longer dying, a protracted chapter
Of accidents and discarded product:
The slaughter of utensils, the annihilation of weapons,
Carcases of tools, scattering of stones,
Lifted into the air by the grovelling shovel, and held
Here in the obsolete point that missed the target to
'Remind those who find it
                  to talk of me forever.'

VIII

And so it does,
Though not as you meant it,
Not knowing beyond Nara
The islands and mountains
Or seeing forever
Stretch to this point. Yet
Your poem contains
Its own assurance,
A blind inheritance
We share, in going on
Because we must,
Surviving destruction,
Valuing the dust.

New Confessions (1974)

'How do they know, when they hear from myself of myself, whether what I say is true?'
AUGUSTINE

Prefatory Note

For some years I have been fascinated and puzzled by the figure of St Augustine of Hippo (AD 354–430). I was led to him partly by my reading of Synesius of Cyrene – that other, lesser father of the church, a Greek African rather than a Roman African, whom I commemorated in my 'Letters of Synesius'. Towards the end of 1971, I began to see the faint outlines of the present book: an inner commentary on Augustine's words – from the *Confessions, The City of God*, the sermons, and elsewhere, partly in verse, partly in prose, which would be written in the margin, as it were, of Augustine's writings, but which would also be a personal book of meditation and transmutation. The brief notes at the end are chiefly pointers to sources.

I

It begins.
In the beginning.

Between the splayed thighs, excretion of blood and mucus, the miracle
is performed. It is an aggrandisement, a conquering, and the passion is
enacted, the victim punished. I am the triumphant blind bully of the
bloody dunghill. Wreathed in my scarlet sin, badged with my grisly
robes, I come among you, greet you with a cry.

II

Vast cloisters.
Redolent curtained rooms.
Sponge gravid with vinegar.
Creases and folds in the brain's wet linen.
Serpent biting its tail, baked to stone, become ammonite.

Thagaste, where among mountains a crossroads establishes a grid
among drifts of sand: where nothing happened that I can remember
happening. Or rather I became everything that happened to me,
without remembering.

There is a row of red brick houses. A cello is being played by someone
I call aunt, but who is not. I fall over, bruise my nose, smell vomit. Or
that may have been later. Look, here is a picture of the house, the
garden, the girl who helped my mother. I am there. I am no taller than
the weeds and flowers I have indiscriminately plucked from that narrow
garden. I was punished, I think, for that uprooting, but cannot remem-
ber how. I was uprooted, but that was not a punishment.

That one is long dead, but I am alive.

We skulked in a corner of the playground, near a manhole cover as
broad and round and solid as a shield. Below it, we pretended villainies.

I followed at the heels of Big David, who was seven. The path by the playground was made of loose chippings of green conglomerate, imagined gems. There was privet, and a room full of shoes. The tram that carried me home had glass steps. Waiting for the tram, I had my cap snatched off by a girl and thrown in the road. On Saturdays, I avoided walking by the house opposite our house. Jews lived there. They would force you to cook their dinner for them, my friend told me. I was chosen to present flowers to the headmistress on Speech Day. I wanted to excel, to be noticed. There was an order in these things, but I cannot see it now. Where do I belong? I was sometimes afraid, and sometimes am afraid now, and always with good reason. Or so I persuade myself.

III

Under the long brown crag running eastward,
Where the track comes down to olives, cattle, corn,
And the farms are husbanded and the families keep
Company with themselves, and peace is cultivated –
There is my place: or here, in a greener country
Where heaped fields stretch to the horizon
And the wind lifts the heads of the trees
And tosses them like horses, where hedges
Throb and rustle with pheasant, partridge, hare,
An ordered beneficence. But, here or there,
My spirit has no husbandry, no order,
Runs all ways raggedly, stumbles in sand,
Wades through tall lashing weeds, is lost in dunes.

The burden is in me, the heavy child of sin
Weighing my body to an ape's dull stoop,
Thickening the tongue, furring the eyes,
Falling down to the dust with the serpent's uncrushed head
And lying there unraised.

IV

Rationes seminales: they allow for the mutable within the immutable, so that we change and the world changes, yet all is the same.

But of course I would put it differently. I understand nothing of the physical laws: they perform their own operations without my understanding, and will go on doing so whether I understand them or not. In the same way, I feed on my memories without knowing what they are, without even knowing I do so. I dream, and interpret my dreams, and go on dreaming.

V

Pure is water, and a balm to many.
Pure is the sea: its salt heals many wounds.
Pure is the lamb that sucks its mother's teats,
White as mercy, whiter than mother's milk.
Pure is the steep mountain: in its air is found salvation,
And high on the mountain the tablets of God's word.
Pure is the black midnight of sleep without dreams . . .

VI

For dreams are memories and anticipations
Nourished on memories. The tempter slips
Into your bed and promises sensations
Half-known till now. Total the dark eclipse
Of the all-seeing and all-brightening sun.

When her thick stifling tapestry is spun
Your body is cocooned in its own dark,
Forbidding entry to all light but one
Struck smouldering from a quick and urgent spark,
An atom hot with elemental power.

It is the waking moment at an hour
When nothing fills the room but bloodless shades.
The watchman calls remotely from his tower
As day piles up and spreads, and light invades
Your dreams and memories and anticipations.

VII

The transient shadowplay
Neither sent from heaven
Each makes his own
Lies heavily in sleep
Floats without effort
The day's performances.

Who has put to the torch
    citadels
Infantry in retreat,
The lawyer in his version
The miser, having buried riches,
The huntsman with his hounds
The sailor dreams of drowning,
The girl scribbles a note
Sends her a present. The dog
Follows the tracks of the hare . . .

Secret desires, ambitions,

mocking the mind,
nor flying out from temples:
when on the bed the body
and the untethered mind
enacting in the darkness

The conqueror of cities

sees flying javelins,
kings slaughtered, bloody.
sees the court, the high bench.
finds the gold dug, vanished.
harries the thick forest.
claws at the tilted prow.
to her lover, who furtively
twitching and barking in frenzy

All our remorse, misery,
follow us into the night.

VIII

Old reprobate, you described it all, but made no judgements. How could
you, in your profound darkness? Where do they come from, then, these
night-mists, these damp exhalations? And what do they tell us? Or fore-
tell? My whole upbringing would have me acknowledge them as serious
messages from beyond this world, only arcane because we lack the

means to measure and assess them. Yet would God speak to us in such a primitive way? Does he seek to degrade us with lewd fancies, and then lead us by a thread of hypothetical interpretations, strung together like cheap beads on a necklace, to know him through these baubles? It cannot be. Yet they burden me with their beseechings . . .

IX

I suppose he would have seen things like that. But what was he really dreaming at fifteen? Anticipations of warm mouths and secret hot places, touched and enjoyed? In some corner of Madaura, away from school, now frayed hewn rock collapsed in tawny sand, he saw a donkey fucking a girl: something like that. A crowd was watching, intent and giggling. He saw it later in a dream. But this time the donkey was himself, young Punic stallion staggering and thrusting. The girl was the same.

Lord, make me chaste.

X

But not yet . . .
There is still time
And the opportunities offering themselves
(For where is the initiative, who is the predator
In this excessive hunt?). Secretly I number them,
Catalogue inwardly their special favours,
Relish again and again their tender memories,
Or recollections that have no tenderness in them
But only fierce ardour and exultation.

XI

The adept tongue that trembles on the body,
Delicious in its searchings, moist with fire,
Accepts the flesh's wafer and the juice
Sucked from the swollen membrane of the grape.
There are ways of ecstasy, and ways, and ways
Among dark harbour streets, nocturnal, secret,
Where stalls are lit by flares and in the glow
Young faces shine with promises, a sweat
Of expectation, longing, guilty, poised
Above a drop that plunges to the sea
Where Carthage boils, from frying pan to fire . . .
I am stunned like an eel in a skillet with pure desire.

XII

A promising boy, though weak in mathematics. He has imagination and
a feeling for words. An able speaker. His efforts at Greek are sporadic,
but with application he can show up perfectly good work. His hand-
writing needs attention. Altogether he should give a good account of
himself at university.

. . . It is this that leads me to stay awake in the night's silence,
studying how by choosing the correct words and exercising the art of
the poet I can display to your mind a clear light, by means of which
you can gaze into the heart of things hidden.

XIII

I have spent too long peeling and paring the skin,
Being skilful and busy with words –
The discrimination of words, the play of rhetoric,
The persuaders smoothing the way for quick profits,
The inscriptions, descriptions, repetitions

(Those on stone built into structures
That will last longer than the uttering tongue).
I admire the articulate, am indeed scornful
Of the barbarous mouthings of students determined to show
How far they are from the poised epithets of their fathers:
But now I look for a commerce beyond sermons,
Without texts or precepts or etymologies,
In some garden where theologies are mute
And the explanation is in the ripe fruit.

XIV

How many hours wasted at windows, looking out on changing trees, drifting clouds, a boy and a girl with their arms round one another? Restless, yet still: touching books, papers, ornaments: drumming fingers on the table, like an actor pretending impatience in a play. *Our heart is restless.* Waiting for a letter, for the telephone to ring, for a descent of grace, or good luck, or rain. *Until it rests in thee.*

XV

A glum provincial with a thick
Outback African accent
Arrives in the capital,
A couple of testimonials
Stuffed in his dim baggage.
He buys a street-map, finds digs
Near some terminus or market
Where his fellow-colonials
Squat shivering over braziers,
Tell lies about their prospects,
Get drunk on cheap liquor,
And send home for more money.
In this quarter ('Lion Valley'
To humorous citizens

Who know where they belong)
Our comer-in sits waiting
For letters from his mother
And looks out of the window
At diurnal somethings and nothings
Till another day has passed
Unmentioned in his journal.

XVI

The abrupt convulsions
Of the new musicians,
The insolent stares
Of handsome queers,
The frank abandon
Of the latest fashion
In flaunting the body –
All leave me unready
To hold to my purpose
Or know what it is.

XVII

Among small ancient farms where every day
Morning enlists fields to be ploughed, stones to be cleared,
Fences mended, brushwood burnt, cattle and goats
To be herded from sparse patch to sparse patch,
And each day has its discipline and pattern –
From such ancestral narrowness I come
To find elsewhere no such conscripted labour
But talents scattered in a city gutter
And idleness proliferating like weed
In ways untended and unprofitable.

XVIII

Forms and observances. The tact of ritual, the courtesy of exchanges. The careful editing of rough matter. Everywhere I see such performances, the smoothing out of our barbarities. Not only do I see them, I participate: though provincial, I am urbane. After all, I found myself a place in the established order of things: I put out my sign, and it was recognized. But, putting it out, I put out something else – my small, fitful flame, the insignificant yet authentic tongue of heat and light. Not that it was ever my part to speak with the tongues of men and angels: fiercer men from the deeper desert did that, and my strongest passion seemed to be for reason. And I feed on the thin gruel of abstinence, keeping a head clear for whatever epiphany is chosen, and a body lean and spare for combat. But what if the rigour of the will is only the rigour of death?

XIX

It loosens the tongue, that swollen, unlovely
Instrument of rhetoric, licking the juices
Of grapes or bodies, indiscriminately.
Since I forswore it, I have discovered
Nothing in the thin liquids of virtue
But the same dull man stuck with the old brick wall,
Only now caged in conscious sobriety,
Controlled as a clenched fist is controlled
Till the veins stand out, straining like hawsers, the palms
Sweat in their prison, and, when the fingers part
With a moist, thudding suck, the arm trembles with joy
But only at relief.

XX

And what of you whom I have put away, put out of mind – except that twenty times a day, and more often in my dreams, you pierce me with your presence? It cannot be mud that splashes across my memory, remembering my second nature, which was you. But I must bury you deeper still, and leave the place where you lie.

XXI

There might have been a wedding
Some other year, in another place,
Blessed no doubt, a complete sacrament,
Just like the real ones that happened
And go on happening. There might have been
Such a joining, such a marriage,
Such a bringing and keeping together
That God himself would have approved.
(Though you would not accept such an extravagance,
And as for me – I grant you an emptiness.)
But whatever disposes such matters chose
To settle our pasts and our futures differently,
To go our different ways.
                We settle
For what we have, and keep our separate pledges
Made to our alien, ignorant partners, whose love
Binds us and separates us and will not let us go.

XXII

Harbinger, prolegomena to the great work: for almost thirty years I have travelled with you, but only as an outrider, a figure on the scene, an agency for the promotion of others. I must set off now, on my own journey.

XXIII

No one has known I have been in this city,
For twenty-four hours doing my secret business
Among suburbs preoccupied with their own secrets –
Silent betrayals, assignations, adulteries.
If I said that I saw my life suddenly changing
In a way that will have no room for what we have shared,
You would suspect I had found someone else
And was making elaborate excuses for a disappearance
To another country with my infatuation.
That would be a mistake: to suppose
Liberty exacts only gifts of selfishness
Or secrecy always shrouds something disreputable
Is to miss the will's strange armoury of chances.
I am committed to a choice I made
When chance suddenly threw in my direction
Dice that fell in unalterable patterns.
The web of subterfuge was broken and blew away,
And I was released to play a different game,
A role I never knew I was capable of.
I am an agent devoted to working out
The secret will of powers not my own.
I draw no pay, am not rewarded
With the unaccountable munificence that is given
To other spies. But what I do is dangerous,
Acts as furtive as theirs, meetings as charged
With all the possibilities of abrupt
Discovery, interrogation, death.
And now, as I leave the city late at night,
Among other travellers who ignore my presence,
I must tread with circumspection through fact and fact,
An alibi glib at my lip for every
Contingency tomorrow's dawn may bring
To ambush, and the questions on the road
I must learn to answer darkly, if at all.

143

Deviousness of collapse. Weeping, in the suburbs, arid, broken, chest cramped with sour liquids, in extremity. Forsaken.

XXIV

Across dry gardens wrinkled leaves are blown
To lodge in corners where they stir and creak
Dryly together, like old men who speak

Only of what is dead and past and known
Too long for speech. I sit beneath a sun
Grown cold and white as a wind-whitened bone.

Somewhere a child's voice calls, a tune ascends
Through notes as shrill and liquid as a thrush.
Half of my life begins as one half ends.

A cloud moves. A weight presses me, is gone.
What would both lift and lighten me, yet crush
My spirit like a thunderbolt from the sun?

And all I have lost is suddenly made one.

XXV

He recorded in his book how it happened, how whatever it was – revelation or awakening – came to him, struck him down, made him new: how after that nothing was the same. It is the turning point, the still centre – all the other dead metaphors we use to keep alive an experience we do not want to die. Ten years fell between the conversion and the confessions. I sit here in the garden, at his recorded and recording age, and watch a squirrel worry the fallen apples of a good harvest. There is nothing left to gather. The dropped fruit will rot. There will be winter, and then spring. I read 'the self-portrait of a convalescent'. My sickness is a nervous tic in my right eye, and the doctor prescribes sleep. *Peritus . . . periturus.*

144

XXVI

By the decay and succession of things the beauty of the age is woven.

The salt at Agrigentum
The Garamantian fountain
And that at Epirus
The Arcadian stone
The fig-tree in Egypt
The apples of Sodom
The Persian pyrites
And the Persian selenite
The mares of Cappadocia
The trees of Tilon

Thrown in the fire turns liquid,
In water crackles as if on fire.
So cold by day no one can drink it,
So hot by night no one can touch it.
Quenches lighted torches
But lights those that are quenched.
Once lit cannot be put out.
Sinks to the bottom but, soaked,
Rises again to the surface.
Ripe in appearance
But dust when bitten into.
Burns the hand. Waxes and wanes with the moon.
Impregnated by the wind.
Never losing its foliage.

XXVII

These quiddities, these inscapes, are foreign to me: I must transpose
them. But in the transposition lies all the knowledge I have, and all the
knowledge I have of what I do not know.

The observations of *otium liberale*.

XXVIII

The reticulations of the centipede
The ripe haze of the clogged orchard
The brief gamut of rain sounding in gutters
The moss still warm in the quail's empty lair
The thin crushed touch of gravel to the nostrils
The spectrum smeared on the narrow paths of snails
The wind heaving the canvas and bracing it taut
The pierced arrow from which stormclouds bleed light
The nipple rising in its stippled disc –
                                        Ask
What binds them in perfection, each perfect,
Distinct in harmony, joined in separation,
Poised to admit, administer, reject,
Supple in passiveness, precise in action . . .
                                    Question
How each maintains its place, follows its destiny
Through maze of choice, through labyrinth of error,
Unhindered in its rapt scrutiny
Of its own selfhood in its selfhood's mirror . . .
                                    Enquire
What chooses each one's scale and range, duration
In centuries or seconds, when each dies
Or each gives birth, where bounds are set to function
And how something of each survives and stays . . .
                                    Then praise

146

Your scrupulous, enquiring ignorance
That weighs, notates, equates and calculates
Through instrument and seminar to advance
Knowledge compounded of ciphers, digits, dates,
Curves of progression, graphs of incidence,
Footnotes to texts, glosses to notes on notes –
And in the end, triumphant, shrugs to advance
The notion that all this depends on chance,
A blizzard of randomness where each separate flake
Whirls in its own six-sided snowy quake,
Starting from nothing, ending in nothing, blank
As untouched drifts of snow, without meaning till
Footprints mark out the power of man's will:
Neat as the rhyme in perfect measured lines,
Technique ascends, the universe declines
To fall through holes in space that no one knew
Existed till professors told them to . . .

The reticulations of the centipede
Move effortlessly, thriftily, at speed.

XXIX

Step down.
        Under the pavement, under the thronged road,
below the weight of earth, the cave of origin
opens and claims its chosen one: *fons
et origo*. Water, wrapped and lapped,
in a stone chamber, cold and salt with tears.

XXX

This Certificate of Baptism holds nothing but the official calligraphy of
a diploma, the copperplate of institutions, according to which we are
born, marry, and die. Would things have been different if I had stepped

down into some hygienic font or swimming bath several decades later, or had clapped hands like a Jesus Freak in a euphoric torrent of adolescent amorousness, lost and found? Instead, I yelled in my parsonical grandfather's arms and knew nothing about it.

XXXI

Where were you? I was where I always was
But you were absent or absconded. Who
Housed you or hid you, in whose unknown face
Did you assume the features that I knew
But did not know? And for how many days
Did you desert me when I looked for you?

I too was where I was, and looked for you
But you were elsewhere, out of sight because
A shade or phantom was the thing you knew,
Error of sight, of judgement and of place,
And I was distant to a seeker who
Sought everywhere but in my open ways.

XXXII

The prodigal returns, is rich with gifts.
Shriven and blessed, come home to his own sty.
Purpose is single, husks will turn to grain.

The shore approaches, the beaked prow drops and lifts.
God looks down from the sun and blinds his eye.
The prodigal inherits his domain.

XXXIII

An exercise of virtue, that unused muscle or useless appendix, atrophied limb and difficult translation. Rhetoric of volition, speech of will. Illuminated, mad. Henceforth politician of the enlightenment, custodian of the lunatic: patron of the Inquisition, rubric of the Reformation, scourge of the schismatic, prosecutor of the heretic. The bitter sea of humanity floods through the dykes. In its wake is salt.

XXXIV

Erudition. Admonition. Discipline. Or, looked at in another way, Believe, Obey, Fight. The will is weak and often devious: it finds stones in its path and trips easily, it looks for obstacles where none exist. It must be taught, warned, and if necessary punished. 'From the canes of the schoolmasters to the agonies of the martyrs' is a progression. What we have to do to those who refuse to be persuaded may seem harsh. So it is. I do not pretend otherwise. But consider the casuistries of these recusants, by which they themselves excuse their own harshness, their own fanaticism, their own violence. They look at history, and make history their justification: certain supposed acts, certain presumed treacheries. There were men, years past, who may or may not have compromised with the temporal power: today, these vigilantes would exhume their bodies and defile them. There were battles, long ago, which – it is said – were fought to set such matters to rights: today, these vigilantes would fight them all over again. Other men say, in what they suppose is a spirit of tolerance: 'Let us put it to the vote – let us reconcile our differences with a referendum.' But matters of faith are not to be settled by casting a scribbled scrap of broken pot into a leather bag. To fight the strength of evil we must ourselves be strong. 'Know what you are fighting for, and love what you know.' Put on the whole armour of God. And as you go into battle, sing. The vigilantes have their own songs, wild ravings and rantings about the True Faith. Very well: answer them with your own song.

XXXV

Your vigilante brother
Is full of pious deeds.
He'll take his Catholic mother
And scourge her till she bleeds
Because her father's father
Was maybe short on faith
And possibly would rather
Have saved his mortal breath
Than stand with sixty others
In the hallelujah tent
Shouting to a God that bothers
About what Donatus meant.
O the wicked sins of the mothers
O the temple veil is rent.

Your vigilante stalwart
Enjoys himself at night.
Tying a rope true-love knot
May seem a mild delight,
But your vigilante ties it
Round necks and pulls it till
The victim chokes and cries 'It
Is true about God's Will!'
After which the poor old sinner
May have a moment's peace
Before a sword is in her
And she's bleeding on her knees.
O the true Lord is a winner
O God's Adversary flees.

'Now gather round, my bullies',
Your vigilante cries,
'We must revenge old follies,
And he who wavers dies.
Up with the true religion,
Up with the holy books,
The dove is not our pigeon,
Carry daggers in your looks.
For wasn't it Our Lord himself
Who said he brought not peace
But a sword – so take it off the shelf
And give your souls release.'
O judge what's true, each for himself
O you who joy in peace.

XXXVI

But the wounds. The blood not figurative, the cries not metaphorical. An armoury of weapons and a cell of torturers. When a man stands up and says 'If necessary, we are prepared to fight', he is either drunk or mad. Or innocent. Never to have seen a human being kill or be killed is a gap in one's experience, but it can easily be closed, like the innocent eye. What he wanted to be done and what this involved actually doing – between the two lay a gulf much wider than the narrow sea he had crossed with such exuberance.

Filled with fear myself, I fill you with fear.

XXXVII

No one had told me this was what to expect:
The mouth full of ashes, still warm from the promised feast,
And the slivers of bone hacked from the offered beast
And the dry knot in my gullet not wanting to swallow.
No one told me. Released
From condign ambitions, from words of a worldly text,
I stand on this spit of sand, pointing north from home,
Stale spit sour in my mouth, the devils brought low
In front across tracts of livid disordered foam
And behind across still deserts, unsettlable waste.

Without dignity, without position
Except to keep upright, propped between day and night,
The refugees crowd wanly out of sight:
But I know they are there, unsummoned to the feast,
Without fire, without light,
In attitudes of abandon or contrition.
They have suffered: suffer: the losers, they pay
For their leaders' heresy, the mark of the beast
Branded yesterday, confirmed today
To go on suffering, until proved contrite.

Carthage, you too were brought low, garnished with salt,
A triumph of waste, defaced for your impudence.
I have seen our enemies burned for their vile offence,
Should find it just, should applaud the divinity
That has wrung the due expense
Out of that proven vileness. Scrupulous to a fault,
I measure the given word against the deed
And find the blistered child on its mother's knee
Wrings something out beyond justice: makes me bleed
For something unassurable, for innocence.

But I am committed. I accepted the thorny crown,
The stigma of blood, the word in the desert, the thrall
Banishing all but the doctrine that those who fall
Fall through the truculent will, gone wild and free.
There is no parable
Our Lord told that has set these scruples down
As I would wish them. Committed to this war,
I must accept devout belligerency.
And yet as the desert winds and the waves roar
Across this headland, I pray for some sure call
To deafen our hymns, to rise and drown us all.

XXXVIII

Luther on Grace. Calvin on Predestination. Torquemada on Coercion.
Newman on the Secret Power of God. A full billing, with Augustine's
name among the small credits at the bottom: 'Based on an idea by . . .'
Credit where some would say discredit is due.

> The baths at Carthage. Flesh and heat. Great robes
> To be cast aside to show the corpse beneath.
> Gold. Marble. Mosaics in darkness, darker glow
> Of reliquaries, plumes of candles. Strong-voiced,
> The Requiem treads down the ashes, prayers
> Pre-empt and empty out what justice means.
> Power is anguish to the trodden neck,
> Is exultation to the heel that grinds:
> Between them dust is blown to the four winds.

Let falsehood, once detected, bow its neck to truth made manifest.

You are with me in the night, as I lie awake and feel my age absorb its
sustenance of vinegar. The streets still throb outside my window,
reminding me of all my accretions. As I remember disputations, trans-
actions, admissions, confessions, absolutions, I remember also journeys,
searches, moments of abandon, moments of blankness. The smell of

honeysuckle, the taste of figs, the sight of a lizard quick on a wall, the touch of sand under the fingers, the sound of the sea wind knocking the canvas. I am trapped by them all, moment by moment, until the whole well of myself is replete with them, the heavy liquid of selfhood. I flow over with incident and token, sign and experience. And in this flood of randomness, where am I but in the separate drops and moistures you have chosen for me, an amalgam of your mixing, an alembic for your experiment?

XXXIX

Night of commemoration and celebration, a triumph, a carnival. Heaped fires smoulder and explode on the swart horizons of a winter night, and the sparks are lobbed upward above shadowy and flaring trees. Dazzling, consumed in brilliance, fitful among the stars, driven to the perimeter of their own light, extinct. The faces of children are reflected in them, a pristine torrent, a former glory. Transfigured martyrs, clasping the once kindled crucifix, bow and topple into the purging rubbish. And the meadow is littered with spent tatters and smudged casings, soggy among nettles and trodden turf under the mist that elbows in through the deserted fields. The psalmists are silent, the prophets' mouths are stopped. The brief imperial holiday is over, and all the pyres burn level with the earth. Victories are vanquished, the dux is acquainted with defeat. The remembered smell of flames rises like grief to the horses' nostrils, and the imagined sting of smoke brings tears to men's eyes.

Small and unseemly memories of men discomfited, their trivial posturings mocked and proved fatuous. Is this my cardinal sin, to enumerate them secretly and glow at their number? They will never be the villains of repeated feast-days but footnotes in history, the scurf of scholarship.

XL

Old lizard-face, gloating over the loathsomeness of sin, sanctimonious adversary, apostle of the Manichees, slobbering in the confessional. Spiritual teaser, *allumeuse* of the inflamed conscience. Thus I recall you. Or that other one, so bland and reasonable, inclined above the sherry glasses, nodding agreement at the polite and deferential questions of ladies unready to acknowledge even the existence of sin. You too I remember. For I subjugated both of you. And I have my pride.

XLI

But there is a darkness beyond all this, and it still prevails. Beyond the smug indulgences of the *urbs*, beyond the indifferent justice of the *civitas*, beyond the pitiful gestures of the *ecclesia*, lurk the ten thousand gods, the ten million demons, the plagues, the devastations, the elemental disasters, the deepest and darkest nature of man. And the priests who dissemble it.

> The countenance of God: is the muzzle of Baal.
> His gifts are the udders of Tanit: flowing to our lips.
> His sacrifice is comely: in the dances of women.

> The countenance of God: is the belly of Baal.
> His gifts are the mountains of Saturn: whose clouds shed fear.
> His sacrifice is comely: in the slaughter of animals.

> The countenance of God: is the loins of Baal.
> His gifts are the knives of Vulcan: flashing like lightning.
> His sacrifice is comely: in the blood of children.

XLII

Numidian mornings, when the sun is still furred with mist, cool for journeys. Beyond the city wall are neat fields sopping with dew, and hills that are this side of danger. Peasants are bent-backed between vines, busy among orchards. Far from the briskly trod marble of the basilica and the rough trade of the market, small birds bubble and clack in groves of juniper and pastures of myrtle. Or elsewhere, in a river landscape of glebe, copse, moorhen and kingfisher, unhindered yet possessed. But a tumulus looms across meadows, low burden of old sacrificial compulsions, plundered relic of vanquished theologies. Stone knife, bronze dagger. As the builders' men move in, under the hearth or by the lintel they uncover a stone salt-glazed jar, whose grimacing mask warns of a lock of hair, a handful of nails, a stain of urine, a pierced heart cut from musty cloth. The heat of the winter sun chills to an icy meteorite, as men believe in witches and old women die in fire.

XLIII

Arguments, purges, assassinations, invasions,
The Gothic disaster: so the dragon hovers
Unseen above your head in muddy dreams.
The potter's wheel spins on.

Unde hoc malum? From the Devil's tree
Ripe fruit is shaken. We tread Paradise
By slippery ways, pursued by eager fears.
The potter's wheel spins on.

The gospel of madness is preached by doctors. Both
Chance and necessity are blunderings.
A troupe of jingling pilgrims wails with joy.
The potter's wheel spins on.

The expelled are patronized with charity.
The unborn are damned before they reach for breath.
Go to the ant, but hear the termite eat.
The potter's wheel spins on.

The cricket chirps: the swan is silent, scum
Thickens across the river's slow descent
Through choked effluvia, discarded trash.
The potter's wheel spins on.

XLIV

Occupied with affairs, busy with deliberations, something within me
dries at the root, shrivels to a slow and parching dust. There is the world,
and there it is: to be negotiated with acquired skill, or plunged into and
crossed with inherited courage. Which is the proper choice, if there is
still time to choose? For no doubt the choice has already been made, or
was made long ago, when I was dully and dutifully making my consci-
entious efforts to advise, exhort, chastise, illuminate, discriminate. Such
small gifts, talents reduced to a degenerate coinage by inflation. Men
furtively bury their wretched hoards in the footings of walls, under
hearthstones or thresholds, stamping down the disturbed earth, easing
back the shifted masonry, secure as moles in their darkness, and as blind.
So it seems with my less ponderous talents, debased small change that
issued from no exchequer. When the treasure is dug up, it is no longer
treasure, but an obstruction to the blunt hoe of a peasant I shall never
see and to whom my judgements will be as unapprehensible as the
desert wind that blisters his trees and cannot be trapped or tamed or
even understood. And that hot wind is the same that has scorched my
spirit to this dry pinch of inert matter I hold between my finger and
thumb. I say to it, Arise, and the dust blows away, leaving my hand
empty.

XLV

If, of those two companions on Golgotha, one was saved and the other condemned, is my God indeed the God of Manes, holding the inexorable balance between dual forces? A duel between equals, never to be won? The play on words becomes a mad contest with swords, for every word I use can draw blood, and many a sentence is a sentence of death.

XLVI

The masons split cold marble with iron mallets.
The carpenters swarm over their wooden carapace like ants.
The wells are dug deep and girdled with basketwork.
The harbour is fashioned into the sea's embrace.
Below, the chips of mosaic litter new floors.
Above, the finials glisten over new roofs.
But everywhere nothing prospers
Unless the Lord wills it, of the house as of the city.

High on the hill the basilica shines in its glory.
Low by the sea the bollards capture the cargoes.
Columns are ranked like harp-strings by temple and forum.
Avenues strike like arrows to east and to west.
The market is busy with cries and acquisitions.
The workshops are quick with skills and intricate craftings.
But everywhere nothing prospers
Unless the Lord wills it, of the house as of the city.

Even the greatest of cities, Rome, is abandoned:
Her citizens come among us, fled from the deluge.
Where is a refuge, here or beyond the Pillars,
Safe from the envious swords, the curt invaders?
Rome is an emblem, woven into our banners,
Fading in sunlight, falling so as to prove us
Comfortless in our error
Unless the Lord wills it, of the house as of the city.

XLVII

So much I have hidden, so much I have buried in you, city of my episcopacy, garden of my generation. Vaults and cisterns echo to my funerals, my inhumations: plots and allotments house my husbanded roots. Men are succeeded by men. Gildo yields to Boniface; but the rooftree does not yield. Across the narrow straits the helmeted and inspired warriors come in their thousands, the Counts of Germany. But Genseric is a man: though his god may be the god of battles, they are battles fought on earth – on dunes, across plains, in dusty streets, among the blood and offal of an earthly topography. Nomads give way to Goths, Goths give way to Vandals. Donatus perished, Pelagius was banished. These things passed: this may also. So much I have hidden, so much I have buried in you, earth of my earth, wonderfully wrought.

XLVIII

In the alleys of Hippo, Freud examines the voided rubbish: the discontents of civilization; the gross matter of dreams. In the forum, the fathers of sociology consult with the fathers of the church. Gibbon and Toynbee measure out their trial-trenches under the olive trees. A sliver of discoloured bone, presumed relic, is borne from Pavia by monks and hutched in Carrara marble below the high altar. Pamphlets and thumb-screws, off-prints and imperial insignia descend in volcanic ash on market-place and harbour, a detritus of theologies, speculations, dogmas. Barbarous manglings, provincial syllogisms. Shelves light with your lucidities, heavy with your superstitions. The tremendous doors of libraries groan on their hinges, plated timbers echo to knocking. But what is opened to us?

XLIX

I take it up and read it, and I see
Ink and papyrus melt under my gaze.
The verses blur, the luminous syllables
Lapse into darkness. In these latter days
The hills like a broken comb against the light
Scratch at each dawn and dusk, a restless music
Compounded with cicadas, crickets, flies,
Frettings of grasshoppers, the viper's hushed
Swarm down the walls and conduits: siftings, poised
As this whole town is poised, on the edge of silence.

From floor to ceiling, penitential psalms
Repeat their abject praises. Thou, Lord, art just
But justice will be done among men too,
And out beyond the walls and out at sea
Our judges gather to administer it.
Nevertheless, Thy will be done: the church
Fills with your citizens, who will not hear
My voice again, which forty years have brought
To this thin whisper. Silence claims me too.
The shelves of manuscripts entomb my tongue.

The sharp prow rose and fell into the sun,
Carrying me busily on Christ's brisk errands.
Heretics fell in disputation, laws
Were balanced on the scales of my regard.
Now at the jetty no craft waits for me
Or anyone. Again I lift the book,
And close my eyes, and see a city rise
Above all brick and marble ones. Below,
Where men are fearful and their fear is just,
A gorgon mouth yawns open and breathes fire.

L

Stern father, with your unknown face,
Trouble me in whatever place
I try to shun your iron grace.

Curious to know how others live
Yet slow to mend the broken sieve
That is myself, to you I give

Whatever holy residue
Remains of what is good and true.
Keep it, as I come close to you.

It ends.
It is finished.

Notes

II 'All this goes on inside me, in the vast cloisters of my memory.' *Confessions* X:8. Thagaste (modern Souk Ahras) was Augustine's birthplace. It lies two hundred miles inland, in what is now Algeria. Its topography is suggested also in Section III.

IV '*Rationes seminales*': from *On Genesis*, IX. Some commentators have seen Augustine's remarks about the pattern of change as an anticipation of the theory of evolution.

V–VIII The Manichees, the Donatists, and the Neo-Platonists all attached great importance to dreams. Augustine was more sceptical: see, for example, *On the Trinity*, XV – 'For who does not know that what people see in dreams is precisely like what they see when awake?'

VII This is an adaptation of one of the 'Fragments' attributed to Petronius (died AD 66). I have no evidence, of course, that Augustine ever read Petronius, but 'old reprobate' (in VIII) would have been a possible way for him to have described the pagan author of *The Satyricon*.

IX Madaura (modern Mdaourouch) lies about thirty miles south of Thagaste. Augustine was at boarding-school there between the ages of fifteen and sixteen. The ruins of the town are still considerable.

IX and X 'I had prayed to you for chastity and said, "Give me chastity and continence, but not yet."' *Confessions* VIII:7.

XI 'I went to Carthage, where I found myself in the midst of a hissing cauldron of lust.' *Confessions* III:1. Augustine plays, in Latin, on the place-name and on a semi-homonym meaning a type of cooking-pot.

XII The second part of this section is taken from Lucretius, *Concerning the Nature of Things*, Book I. If Augustine ever read Lucretius, he no doubt disliked him.

XIV 'Thou hast made us for thyself, and our heart is restless until it rests in thee.' *Confessions* I:1.

XV Augustine sailed for Rome, by himself, in 383, and spent an unhappy year there. *Confessions* V:8–12.

XVIII Symmachus, Prefect of Milan, appointed Augustine as professor of rhetoric for the city in 384. It was Symmachus who once wrote: 'The highroad to office is often laid open by literary success.'

XVIII–XIX On abstinence, see *Confessions* X:31.

XX–XXI 'At first the pain was sharp and searing, but then the wound began to fester, and though the pain was duller there was all the less hope of a cure.' *Confessions* VI:15. The name of Augustine's mistress is not known. 'She went back to Africa . . .'

XXIII–XXIV *Confessions* VIII:12. For his '*dolor pectoris*', see *Confessions* IX:2.

XXV Augustine experienced his conversion in August 386. He probably began the *Confessions* in 396, when he was forty-two years old.

'the self-portrait of a convalescent': Peter Brown's description of *Confessions* X, in *Augustine of Hippo* (p. 177). '*Peritus . . . periturus*': 'I used to talk glibly as though I knew the meaning of it all. . . . Had I continued to be such an expert, I should have died.' *Confessions* VII:20.

XXVI For the 'innumerable marvels', *The City of God* XXI:5.

XXVII '*otium liberale*': cultured retirement; see *Retractions* I:1 ('*Christianae vitae otium*'). Also *Confessions* IX:4 for Augustine's retreat at Cassiciacum, not far from Lake Como.

XXIX–XXX Augustine was baptized by Ambrose in the baptistry now below Milan Cathedral at Easter 387.

XXXII Augustine returned to Africa to take up his ministry in 388, first to Carthage, then to Thagaste, and finally to Hippo.

XXXIV Needless to say, this 'sermon' is as anachronistic as much else in the present work. Nevertheless, Augustine's '*eruditio*', '*admonitio*', and '*disciplina*' are not idly seen as analogous to Mussolini's '*credere*', '*obbedire*', and '*combattere*'. For 'the canes of the schoolmasters . . .', see *Confessions* I:14. For the whole matter of the Donatists and *circumcellions* (here 'vigilantes'), see Peter Brown *op. cit.*, chapters 19–21, and W. H. C. Frend's *The Donatist Church: a movement of protest in Roman North Africa*. 'Know what you are fighting for . . .' is an adaptation of Cromwell's supposed remark on his Ironsides.

XXXV In reply to the 'wild ravings and rantings' of the Donatists, which were frequently cast in the form of popular songs, Augustine himself did in fact compose an 'A.B.C. against the Donatists': the refrain to the third stanza is taken from it.

XXXVI 'Filled with fear . . .': from a sermon by Augustine on the text 'Do not be slow to turn to the Lord, nor delay from day to day, for his wrath shall come when you know not.'

XXXVIII In 410, the Emperor Honorius ordered a debate to be held between the Donatists and the Catholics, led by Augustine. This took place at the great baths in Carthage in June 411. Augustine triumphed: 'Let falsehood . . .' was the judgement of Flavius Marcellinus, who presided over the debate.

XL One could think of Faustus the Manichee and of Pelagius, among other apologists and moralists.

XLI The worship of Baal, Tanit, and other Punic deities was common among the pagans of Numidia.

XLII 'a stone salt-glazed jar': see Ralph Merrifield's 'The Use of Bellarmines as Witch-Bottles', *The Guildhall Miscellany*, no. 3, February 1954.

XLIII *'Unde hoc malum?'*: see *Augustine of Hippo*, p. 394. For the potter's wheel, *Lamentations* 4:2 is one of a number of Biblical references.

'The cricket chirps . . .': said by Eraclius, Augustine's own appointed successor as Bishop of Hippo, in his first sermon in 426.

XLVI Rome fell to Alaric and his Gothic army in August 410. Many refugees fled to Africa.

XLVII Gildo, the Moorish Count of Africa, usurped Numidia in the late fourth century, until he was suppressed by the Emperor Honorius. Boniface, at the head of Gothic troops, had become Count of Africa by 423. Genseric, King of the Vandals, completed the subjugation of Roman Africa during the next decade.

XLVIII The only tangible relic of Augustine is a fragment of arm bone, brought from Pavia to the Basilica of Hippo in the nineteenth century and placed inside a marble effigy of Augustine behind the high altar, where it remains to this day.

XLIX During his final illness, Augustine ordered 'the four psalms of David that deal with penance' to be copied out and hung on the walls of his room. He died on 28 August 430. A year later Hippo was sacked.

from *A Portion for Foxes* (1977)

136   *The Unnameable*

It creeps away to die, like animals,
But does not die. It burrows in the thick
Compost at ends of gardens, fetches up
Pecking at attic skylights, with the lock
Turned tight with rust, unable to escape.
It frets and rustles, uttering frail calls.

Nothing can heal or help it. Seek it out,
It will go deeper, further. It won't want
Your rescue or your comfort, knowing best
What finds may ferret out, what cures may kill.
You recognize the sounds, you smell the scent:
More, you too crouch in darkness, where an animal
Crawls on all fours, head down, the collapsing tunnel.

137   *The Procession*

And when you have waited there so patiently
And at last the great procession passes by
With those sad, slow tunes you hummed interminably,
How will you join them? Will you somehow try
To draw attention with a slogan scratched
Hurriedly on a bit of paper, sound
A trumpet from the window where you watched,
Hope that by standing by you will be found
Among the million others? None of these.
No matter how confused and large the crowd,
Or how well-disciplined and separate
Those solemn marchers, you will step with ease
Down from the jostling pavement, be allowed
To join them. And you will not hesitate.

138 *By the Sluice*

It pulses like a skin, at dusk
Is shaken like dusty silk. The current moves
But takes its impetus and gathers speed
Only beyond the sluice-gate. Here, the faint
Shudders, the morse of water almost trapped,
Perform half mesmerized, half dying too.

Yet are not dying: those trembling dots, those small
Reverberations, rise from what is hidden –
Scatters of minnows, nervous hair-triggered fry –
Grasping at sustenance, grabbing at what is given,
Submerged ferocities, brute delicacies.

What have I hidden here, or let go, lost,
With less to come than's gone, and so much gone?
Under the gate the river slams its door.

139 *Metamorphosis*

Something is changing.
                    Soft fold on fold of flesh
Loosen, go liquid, swell, are filled with sighing.
The moistened petals melt into a cud,
Are eaten and renewed, let down their rain
Somewhere above, are salt as sea or blood.
The wound opens, closes, aches again.

The body's instruments, the choir of love,
Tremble and falter; stumbling, become one,
Singing of such an ecstasy as can move
Habitual gestures or inert repose
Into the dance of animals, the groan
Dashed from the dropping petals of a rose
As thorns thrust stiffly in a summer wind,
And pulse and impulse, leaping, fall behind.

It was wide, true, but no wider than the straits:
Most of it boulders and pebbles, the water itself
An uneven grey-blue snake, writhing in bursts
Here and there, but elsewhere sluggish with puddles.
It was not the size of that river, or the distance they'd come,
Or the men dead with delirium, or those killed in battle,
Or the exhaustion of a long campaign. But was it
Fear of the mountains rising red from the plain,
Fear of the unknown tribes on the other side?

No,

However the legends go, or the histories patch it together,
The place was not ready. Over the other side,
Whatever travellers had come in their ones and twos
Over the centuries, was a possible paradise,
Untouched, immaculate, the dreamt-of place
(Though not for those who lived there: it never is).
We hesitate at those portals, whether Greek or Jew,
Bond or free, freethinker or devout, and are quiet
When, for a moment, history comes to a stop.
The regimental commanders muttered together; the battalions

rested;

The leader was informed.
The bend of the river waited, and went on waiting.
The mountains, the buzzards, the plain, and the other side
Waited. The signal was given.

Then they turned back.

141   *A Moment in the South*

How different the day when the great composer
Arrived with carriages in the white piazza,
Advanced through avenues of oleander
To where his willing host, full-bearded patron
Of ancient lineage, greeted him on the loggia.

This was the place (the genius knew at once)
Where he would set that awkward second act:
A hanging garden under which the gulf
Spanned sun and haze in a long breadth of blue.
Such was his exclamation to the Count.

The tourists' brochure throbs with reverence
At this munificent and thrilling scene,
Enacted among fragrant southern trees,
When in the white piazza old men sat
Watching the dust rise from those carriages.

142   *At the Ironmonger's*

To: Messrs Trew, 12 sets no. 2 Domes of Silence, 8p per set . . .

Cabinet-hinges, casement-fasteners,
Mirror-clips and drugget-pins,
Ball-catches and bale-latches,
Curtain-hooks and curtain-rings,
Brass cabin hooks and brass escutcheons,
Cotter-keys and trammel-wedges
And, in the bottom drawer,
The domes of silence.

Coffin, casket, mausoleum,
Headstone, crucifix, monumental
Lettering etched in Latin, Hebrew,
R.I.P., Kyrie Eleison,
Sword of faith and star of David,
Ritual pyre and epicedium
And, in the bottom drawer,
The domes of silence.

143   Stereoscope: 1870

A trick of cinematic archaeology,
A wooden toy to gaze in, among views
Where rigidly the poses now amuse
A casual audience that gasps to see
How three-dimensional such people were,
With different clothes and different hair, but all
Clear in their different rooms as we are. Tall
Men lean on mantelpieces; children stir,
Or seem to stir, restless at nursery tea;
A wife works at her crochet in a chair:
And all live in a world at which we stare
Because we recognize perspective, see
How everything is close or distant, not
Smoothed to the level pages of a book.
It is at that we almost dread to look,
Such depths, such closeness, rooted to the spot.
Peer through these eyepieces: the past goes round
Like mill-sails turning where no breezes blow,
And where we were a hundred years ago
Tugs us as something lost, not to be found,

Or sought elsewhere a hundred years from now.

'Increasingly our attention is being drawn
To carvings set up to the Veteres.
(We give the word thus, though singular occurs
As much as plural: masculine and feminine
Forms have been found indifferently.
The spelling, too, varies enormously.)
We take it these mysterious deities
May be equated with the equally
Mysterious triads known by Dr Ross
As *genii cucullati*, "the cloaked gods",
Whose distribution also runs across
The northern frontier.'

                              My attention nods
Over the pamphlet and the photographs
Of rough-hewn altars, each one posed and lit
As if some cack-thumbed Michelangelo,
Possessed – though self-taught and illiterate –
By things outside himself, should this way show
His genius to a universe that laughs
At transcendental posturings like these:
'To the Gods, the Veteres . . .'

                              Under my eyes
Carved word and image flow together, merge,
Spreading across the scholar's cautious prose
To reach the dark rim of the very edge
That lies beyond the window's frontier:
Where Paul in Athens stooped to read the words
Inscribed upon the superstitious stone,
'To the Unknown God', and felt a moment's fear,
Possessed neither by Christ's words nor his own.

145   *Rescue Dig*

In a fading light, working towards evening,
Knowing next day the contractors will be there,
Impatient earth-movers, time-is-money men,
And the trench, hastily dug, already crumbling
(No leisure for revetments), you're suddenly aware
Of some recalcitrant thing, as when your pen
Stubs at the page
And slips stubbornly, tripped by a grease-spot, dry
Shadow-writing. The trowel hits the edge,
Solid against solid, perhaps pottery,
Perhaps bone, something curved and flush
With earth that holds it smooth as yolk in white
And both within their shell. Feel round it, go
Teasing its edges out, not in a rush
Of treasure-hunting randomness, but quite
Firmly yet tactfully, with a patient slow
Deliberation, down
Round the bounding line that holds it, up
Its cupped outline (grey or brown?
The light is bad), letting the soil slip
Smoothly away. Too quick in your eagerness
And you'll fracture its flimsy shape, be left with scraps.
What are these folds on it? A skull's brow-ridges,
Lugs at a pot-rim? Let your hand caress
Its texture, size and mass, feel for the gaps
That may be there, the tender buried edges
Held by the earth.
Now what you want is time, more time, and light,
But both are going fast. You hold your breath
And work only by touch, nothing in sight
Except the irrelevant spots of distant stars
Poised far above your intent groping here.
Exasperated, suddenly sensing how
Absurd your concentration, your hand jars
The obstinate thing; earth falls in a damp shower;

173

You scrabble to save it, swearing, sweating. Now,
In the total dark,
You know it's eluded you, broken, reburied, lost,
That tomorrow the bulldozers will be back;
The thing still nameless, ageless; the chance missed.

146   *Witch Bottles*

Tiger-striped or leopard-spotted – thus
The usual label of the connoisseur:
But more like a toad's metallic mottling,
And having that granular coldness.
There is a heaviness, something of the earth.

Found in London clay, ten feet down,
Or on Thames mud in fragments, sloughed skins,
Nothing so sinister there. It's when they squat
Under some old cottage's hearth or threshold,
Revealed by the wreckers, that they chill the air.

The mask, with its hourglass mouth, runs with sand
And in its belly rusty pins transfix
A chopped-out felt heart, musty in its faint
Stink of phosphate, mingling plucked hair and piss.
Charmless, a talisman exposed and shrunk

To this coagulated baleful mass:
Corroded brass, nail parings, thorns, the scum
Gathering and thickening, and now dispersed.
Somewhere a gaunt crone shrieked in the fire's heart,
Grey flesh annealed to stone, its smeltings here.

147 *At Ely*
(John Tiptoft, Earl of Worcester, d. 1470)

Among the floating passengers below
This starry lantern, hale in effigy
Tiptoft lies by his brides, immaculate:
Serene and resurrected trinity.

Restored by art, cosmetic in his grace,
Watch him embrace the pure November chill,
Who at another time, alone, knelt down
And felt the axe descend on Tower Hill.

148 *Eccles*

Cliffs sifting down, stiff grassblades bent,
Subdued, and shouldering off thick sand,
Boulders – compacted grout and flint –
Jut from a stranded beach, a land
Adhering thickly to the sea.
Tide-drenched, withdrawn, and drowned again,
Capsized, these buttresses still strain
Towards perpendicularity.

The place-name mimes the fallen church,
Abbreviated, shrunk to this
Truncated word, echo of speech,
A Latin ghost's thin obsequies
Carried by wind, answered by sea –
Ecclesia: the syllables
Curtailed, half heard, like tongueless bells
From empty steeples endlessly.

He crossed the dry ford and the rock-strewn course
Coming towards the city: Taxila.
Behind him, to the West, a slow loss
Of blood, not his, a show of open wounds
Not yet to be healed. He had come so far
Language had left him: he conversed in signs,
And heard replies in meaningless grunts, rough sounds,
Yelps and choked gutturals, as a dog that whines
Under a bully's blows.

                How could he bring the word
To aliens like these? What wordless miracle
Could his dubiety raise and reveal?
Practical skills, the trade of strain and stress,
The palpable structure planned in wood and stone –
These were his passport. He had come so far
Commissioned and professional: the king's messengers
Insisted on his foreign competence,
His smart outlandishness. A palace, wrought
Out of daedalian magnificence . . .
He passed between the city walls, alone,
Trusting his still invisible harbinger,
And found the king.

                The man who wanted proof
And touched those dripping hands, that leaking sore,
Laid out his stylus and his plans before
A king of men, and pitched the palace roof
High up in heaven, a mansion without walls,
Unprovable, unseen, where the rooftree falls
Down to its cloudy base, its starry floor.

150 *A Portion for Foxes*

Psalm 63: 10

One streaked across the road in front of us
At night – a big-brushed grey one, almost a wolf
I liked to think – somewhere in the Punjab,
Close to a village where no doubt it scavenged.
And then back home, in England,
To see what our cat brings in –
The heads of sparrows,
A mole's pink paws, the black and marbled innards
Torn from a rat, a moorhen's claws:
Rejected spoils, inedible souvenirs,
A portion for foxes.

But here there are few foxes, no wolves,
No vultures shuffling scraggily in treetops,
No buzzards drifting in sunlight, or jackal wailing
At the edge of the compound. Only a ginger cat,
Ferociously domestic, stalking the meadows
For small and lively prey, far from those borders
Where 'fall by the sword' is no Sunday metaphor
Echoed antiphonally down gentle arches,
Where even now the gleam on a raised blade
Brings back the unspeakable, the mounds of fallen
Lying in lanes, in ditches, torn, dismembered,
A sacrifice to the wrathful god, or gods:
A portion for foxes.

151 *Marriages*

How dumb before the poleaxe they sink down,
Jostled along the slaughterer's narrow way
To where he stands and smites them one by one.

And now my feet tread that congealing floor,
Encumbered with their offal and their dung,
As each is lugged away to fetch its price.

Carnivorous gourmets, fanciers of flesh,
The connoisseurs of butcher-meat – even these
Must blanch a little at such rituals:

The carcasses of marriages of friends,
Dismemberment and rending, breaking up
Limbs, sinews, joints, then plucking out the heart.

Let no man put asunder . . . Hanging there
On glistening hooks, husbands and wives are trussed:
Silent, and broken, and made separate

By hungers never known or understood,
By agencies beyond the powers they had,
By actions pumping fear into my blood.

152 *Spool*

Envy and sloth, envy and sloth:
The two-pronged pincer and the shortened breath,
The sour mouthful, the finished youth.

On the empty platform, in the full sun,
The chattering accusations begin,
And begin again, and begin again.

Too late now for the Grand Tour,
Canals and villas in the blue air.
All journeys end on the way here.

Scratching such words on an envelope,
There is nothing to capture, nothing to keep,
And the words revolve on a loop of tape:

Saying envy and sloth, envy and sloth,
The two-pronged pincer and the shortened breath,
The sour mouthful, the finished youth.

153 *'Life and Other Contingencies'**

Here is the set text – neat tabulations,
The bracketed asides of algebra.

Not that I understand them, but formulas exist:
The actuary tells you what they are.

At age 46, this and this are known.
Friendly societies have experience.

What happened earlier will recur, given
Similar circumstances. It's common sense.

Two volumes on the shelf. Now take them down:
Open at any page, at any line.

Portions of me are money. What I leave
Will prove the logic, confirm the whole design.

What cannot be accounted for is not
The text's concern. It tells you what is what.

*By P. F. Hooker F.I.A., and L. H. Longley-Cook M.A., F.I.A.,
F.C.A.S., A.S.A., Cambridge University Press, two vols.

154 *'Tell it Slant'*

Precisely enigmatic. So
You draw the line: scrupulous words
Draping the naked mysteries.

Take care not to let them go.
Thoughts rise like startled birds.
Fall back on the histories.

Meticulous runes. A fearful hint
Suggested in what is not said.
Move warily among the dead.
Strike a dry spark from a flint.

Truth is partial. Name the parts
But leave the outline vague and blurred.

Mistress of passion, master of arts –
Degrees won from a cheated word.

155 *Simple Poem*

I shall make it simple so you understand.
Making it simple will make it clear for me.
When you have read it, take me by the hand
As children do, loving simplicity.

This is the simple poem I have made.
Tell me you understand. But when you do
Don't ask me in return if I have said
All that I meant, or whether it is true.

I like this more than that.
That is better than this.
This means this and that.
That is what this one wrote.
This is not that at all.
This is no good at all.
Some prefer this to that
But frankly this is old hat.
That is what Thissites call
Inferior this, and yet
I hope I have shown you all
That that way lies a brick wall
Where even to say 'Yes, but . . .'
Confuses the this with the that.

Instead, we must ask 'What is this?'
Then, 'Is that *that* sort of this,
Or a modified this, or a miss
As good as a mile, or a style
Adopted by that for this
To demonstrate thisness to those
Who expect a that-inclined prose
Always from this one – a stock
Response from readers like these.'
But of course the whole thing's a trick
To make you place *them* among those
Who only follow their nose,
Who are caught on the this/that spike
But who think they know what they like.

157   *On Consulting 'Contemporary Poets of the English Language'*

Dannie Abse, Douglas Dunn,
Andrew Waterman, Thom Gunn,
Peter Redgrove, Gavin Ewart,
Susan Fromberg Schaeffer, Stewart
Conn, Pete Brown, Elizabeth
Jennings, Jim Burns, George MacBeth,
Vernon Scannell, Edwin Brock,
Philip Hobsbaum, Fleur Adcock,
Brian Patten, Patricia Beer,
Colin Falck, David Rokeah,
Peter Dale and David Gill,
David Holbrook, Geoffrey Hill,
David Gascoyne and John Hewitt,
William Empson and Frank Prewett,
Norman Hidden, David Wright,
Philip Larkin, Ivan White,
Stephen Spender, Tom McGrath,
dom silvester houédard,
A. Alvarez, Herbert Lomas,
D.M., R.S., Donald Thomas,
Causley, Cunningham, Wes Magee,
Silkin, Simmons, Laurie Lee,
Peter Jay, Laurence Lerner,
David Day, W. Price Turner,
Peter Porter, Seamus Deane,
Hugo Williams, Seamus Heane-
y, Jonathan Green, Nina Steane,
C. Busby Smith and F. Pratt Green,
Fullers both and Joneses all,
Donald Davie, Donald Hall,
Muldoon, Middleton, Murphy, Miller,
Tomlinson, Tonks, Turnbull, Tiller,
Barker, Brownjohn, Blackburn, Bell,
Kirkup, Kavanagh, Kendrick, Kell,

McGough, Maclean, MacSweeney, Schmidt,
Hughes (of Crow) and (of *Millstone Grit*),
Sir John Waller Bt. and Major Rook,
Ginsberg, Corso, Stanley Cook,
Peter Scupham, John Heath-Stubbs,
Fenton, Feinstein, both the Grubbs,
Holloway G., Holloway J.,
Anselm Hollo and Peter Way,
Logue, O'Connor, Kevin Crossley-
Holland, Hollander, Keith Bosley,
Matthew Mead and Erica Jong,
Henry Reed and Patience Strong,
Kunitz, Kizer, Kops, Mark Strand,
Creeley, Merwin, Dickey and
The other Dickeys, Eberhart,
Bunting, Wantling, Pilling, Mart-
in Booth, a Dorn and then a Knight,
A Comfort following on a Blight,
Skelton (not the Rector of Diss –
The Poet's Calling Robin, this),
Alistair Elliot, Alastair Reid,
Michael Longley, Michael Fried,
Ian Hamilton (twice – the Scot
With 'Finlay' at the end, and the other not),
Adrians Henri, Mitchell, Stokes,
Lucie-Smith and Philip Oakes,
Father Levi of the Soc-
iety of Jesus, Alan Ross,
Betjeman, Nicholson, Grigson, Walker,
Pitter, Amis, Hilary Corke, a
Decad of Smiths, a Potts and a Black,
Roberts Conquest, Mezey, Graves and Pack,
Hugh MacDiarmid (C. M. Grieve's
His real name, of course), James Reeves,
Hamburger, Stallworthy, Dickinson, Prynne,
Jeremy Hooker, Bartholomew Quinn,
Durrell, Gershon, Harwood, Mahon,

Edmond Wright, Nathaniel Tarn,
Sergeant, Snodgrass, C. K. Stead,
William Shakespeare (no, he's dead),
Cole and Mole and Lowell and Bly,
Robert Nye and Atukwei Okai,
Christopher Fry and George Mackay
Brown, Wayne Brown, John Wain, K. Raine,
Jenny Joseph, Jeni Couzyn,
D. J. Enright, J. C. Hall,
C. H. Sisson and all and all . . .
What is it, you may ask, that Thwaite's
Up to in this epic? Yeats'
Remark in the Cheshire Cheese one night
With poets so thick they blocked the light:
'No one can tell who has talent, if any.
Only one thing is certain. We are too many.'

158 *A Girdle Round the Earth*

'King Rear was foorish man his girls make crazy'
Says something certainly about the play.
'Prutus fall on sord for bolitical reason'
Is unambiguous, though not the way
We native-speakers might have put it, who share
A language with the undoubted global poet.
In Tokyo or Benghazi, he abides
Our questioning syllabus still, will never stay
For an answer as the candidates all stare
Into the glossaried cryptograms he hides.

O Saku Seppiya, Shakhs Bey-er, O you
Who plague the schools and universities
From Patagonia to Pakistan,
From Thailand to Taiwan, how would it please
Your universal spirit to look down
And see the turbans and burnouses bent
Above your annotated texts, or see
Simplified Tales from Lamb by slow degrees
Asphyxiate the yellow and the brown?
To pick up the quotation, 'thou art free' –

But Matthew Arnold, schools inspector, who
Saw you 'self-school'd, self-scann'd', could not have known
How distantly from Stratford and the Globe
With British Council lecturers you've flown:
Midsummer Nights in Prague and Kathmandu,
Polonius stabbed dressed in a gallabiyah,
Shylock the Palestinian refugee,
And Hamlet's father's Serbo-Croat groan,
Dunsinane transported to Peru,
Kabuki for All's Well, Noh for King Lear.

'To be or not to be. Is that a question?'
The misquotations littering the page,
The prose translations fingermarked with sweat,
You prove again, world-wide, 'not of an age
But for all time', the English Ala' ad-Din,
The Western Chikamatsu, more than both
And different from either, somehow worth
Those sun-baked hours in echoing lecture-halls,
On torn tatami or dune-drifted stage:
'Lady Macbeth is houswif full of sin',
'Prince Hel is drinkard tho of nobel berth.'

159 *My Oxford*

. . . memories of vomiting blindly from small Tudor windows
(Philip Larkin: *All What Jazz*)

Trinity Term . . . From somewhere down the High
A gramophone enunciates its wish
To put another nickel in, and I
Am going to have drinks with Ernle-Fyshe,
A Merton man who had a poem once
In *Time and Tide*. The future has begun.
Over by Magdalen Bridge the tethered punts
Knock at the jetty. I am having fun.

Upstairs I hand my bottle over, take
A mug of rhubarb-coloured punch, and wave
A sprightly hand at someone. 'I just make
Whatever's made from what you bring.' A grave
Critic from Keble, aged nineteen, says why
The only man is Mauriac. And then
A girl in peasant dirndl, dark and shy,
Asks me to tell her about Origen.

My bow-tie chaste, my waistcoat green brocade,
I lay the law down, and another drink.
Bells clang from colleges, her hair is swayed
By breezes at the open window. Think
How much there is to do (that villanelle,
That *Isis* piece, that essay for A4) . . .
But confidently thinking all is well
I gulp another, sinking to the floor.

Someone recites his latest poem, while
Tom Lehrer's lyrics sidle through the haze.
'What John Crowe Ransom has is purely *style*.'
'Auden is only passing through a phase.'
The girl has turned elsewhere. My head goes round.
Let Mauriac and co. do what they like.
I lean from the embrasure. There's the sound
Of copious liquid drenching someone's bike.

O Golden Age! O Nineteen Fifty-Three,
When the whole world lay wide in front of me!

160   *For Louis MacNeice*

Your long face, like a camel's, swivels round
The long bar of the George, and stops at me
Coming in like bad news. The BBC
Recruits young graduates to rescue Sound
From all that bright-lit, show-biz sort of stuff
And I am one of them, arrived too late
For the Golden Age (the exact date
October Fifty-Seven), though enough
Remains like a penumbra of great days
To sanctify our efforts. There you stand
Aloof and quizzical, the long bar scanned
For friends or enemies, a scornful phrase
Poised to put down the parasite or bore;
But underneath that mask a lonely man
Looks out, lugubrious comedian
Or elegiac dandy, more and more
Driven into the corners of yourself.
Uncertain of your mood, after an hour
Of a shared office going slowly sour
With cigarettes and hangovers, the shelf
Above your desk capsizing with its load
Of scripts that date back sixteen years or more,

I try the Twickenham ploy, the sort of war
You relish, England-Ireland, worth an ode
Better than J. C. Squire tried long ago.
That does it. You prefer such stuff to bleak
Intensities of bookishness, and speak
With passion of who scored, and how, and know
Each quiddity of form and style and skill.
And yet I play this game only to thaw
That icy stare, because I'm still in awe
Of your most private self, that self you spill
Into the poems you keep locked away.
Looked back on now, how much I must despise
That Boswell-type with deferential eyes
Who saw you as a lion on display!
The living man eluded me. Though praise
Bitten out from those pursed, laconic lips
Astonished me, dismissal could eclipse
My universe for hours, even days.
Now that you're dead, I read you and I hear
Your nasal, almost strangled voice recite
Poems you wrote in loneliness at night,
Far from the George and parasites and beer.
My glum prosaic homage comes too late,
Ten years too late, for your embarrassment,
And yet those truant hours spent and mis-spent
Off Portland Place I humbly dedicate
To a Muse who watches, listens, is aware
Of every sell-out, every careless word,
Each compromise, each syllable that's blurred
With vanity or sloth, and whose blank stare
Chills and unmasks me as yours used to do.
Forgive me, Louis, for such well-meant verse,
Such running-on where you would have been terse,
And take the thanks I meant to give to you.

161 Mr Warrener

. . .born in Lincoln and studied
at Lincoln School of Art, and
in London. For a time he worked
in Paris where he became a friend
of Toulouse-Lautrec, but in 1904
he returned to Lincoln to take
over the family coal merchant business.
                Note in the Usher Gallery, Lincoln

Attics and absinthe, girls in shadows
Along the Seine under the gaslight,
And canvas after canvas covered
With botched-up images that hovered
In air for me to get them right
Before those placid flats and meadows
And that safe city on a hill
Beckoned me back again. And still,
Here at the roll-top desk where orders
Are neatly stacked for coke and cob,
Deliveries to Brigg or Bailgate,
The lamps all lit, and working late,
I feel my pulses leap and throb
Remembering art's old disorders.

162 *At the Shrine of Santa Zita**

What are you doing here, quiet under glass,
White frills and flowered chaplet, open mouth
Hard-beaked as a tortoise?
Your leathery hands have done with knitting, baking,
Wiping and dishwashing and mending cast-offs.
You have put your feet up.

Odd at first sight that you should be presented
Thus, like a girl dressed for her confirmation,
Weary of miracles.
Yet the brown mummy spruced so smart and tidy,
Dry skin and bones made housewifely and decent,
Is a true emblem.

Seven hundred years of labour-saving gadgets
Weigh little in the balance put against you,
Gaunt patroness of habit.
It would be pleasant if such daily order,
Such steady working at routines and drudging,
Were always framed so.

Parcelling up the garbage for collection,
We catch the reek of everything neglected
Shoved into corners.
The sweeper-up we do not care to mention
Sets to his chores more ruthlessly than you did,
And sifts no rubbish.

But here you lie in your ridiculous canopy,
An old crone in a little girl's white finery,
Your left hand resting
Restlessly on the lace, as if impatient
To pick a rag up from the floor beside you
And go on dusting.

*patron saint of domestic work, b. 1218, d. 1278, in S. Frediano, Lucca

163 *Jack*

She tells her grandchildren how her brother went
Off in the ambulance, his big laced boots
Heavy on the stretcher at the ends of legs
So white and thin. A family event,
The prelude to a funeral. She puts
A storyteller's shape on what she says,
And what she says holds them and makes them see
That Yorkshire street, those other, different days.

At nine years old her brother went, when we
Were nowhere, her grandchildren further off
Even than that. An accident, a death.

She pauses suddenly. The unwilled tears come,
She drops her face, and with a little cough
Stops the recital. Round the shadowy room
Children and grandchildren are silent too,
Life standing like a weight we cannot move,
Unmuscled by the thin, sharp shaft of love
That still must wound, and still the wound must show

And all that happened sixty years ago.

The mountain meadow tilted back
Among white rocks and sprawls of berries.
We panted up the mountainside,
Plucking at clumps of grass and pausing
To catch our breath at level places.
And suddenly there, above the meadow,
Through a thin screen of trees, the sky
Exploded with a hundred swallows
Plundering the blue air's farthest reaches,
Threading and stitching side to side
Silently in the silent pasture:
A fuming swirl of wings and bodies,
Violent, disciplined, alien,
A wildness, wilderness, pure and strange.

And vanished then. The empty sky
Ached, and a stunning absence filled
Those lost and vast and cloudless spaces.

165   *Called For*

Emily's

Tonight we drive back late from talk and supper
Across miles of unlit roads, flat field and fen,
Towards home; but on the way must make a detour
And rescue you from what, half-laughingly,
We think of as your temporary world –
Some group or other, all outlandishly
Named and rigged up in fancy dress and loud
With adolescent grief. Well, we're too old
For alien caperings like that. The road
Runs towards home and habit, milk and bed.

That unborn child I locked up in neat stanzas
Survives in two or three anthologies,
An effigy sealed off from chance or changes.
Now I arrive near midnight, but too early
To claim you seventeen years afterwards:
A darkened auditorium, lit fitfully
By dizzy crimsons, pulsing and fading blues
Through which electric howls and snarled-out words
Isolate you (though only in my eyes)
Sitting among three hundred sprawling bodies.

Your pale face for a second looms up through
The jerking filters, splatterings of colour
As if spawned by the music, red and blue
Over and over – there, your face again,
Not seeing me, not seeing anything,
Distinct and separate, suddenly plain
Among so many others, strangers. Smoke
Lifts as from a winter field, obscuring
All but your face, consuming, as I look,
That child I gave protective rhetoric.

Not just this place, the tribal lights, the passive
Communion of noise and being young,
Not just the strident music which I give
No more than half an ear to; but the sense
Of drifting out into another plane
Beyond the one I move on, and moved once
To bring you into being – that is why
I falter as I call you by your name,
Claim you, as drifting up towards me now
You smile at me, ready for us to go.

Victorian Voices (1980)

Here at the bench in front of me, the flasks
Ripple and throb with all the simulacra
Providence has provided; the various tasks
Assigned to each and all by their Creator
Perform and are performed. Forests of spines,
Vitals enclosed in hollow boxes, shells
Built of a thousand pieces, glide along
Majestically over rock and reef.
Yonder a *Medusa* goes, pumping its sluggish way
Laboriously, not ineffectually,
Beneath the surface of the clear wave;
A mass of *Millepore*, a honeycomb
Much like the second stomach of an Ox,
Slimes, reappears, retires, appears once more;
And there, that massive shrub of stone, the coy
Calcareous atoms of the *Madrepore*,
Short branches, branched and branched again, pierced through
With holes innumerable, threaded with tentacles.
Ha! Here is the little architect
Ready to answer for himself; he thrusts his head
And shoulders from his chimney-top, and shouts
His cognomen of *Melicerta ringens*.
Look! He is in the very act of building
Now. Did you see him suddenly
Bow down his head and lay a brick upon
The top of the last course? And now again
He builds another brick; his mould a tiny cup
Below his chin, his sole material
The floating floccose atoms of his refuse. So
Prochronically pellets build to bricks,
Eggs from their chambers, sharks from embryos,
The hollow cones that are the present teeth
Of crocodiles, the tusks of elephants
Refined through layer after layer until
Centuries are accomplished year by year –

And then, after the pulpy fibrous doors
Knocked on in the vegetable world,
The lower tribes, the higher forms – then Man,
Our first progenitor, the primal Head.
What shall we say, we who are chyle and lymph,
Blood, lungs, nails, hair, bones, teeth, phenomena
In the condition of the skeleton
Distinct, the navel corrugated here. . .?
I ask you this: could God have made these plants,
These animals, this creature that is Man,
Without these retrospective marks? I tell you, no!
A Tree-form without scars limned on its trunk!
A Palm without leaf-bases! Or a Bean
Without a hilum! No laminae
Upon the Tortoise plates! A Carp without
Concentric lines on scales! A Bird that lacks
Feathers! A Mammal without hairs,
Or claws, or teeth, or bones, or blood! A Foetus
With no placenta! In vain, in vain,
These pages, and these ages, if you admit
Such possibilities. That God came down
And made each each, and separately, and whole,
Is manifest in these. Let us suppose
That this, the present year, had been the special
Particular epoch in world history
God had selected as the true beginning,
At his behest, his fiat – what would be
Its state at this Creation? *What exists*
Would still appear precisely as it does.
There would be cities filled with swarms of men;
Houses half-built; castles in ruins; pictures
On artists' easels just sketched in; half-worn
Garments in wardrobes; ships upon the sea;
Marks of birds' footsteps on the mud; the sands
Whitening with skeletons; and human bodies
In burial grounds in stages of decay.
These, and all else, the past, would be found now

198

Because they are found in the world now, the present age,
Inseparable from the irruption, the one moment
Chosen, the constitution, the condition:
They make it what it has been, will be, is.

The flasks ripple, subside. I am tired. And miles away
I know who sits and writes and tests and proves
Quite other things and other worlds. I fix
My microscope on *Case-fly* and on *Julus*,
The field left clear and undisputed for
The single witness on this other side,
Whose testimony lies before me now:
'In Six Days God Made Heaven and Earth, the Sea,
And All That In Them Is.' Amen. Amen.

167   *A Literary Life*

I tried to open up so many eyes
To the great minds of all humanity.

I thought he liked me, thought I knew him well,
Twin strugglers through the London labyrinth,
Scribblers who learnt the scribbling trade with care –
Though he was never 'Varsity, of course:
How he arrived is something he keeps dark.
A Third in Mods, Second in Law and History,
Is all I have to boast of, but it was
Balliol, with Lang and Mallock, Nettleship,
Prothero, Milner, Rawnsley, Asquith, Cluer . . .
And then my disinheritance (that uncle and his schemes
Of 'business', and my Battels and my cheques,
And mischief in the breach, and no more cheques) –
Well, 'coaching' might have kept me, scraps of Greek
Shoved down the throats of ninnyish nincompoops;
But on that day I strayed into St Giles,
Facing the lectern, opening up the book,
Placing my finger with unopened eyes –

Those words (Acts Nine, Verse Six): 'Arise and go
Into the city, and it shall be told thee
What thou must do.' Nothing in view, alone,
Without inheritance, and penniless,
I came to London.
                            December Seventy-two –
The 'turnover', my first, a causerie
Of thoughts on 'End of Term' – oh guineas earned
Deliriously, scribbling eight hours a day
Fusty and musty in a dear old garret
Off Temple Bar, addressing envelopes
For half a crown per thousand for the *Globe*;
Letters from Swinburne about Tourneur ('if you should
Run up here sometime may I have the pleasure
Of seeing you in these rooms . . .' – the very words!)
So I aimed high, and higher, up and up –
With Leslie Stephen in the *Cornhill*, Smith
Taking my 'Dryden' for the *Quarterly*,
And work, and work, and work . . . I must jot down this:
That evening, out at Putney, A.C.S.
Invited me to hear him read his new
Volume of poems. Dobson, O'Shaughnessy, Watts,
William Rossetti, Marston – The Pines was full
Of singing birds, and I among them all.
What bliss to see them, hear them, watch the frail
Outlandish Swinburne leap and shriek and moan
Immortal verses! But it could not last.
Another year or so, and we fell out.

Extension Lectures down at Brixton, Richmond
(Frequently honoured by the Princess May,
Later to be our Queen, Duchess of Teck,
And other notables), Hackney (in Lent
Of Ninety-one, 'The poetry of Browning'),
Anerley, Ascot, Balham, Battersea,
Crouch End and Cheshunt, Highbury and Lee –
An interview with Browning, one with Froude,

And then, and then – the Chair at Birmingham . . .
But nothing quite right yet: others made way,
Climbed ladders, set their mark, were darlings all
Of quarterlies and salons and the most
Important colleges – such as my long-time friend,
Or so I thought him, one-time, some-time friend
Who gave those Cambridge lectures – tall and sleek
And full of names dropped, fudge upon the page,
And errors, errors, errors by the ton.
To say so in the *Quarterly Review*
Was – surely? – a good office, what a straight
Purposive fellow ought to say, in truth:
No personal attack – here was a book
(All pasted up for lectures) which was gross
With slovenly facts, deplorable and low . . .
But that I said so – this was beyond the pale,
Though Gladstone, Huxley, Arnold, took my point:
I think they did . . . The truth is hard to find.
What lodges in my skull is that fine phrase
They say the Laureate uttered to my friend
(My one-time friend) – 'You want to hear my view
Of that man J.C.C.? I tell you this –
A louse upon the locks of literature!'

After that, Birmingham, books, and Conan Doyle,
A touch of the old trouble – a low state
Of worn depression, sometimes several days –
And finally, the School of Journalism
To be my final crown . . .

Well, there it was, and here I am, a man
More sinned against than sinning, waking up
At ten to ten in Lowestoft, and going
Out for a walk a little dizzily
(A sleeping draught perhaps), and stepping in
To four foot six of water and thick mud.

Among the many papers found on me
A stained sheet with some careful jottings made
For the forthcoming Johnson Celebrations,
And these words too, which need no note or gloss:
'Poems in couplets written so that each
Couplet has two or three emphatic syllables,
Two or one in the first line, one in the second
Commencing with the same – this is also
The initial of the chief emphatic syllable
In the second line: thus, "I was wearie of wandering
And went me to reste
Under a brod banke
Bi a bourne side."'

And scholarship, and literature, live on:
As once I heeded, heedless others stray
Ennobled in their errors. Here I lie.

168   *To a Girl of the Period*

Will the bent bow spring back, the strained cord break?
Will temperament and long usage prove too strong?
But three months married, and I ask how long
All this will last . . . Before him, other men
Seemed apt to take me gladly: I refused,
Notoriously unanchored, a free woman
Convinced that all society is built up
By process of experiment, that the last
Word has not been said on anything.
These were the very phrases that I used,
Intent to build the future with a past
Weighed, sieved, rejected if the test so proved.

*

And was it then for pity that I loved,
Or thought I loved? Those boys and girls of his,

Quaint scoffed-at relics, an eccentric's toys –
All dressed in coarse blue flannel, Nazarenes
With love-locks to their shoulders, picturesque
As Botticelli's angels. One forgave
Thoughts of unfitness for their beauty's sake –
And so their father: his face the face of Christ,
Believing revolution was at hand,
When wars would cease, when justice without flaw
And abstract right would swiftly take the place
Of mere expedience, when the reign of peace
And truth and purity of life – alike
For men and women – would begin at last.

So I have walked the wood, and have picked up
The crooked stick. But wherein lay the flaw,
As it still lies? For he was sweet in word,
His manner acquiescent, and he smiled
To be compliant – indeed, did much I wished
Because I wished it. But I never touched
The core. The shortcomings, the weaknesses,
Lay all about. The intimacy of marriage
Forced them upon me.

                    We kept open house –
But open to our opposites: round him,
Poor patriots and penniless propagandists,
While those whom I invited he pronounced
'Worldly, ungodly, frivolous, fashionable'.
For him, my taste in proper sense of dress
(Off with the children's medieval rags
And on with frocks for girls, jackets for boys)
Was dandyism, forethought was faithlessness,
Conventional propriety just 'fashion'.

Was it my money ruined us, dependence
Of the traditional breadwinner on one
Who added to her faults of practical rigour

The graver fault of riches? His engraving
Brought in its fees, but was precarious.
The burden of the children and the home
Fell to my energies, while Utopia
Took all his time. Clean linen tablecloths,
The accurate adding-up of butchers' bills,
Were trivial stuff to him – and to me also,
Yet must be seen to. All my early ardour,
The independence which I sought and won,
Reduced to coaxing, nagging, silences
More terrible than either . . . Well, the parting came,
So gradual that *drifting* is the word
That fits it best.

                  And words are what I have –
Use, now, as my sole weapon – not to call to arms
The Shrieking Sisterhood, Wild Women shrill,
Revolting daughters (as experience
Lived through and suffered might have given me cause),
But to *condemn* them, sexless masks of men,
Hard, without love, ambitious, mercenary,
Without domestic faculty and devoid
Of healthy natural instincts . . . So with spitting rage
Women and men attack me, 'Girl of the Period'
Cartooned and comedied and turned to farce,
The hoyden travesty. No one in the world
Honours and loves true women more than I,
But then they must be *women* – with their faults,
But better than the adopted faults of *men*!
Misrepresented and misunderstood,
I pen another article while I know
Its fate is to be twisted, jeered at, burnt,
Mangled for sermons, told it takes a view
Branding a woman no better than a cow . . .

*

Maternity – that blessèd, blessèd word
Fulfilling womankind, its benisons
Denied to me. With scarcely hidden tears
I tell you that this little rush of Fame,
This famous notoriety, is nothing
Compared with that imagined ecstasy
For which I yearned, for which I was so fitted
By temperament, by body, and by skill.
Babes of my reveries, shawled plumply in my arms,
Products of finest art, of care and love,
You must belong to others. Knowing all
In my own person, all that women suffer
When actively they launch into the fray,
I would prevent with all my strength young girls
From following my own unwilled mistakes –
Guard them, indeed, with my own body from
Such insults as my life has given me,
Teach them to be themselves – and to be free.

The Punjab war is done: in all the land
No man in arms against us. Those who bolted
Ran through the Khyber Pass and go on running.
They came like thieves and dash away like thieves.
The Maharajah and the Council signed
Submission yesterday, the British colours
Were hoisted on the Citadel of Lahore,
The Koh-i-noor surrendered to our Queen,
And the Punjab – each inch of it – proclaimed
A portion of our Empire. What I have done
Is my responsibility. I know it
Just, politic, and necessary; my conscience
Tells me the work is one I pray that God
May bless; and with tranquillity I await
My country's sanction and my Queen's approval.

It is not every day an officer
Adds to the British Empire such a prize –
Four million subjects, and the priceless jewel
Of Mogul Emperors to his Sovereign's crown.
This I have done – but do not think that I
Exult unduly: I do not. But when
I feel conviction honestly that this deed
Is for the glory of my land, the honour
Of her most noble majesty, the good
Of those whom I have brought under her rule,
Fitly I may indulge a sentiment
Of honourable pride. Glory to God
For what has been achieved.

Some other matters:
A curious discovery at Rangoon –
Digging an old pagoda to make way
For army barracks, our men came across
Gold images and bracelets, with a scroll
Showing these things were put there by a queen
Five hundred years ago. In all such places
One or more images are found of Buddha:
Our fellows call them 'Tommies'. There are few
Pagodas to be seen without a hole
Made by ingenious Britons in their search
For Tommies. I am sorry to admit –
Accessory after the fact, you know –
I purchased secretly myself some bits
Of this mythology when first I reached
Burmah.

I have a sad death to report –
Bold as his sword, high-minded, kindly, pure,
Devoted to his calling, Mountain is gone.
A Christian soldier, died as he lived. He rests
In the old cemetery at Futteghur.
His widow's on her way here; he'll go home
By the next steamer.

I have just received
A packet of the rhododendron seeds
Despatched from Kooloo, which the Duchess wished,
And trust they will do well.

The troops have driven
Moung Goung Gyee out of the Irawaddi:
They took him in the jungle – took his gong,
His gold umbrella and his wife. A pity
The man himself escaped. The place is quiet.

From Barrackpore to Simla, from Peshawar
To Kunawar and Chini, from the camp
At Umritsur to Attok, there is peace.
The reinforcements from Madras have come,
So now I calculate 14,000 men
(5,000 Europeans) are there, thirteen
Steamers upon the river, besides marines
And many sailors. Opium stands high –
On each *per mensem* sale the Government
Gains well. The punishment we meted out
To Rani and to Bunnoo is rewarded –
The Rani people whom Sir Colin thrashed
Last May, destroying valley, stoup and roup,
Have just come in with turbans in their hands
Begging forgiveness, offering allegiance,
Submitting to our fortress. Our success
In sowing dissension between tribe and tribe,
'Twixt Mussulman and Sikh, Hindoo and all,
Is clear: suspicion reigns, and union
Is hopeless between any. Peace and plenty!

*

Just as the office mail was going out,
A rising in Bengal among the hills –
Barbarous folk, though usually timid,
Armed just with bows and arrows: some say greed,
Some say fanaticism, some ill-treatment
By those who build the railway. Troops are there
And closing in. The trouble has not spread
And soon should be put down. But what vexation
Just at the close of my career . . .

*

Before I lay this sceptre down, I plan
To show the court in a most frank despatch
What has been done in India these eight years –
And left undone. I look things in the face.
'Opus exegi': taking leave of those
I ruled over, tomorrow I embark.
The Friend of India some months ago
Called me 'not personally popular'.
If that is true – 'tis not for me to say –
Never were full and copious tears so shed
Over a man *unpopular*, wiped away
By bearded men . . .

                    I am quite done; my leg
Gives pain continually. Let Canning do
The best he can: the brightest jewel of all
In our imperial crown weighs heavily.
Less easy every day the burden lies –
Annex one province, two others will rise up
Like hydra-headed monsters, their partition
A parturition. What will be born of this?
Rumours and panics and religious wrath
At a few cartridges . . . and 'hope deferred'
At Delhi, given time, indeed one day
'Makes the heart sick' in England. Blow away
The rebels from our cannons, still there hangs
A cloud of blood above the hills and vales,
Ganges, and Indus, and my lost domains.

Alfred is visiting the Misses Trigg,
Devout old souls whose thread is almost cut;
The girls are at their tasks; and so am I,
A careful mother whose peculiar care's
An infant's pure delight in little things.

O Observation – though restricted now
To Ecclesfield, this room, these walls, this bed –
How I have used you, for diviner use!

In parables and emblems all things spell
Lessons for all of us – my humble gift.
Every true story of humanity
Contains a moral, wrapped and neatly tied
Like an unopened parcel for a child.
We are all children in the eyes of God.
The Crab, the Starfish, and the Bird of night,
The valiant Oak, the Robin Redbreast – all
Teach the inquiring infant to accept
Things as they are, in equanimity.
Red Snow, they say, that falls upon the Alps
(Though I have never ventured from these shores)
Or Great Sea Tangle such as Columbus saw –
Of these I am cognisant, but am more inclined
To nearer things, to close domestic signs.
See how the Bee plunges within the cup,
Fretting its legs with nectar, golden dust,
Always industrious, sweetly employed.
The Long-tailed Tit (*Parus caudatus*), I chose
After a passage by the Reverend Johns
(*British Birds in their Haunts*) – a happy choice
To illustrate 'the happy family':
For from the moment that a young brood leaves
The nest until next mating season comes,
Papa, Mama and children keep together

In perfect harmony – the same tree-clump
Is their society, they choose together
The next place they shall flit, no one disposed
To stay when all depart, molesting no one,
And suffering, as far as one can see,
No persecution. Here is a pattern made
For all young hands to copy.

                   It is true
Nature has crueller ways: the House Spider,
Having secured her web, constructs below
Hidden from view a silk apartment whence
Threads are extended, forming a cunning bridge
To the rayed centre – out, then, rushes she
Like a small thunderbolt, seizing her prey with fangs
Which suck the victim dry of all its juices
And then casts out the skeleton-remains!
I do not dwell on that. The value of hair
As a manure for rose-trees was told me
By a prizewinning gentleman who gave
Credit for his success to this device:
Dig in a sheltered place, go pretty deep,
Place in the hole a bone or two, some hair,
Water with soap-suds – practical advice,
And interesting too, to indicate
Animal assisting vegetable,
As vegetable does likewise in its turn.
Nothing can be more satisfactory
As to results. Neither our confidence
Nor yet our comfort are misplaced; no fear
Of being taken in; in all such matters
We are not at chance's mercy; everything
Goes on with regularity, by rules,
By habit; or, as naturalists word it,
By virtue of some *Law*, firm, definite,
A stringent fixity, the Light of Truth.
It is a will on which we can rely;

From past expressions of it, we presume
The future; so we rightfully say *Law*.

The Dragon-fly Grub – a creature whose appearance
Is most unprepossessing, and whose character
Is hardly amiable – can be kept
Happily in a foot-pan filled with water
And fed from ponds or ditches with live insects.
Observe at leisure Metamorphosis –
How, at the chosen moment, this vile thing
Climbs up the Flag or Iris planted there
For your experiment – a rent appears
Within the Pupa case, the wings expand,
And the winged tyrant of the airy world
Most beautifully ascends.

        O read the book
God's servant, Nature, puts within your ken!
There in these works which seem to puzzle reason
Something divine is hidden, to be discovered
By patient scrutiny. Thus, crickets sing
Loudly, and most troublingly by day,
In damp conditions – as in a cottage here
Where a young mother died by slow degrees
Of a consumption; and it seemed as though
The crickets heralded the sad event.
See on my sun-dial the words I chose,
Hallowed by constant observation – 'Watch,
For ye know not the hour . . .'

        Now, Juliana,
The day's dictation's finished. Kindly copy
My words in your fair hand. My own, disabled,
Aching and helpless must lie here unused
Upon the counterpane. I have employment,
I see the sun, love life. And when you pray,
Pray not that I may have less pain but that
More patience may be mine.

Hockley is turning Papist, so they say:
His set is stiff with incense, and he bobs
Most roguishly in chapel. More and more
The Whore of Babylon extends her sway.
Branston is fiddling with his 'little jobs',
Copying the Bursar's buttery accounts
Into a pocket book he locks away.
In Common Room each night, the floor
Is held by Foxton, face flushed like a plum
About to drop – and we have seen him drop
Drunk as a carter in the smouldering grate.
They are all here, my *Corpus Asinorum*,
Donkeys in orders, stuffed in jowl and crop.
One day it will be said 'He did the state
Some service', when they read my book of fools.

The Master's slack. He does not know the rules.
He is – can't be denied – a natural curate
And would be better suited to the cure
Of souls in Wiltshire, ministering to pigs.
I've seen old Figgins watch him like a ferret,
For Figgins was passed over, and for sure
Preferment went because Enthusiasts
Clamoured for someone without Roman views.
But – pardon me – the Master strokes and frigs
His conscience like a trollop with an itch
Flat on her back and panting in the stews.
All pious mush dressed up as manliness,
Evangelistic canting, keen to bring
Trousers to niggers who don't wear a stitch.
A man's religion is his own. To sing
Barnstorming stanzas to the Lord's as poor
As Newman fluting eunuch fancyings,
His heavenly choir on earth. O that old Whore,
How devious she becomes!

                                        This elm-smoke stings
My eyes at night, when I should be holed up
Snugly behind the bulwark of my oak.
Some more Marsala, or another cup
Of punch . . . What frowsty collared priest is this,
Another chum of Kingston's on the soak
Or snivelling gaitered surrogate from Bath?
Give me your arm – I needs must go and piss.

My colleagues all tread down the primrose path
That – who? – oh, Shakespeare then – put in a play.
I should be even now, I tell you, hard
Pent in my room and working at my book,
Theocritus, my text, my elegiac
Pagan . . .

                    How these chatterers swill and stay!
I'll take a turn with you around the yard,
The farther quad where dotards never look,
Or if they do, then always back and back
To the dark backward and abysm of time . . .
But then we all are backward-lookers here,
If you would understand me: relicts, men
Who hear the echo when we hear the chime,
As Great Tom stuns the silence. In my ear
I sense the falter of the tolling bell,
I hear it boom again, again, again,
Fetching me back and back, not boding well,
And the full moon hangs high across St Ebbe's . . .

Where was I? Morbid, maybe, at this hour
When Master, Bursar, Chaplain, Dean and all
Waddle like corpulent spiders in their webs
To winding staircases and narrow beds,
To livings without life, posts without power,
A benefice without a benefit.
I have you all marked down . . .

Later he wrote: 'On 24th September
Shocked to hear of tragic death of friend
&c': 'keen regret' to him long after
That I and she to whom he was attached
So warmly 'never met or were acquainted
And now would never . . .'

    He was more astute –
Though no less given to subterfuge – than I,
Who saw him first a young, raw, fresh-faced thing.
The 'attachment' that he wrote of was but one
Melded with many others – love-longings
He used as I could not.

    My longings led
Down to the back room of the *Lamb & Flag* –
Brandy-and-water till the dreams took over,
Wafting me back to times when all ran right,
All was about to be, nothing came sour
Against the throat and tongue, nothing looked dark
Against the study-lamp . . . But then the raging,
The boasts and incoherences, the tags
Bellowed or muttered to an audience
That played me for its sport, a thrashing minnow
Swelled to a pike and gorging on the hook.
And, at the last, a brother's troubled arm
Helping me up and out and home to bed,
To toss and twitch and, sweating, sleep it off
Till the next bout would have me in its grip.

The miseries we have become compounded
By those we guess are yet to come, the failings
That magnify to failures. First the sighing
Winds that portend a shower, the scattered drops,
The downpour venting to a steady drizzle
Drenching before and after. So it was:
Small gifts that proved yet smaller, all ambition
Shrunk to a modicum, a way of life.
Workhouse accounts inspected, another novel
Judiciously dissected in review,
A reputation coddled till it smothered.

Onset of autumn – melancholy time
In Cambridge, mists uprising from Coe Fen
Over the causeway, Michaelmas daisies drenched
Drooping their heads in college gardens. Shrouds
Gathered on candles, and foretold a death:
Whose death was supposition – but I knew,
Even as by the mantelpiece I stood
And talked, and heard them guttering; and he
Recognized, too, the sign. And all such signs
Were his to play with, twists and turning points
For fictions, symbols, circumstantial plots . . .

If she I fumbled in hot madness knew
How things had fallen out, our issue growing
Monstrous, strung up as witness of our sin
Though long estranged, the dire inheritance
Of evil warps, repugnant origins,
She would be privy to them. And she knew –
Because she had to bear – the sad beginnings.
I – we – and our son too – we have been used
By one to whom I was mentor . . . yes, and friend:
The dutiful recorder of my trust,
Advice, remonstrance, love. What Homer said,
What Virgil took through labyrinths of metre,
What all my lavished learning broke and spilt,
He bore away, and stored, and deviously
Set out in his inventions. Meanwhile I
Drudged here and there, perpetual ordinand
Not fit to be ordained, my weaknesses
Disguised as scruples or as personal quirks
Familiar to familiars.

                    Yet I loved him
As one untainted by my shameful spells,
As one fit to be fledged – and then he flew!
How far and with what difficulty flew,
Far out beyond me, beyond that grey day
Far from our Dorset heath, our ambulations
Entranced with all my nurturings of talent,
Beyond the too-entrancing Cambridge courts
I lapsed towards, seeking again a brother. . . !

Dear brother in the outer room, you hear
A kind of trickling, a sound you cannot place:
That cold commemorator I encouraged
Will place it, use it, all grist for his mill.
I took the open razor to my throat.

Old pupil, you have new material now.

173   *A Message from Her*
      (Modern Love, v)

                    I

So I dissembled: you dissembled too,
Striving to gain the fame you could not have.
You thought me your importunate young slave.
I thought you fierce to attain the things that you,
You only, could achieve. So we were wrong
In feigning each was only bent on each,
Eyes signalling to eyes, not needing speech.
The labour hence was tortuous and long,
Words broke to sentences, each phrase strung out
Like drunken men striving to stretch their thirst
Into the dawn, or lovers who at first
Believe each touch and kiss a final bout,
And then renewed, renewed . . . And each goes on
Battling, and feinting, reeling under blows
That deaden as the deadly feeling grows
That they are dead indeed; and dead and gone.

II

That gentle painter with beseeching eyes –
He was no menace: not the first, at least.
Some other bore the sign, mark of the beast,
Before he ever came. What sad surprise
When I escaped – more matter for your art!
This was the dizzy sickening of your will,
Sisyphus labouring up the stony hill,
Something that drained the nerves and pierced the heart:
An emptiness that gave me room to breathe
But vacuum to you – and how you strove,
Your lungs protesting, with what you used to love,
Your murderess . . . So our passions seethe,
Spill over, settle, chill. We learn to die
By living our own lives, leaving a room
Furnished like any self-respecting tomb,
The funeral bands disguising vacancy.

III

I left a note: 'He is in tears – I must
Go to him now.' And so the hours went by,
And you, of course, knew I could never lie.
But there I lay, lapped in an alien lust
That you could never understand, nor ever
Satisfy. Those broodings, those inert
And silent pangs that shadowed your sad hurt,
How could you contemplate what came to sever
Mismatched endurances with such a blow?
My love – my once love – you were far away,
Remembering some distant hallowed day
When from my gown I let the loose bands go
And I was Princess to your wandering Prince,
And all was fable, Land of Faery . . .
What you cast out, what you could never see –
That was the simple truth, long vanished since.

IV

No word of me in letters, never a word
Let fall from that point onwards that I shared
Eight years with you, or that I ever cared
Concerning you. Fled like a migrant bird
To climes unknown, in ignorance I became
A footnote to your *opus*, quite cast out
Like the lean scapegoat who must bear the doubt
Because no other creature bears the blame.
And so I sickened – pitiless endless pain,
The swellings and the achings. Pale and weak,
I stumbled into debt, wrote letters, bleak
Day after day. For you, the deadly strain
Was not *my* dying but *your* distant fear
Of sickness and of death. I knew I must
Face on my own the test, accept the just
Reward for sin, and nowhere seek a tear.

V

How strange to be remembered in this way!
A set of almost-sonnets, crabbed yet rich,
Abrupt yet ample, stitch woven into stitch
As line by line you tell the present day
What happened, who kept silent, which one spoke
Words that must wound, how reverie went wrong,
And each verse carrying its bitter song –
Bitter, reproaching nothing but the yoke
That kept us bound together. This is how
Art will remember us, not in the ways
That stretched and broke us through those racking days
But in the mode that's apt and modish now:
Art for Art's sake . . . Forsaken, you set down
A set of tablets permanent as stone.
I was a wisp, a nothing, on my own,
Commemorated with an iron crown.

You think I'm drunk because my Irish voice
Is thick and crapulous – ah, there's a word
You wouldn't give me credit for: you think
I'm thick as peat, sir, thick as two short planks,
Because you hear my stumbling bumbling throat
Expectorate a load of roughened vowels.
Why smoothness, sir? Why should I learn to trim
Words that are mine to suit the vocables
That, polished, come from *your* mouth? I imbibed
Fine terms and cadences from all my tribe,
The Irish minstrelsy.

                        A crippled beggar
For forty years, a beggar before that
Since I could walk – my mother turned me out
To beg, because my father served the crown
In Egypt or some other foreign part
And never came back. I learned no trade. I might
Have learnt the shoemaking, but what's the use?
Fine times I had when the French war was on –
I lived in Westminster, one of two hundred
We called the Pye-Street Beggars, and our captain
Was Copenhagen Jack. Jack's word was law.
Each day he formed us up, gave us our beat:
'Twas share and share alike – the captain extra.
We had our lays – oh yes – the 'blind dodge darkies'
Who played at being blind, 'shakers' with fits,
And shipwrecked mariners who'd never seen the sea,
And men who took a bit of glass to scrape
Their feet until the blood ran – dodging lame, sir . . .

Not like my honest lameness. A horse and cart
Drove over me – well, yes, a trifle drunk, sir.
We lived like lords with Copenhagen Jack –
Fifty'd sit down to a supper, geese
And turkeys and all that, and keep it up
Till daylight with our songs and toasts.

                            Oh no,
There's nothing like it now: the new police
And this Mendicity Society has spoiled it all.
When Jack was 'pressed, his boys got rid of me –
They skinned me, took my coat and boots, turned out
In tatters on the 'orphan lay'. I cried
All day on the doorsteps, with my captain gone.
That won me ha'pence, though, and silver too,
And when I brought the swag home all the lads
Danced round and swore they'd make me captain next.
But when they'd had their fun, they took it all,
Kicked me under the table. I ran away,
Found a new house – St Giles – no captain there,
But better treatment. A hundred beggars,
Two or three hundred more in houses near –
Now all those houses gone, sir, taken down
When Oxford Street, New Oxford, was built up.
Oh we lived well then, St Giles and Westminster –
Eight, ten, fifteen, aye, thirty shillings a day
I've earned a-begging.

                      Not one shilling now.
The folks don't give today as they did then,
They think we're all impostures. And the police –
They won't let you alone. No, sir, I told you –
I never knew aught else but begging work:
How could I? 'Twas the trade I was brought up to.
A man must follow his trade. No doubt I'll die
A beggar, and the parish'll bury me.

A rum, sir? Thank you. And I'll speak you such
A ballad as my forebears left to me
From Holy Ireland. No, not drunk at all –
'Tis but my speech, a cockney Irish yet
The inheritance of kings, of bards, of saints,
Crippled, on crutches, with a tray of laces.

175 *The Studio*

Pale beauties of a former day, lie there
Suppliant slaves attentive to my gaze!
My brush must worship you, large-eyed, bereft
Of all but wisps of gauze and feathered fans
In such a heat, the ancient classic sea
Glimpsed blue through the embrasure. How you strain
Mutely at these constraints I put on you,
Languid on couches, supine by the pool!

How different the view as now I turn
And look on dank back-gardens, dripping walls,
Façades of terraces, a distant spire,
And rank on rank of villas sprawling up
To crown this city fate has given me . . .
If I had been brought up among your groves,
Your temples and your chambers, purple-draped,
Sun-drenched in marble, what might I have been!

And so I use you, distant and ideal,
Maidens of modesty, passionate and still,
To be my paragons. My purposes
Are chaste, exact, sublime, and beautiful,
However men may misinterpret such
Voluptuous offerings – the upraised breasts,
The yearning thighs, the lips that, swollen, speak
Impulses we deny except to Art . . .

Back to the canvas . . . Think – in Manchester
My allegories grace those blackened fanes,
Suggesting a perspective we have spurned
In votes, and bills of lading, and machines
That knit and fret and petulantly stamp
Patterns on shoddiness, an endless wheel
Of usefulness and profit. Yet my shapes –
Lovingly nurtured, individual . . .

They say I make my profits too. 'Tis so –
I tug the heart, the lost inheritance,
And so the purse-strings. Is that shameful, then?
To please with what would else be lost to us?
They speak of *markets*: I am fortunate
In doing best what's best for my design,
Romantic ardour in a classic vein,
The pristine captured and brought down from heaven.

Watch how I mix the umber with the rose,
Tinctures of flesh beyond imaginings,
The dew still on the petal, light of light,
Waterdrops glistening on the lifted arm –
A talent, and a gift: no muddiness,
No crudity, no vaulting after vague
Resemblances, but everywhere my crisp
Edges of excellence, a bounding line.

These Frenchmen and these Dutch – I've heard of them,
But what about them? Vogues will come and go
As they have always done. The test must be
Standards established by the chosen few
Time has preserved for us – Praxiteles,
Phidias, a handful else. Where can Art go
Except in emulation? Here – the pink
Lies on the white, and trembles on the cheek.

Rich bronzes, figured vases, jewellery –
Fruits of my labours, subterranean joys:
My men sit round a dark sarcophagus,
Broken and plundered centuries ago,
And nod at noon. I sift and sift again,
Under the hottest sun, in longest hours
Of sleepy sweltering heat, intent on each
Small shovelful of soil, or sand, or ash.
No matter that the London functionaries
Hold back my proper monies, ignoring letters,
Museum men walled up in bills of lading,
Idly content that yet another consul
Should now and then transmit them treasures. Mine's
A nose for all that's oldest, finest, rarest,
From shy Etruscans to these desert shores
Where Battus first made landfall and the light
Of Greece first dawned in darkest Africa.
White-crowned Cyrene – never have I seen
A Grecian city so commanding, high
On its acropolis, with all around
A wilderness of tombs, deep lintelled caves,
Domes, and hog-backs, and noble architraves,
And hoarded grave-goods (even though despoilt
By brigands old and new) that catch the breath.

Not so this post my lords have given me –
A dreary town stuck betwixt sea and sand,
Salt-lakes, and hovels windowless and low
With stable-yard interiors like middens,
A crumbling castle, one poor minaret,
One grove of date palms, line after line of walls
Monotonously red, the houses unhewn stone
Bedded in mud, and rain, and filth, the whole
Wretched confusion a barbarity
Fit for the Barbary Shore . . . A tail-less lion

Over my doorway, in as quaint a style
As Mycenean, and a flag-staff – these
Alone distinguish my abode as that
Which represents Her Majesty. I hope
I am not doomed to a long exile here
In this *Ulubrae*, sand-girt, dead-dog-strewn.
Smyrna, Palermo – those I covet most . . .

Still, for the present I must grant it has
Greater attraction than it would possess
For many people: diggings established, soon
I hope to make a good haul of antiques.
As for my consular duties, I have borne
In mind your last injunction, that I should
Ingratiate myself among the Arabs. The other day
I visited a powerful tribe in camp –
Five or six hundred horsemen at a gallop,
Brandishing their long rifles, shouted welcome
And honoured me with races, firing muskets.
I am on good terms, also, with the Pasha:
I stood firm to his claims, and he withdrew
Pretentious interferences. I begin
To understand these oriental gentlemen –
I wish I could claim as much for what I know
Of their outlandish languages . . .

                              Many tombs,
Well-furnished I would guess, are even here
Hard by Benghazi, on the salt-lake shore.
More to the north-east, on the Tocra track,
Relieve the barren undulating waste,
Unfreshened by flower or shrub, by leaf or blade.
It is of these I wrote at the beginning,
The Tocra vases, finely beautiful,
Panathenaic some of them. Even more
The port of Apollonia presents
Far richer prizes, if I can persuade

A *firman* from the Pasha. Where I fear
Sole opposition is from the Brotherhoods,
The Convents of Senoussy who keep up
Fanaticism and intolerance
Among the lower Arabs: dangerous men.
Twice in my tour they threatened me with talk
Of 'Nazarene dog', and at Ptolmeita I
Escaped only because my *exequatur*
Displayed the Sultan's signature. Such trials
Do not, however, bring me to despair;
A spice of danger lends a certain relish
To searching for antiquities.

              If Lord Somers
Should be inclined to pay this coast a visit,
I would delight to be his *cicerone*. Did I mention
At Apollonia the numerous columns
Of cipollino, relics of Christian churches,
To which the Turks attach no value, but
Which I am sure would be much prized in England,
Either perhaps to adorn the National Gallery
Or decorate the portico of a church?
May I beg the Admiral at Malta to allow
Some gunboat, on a cruise, to bear me hence
And lift these handsome spoils? Such prospects lighten
The burden of this wretchedness, the whines
Of Maltese litigants, the silences
I long endure from London. My dear Sir,
I beg you not to let me languish here,
Though I am avid for what treasures yet
May be vouchsafed to me.

Can these thick-pelted Calibans, deep in their dripping forests,
Be human as I am, or else collateral
Ancestors, the kin of apes and monkeys?
Such questions exercise the gentle reader
Snug in his study, holding in his armchair
My books of travel: they are not my questions.
Journeying, I best follow the old author –
Humani nil a me alienum puto.
For, from the moment England drops behind me
With all its rules of upbringing and habit,
Sensible tracts, quotidian drudgeries,
And all my dismal memories of girlhood,
I grow another face, become another person.

Travellers, indeed, are privileged to do
The most improper things imagined with
Perfect propriety. The sickly elder daughter
Whose youth was spent reclining on the sofas
In rectory drawing-rooms, with spinal trouble
That nagged through camomile and laudanum,
Now jolts on horseback through the wilderness,
Land of the Rising Sun's most northern island.

Evenings in plaited huts, gulping down rancid stews
(Boar offal, spongy roots, unnameable victuals),
Saké libations to the million deities
Worshipped in mountain, tree and rock and river,
Dim-lit interiors where elders endlessly
Spell out the genealogies of tribe and tribe,
And over all the mystery and the deluge
Descending like a revelation on me.
For God is here, among these (you say) savages,
As instrumental in his signs and wonders
As anywhere in tamer, temperate places.
No, I do not presume the evangelical:

My part is not the preaching of the Gospel,
Though some could only gauge what I am doing
In terms of carrying Bibles to the natives –
Aunt Mary as a missionary in India
Or Cousin Mary among Persian deserts.
These Ainu have no written law or history –
Indeed, no forms of written words among them –
And, placid in their sad, sweet resignation,
Only inflamed by copious potations
Of rice-wine spirits, are uncomprehending
At notions of a Saviour among them.

If you cast doubt upon the seemly wisdom
Of trusting female frailty to the dangers
Exposed by such benighted sole encounters,
I ask you, reader, merely to examine
Your storyteller as she stands before you:
Four-foot-eleven, a stumpy dumpy creature,
At her age – rising fifty – unencumbered
With fancies how her charms might be like tinder.
I trust myself to Ito, my interpreter –
Sharp-witted, vain and bandy-legged, a youth
Hot for his girls, his sweetmeats and his pride.
A foreign lady capable of 'drinking
To the gods' in their intoxicated fashion
Without intoxication, and whose questionings
Seek out the best and not the worst in all men –
They cannot harm me. Diligent and merry,
The grooms who take my horses and are humble
Could not depend entirely on the tardy
And insufficient efforts of the niggard
And selfish Church I grew in and grew up to.
God numbers these in his inheritance:
These heathens puzzled by the word 'salvation'
Will yet be saved – but not by my endeavours.
The gates of Heaven are wide and full of mercy,
Opening to all who follow in their fashion

The instincts they may never have acknowledged,
Whether Hawaii, Arkansas or Yorkshire
(Parishes known or unknown, known to me),
Loosed them to make their world their destiny.
Peevish I may be, briefly, at my portion
(I should have been a man, though would not say it
Except to Ito, who'll not understand),
But this I know – accept – embrace – and glory in –
The freedom of a journey that excuses
All things but cowardice, bad faith, incompetence,
And leaves me free to look at what was never
Revealed before to the sick English daughter
Of a good man who never could envisage
The stumbling trackways she can now exult in,
Far from the rooms she lay in once, alone.

178 *The Potter's Field*

Here, sir, a fine display of bravery
And fortitude, all rendered out of clay –
Here's Caius Mutius holding his right hand
Within the fire, showing Porsenna
The firmness of the Roman character;
On the reverse, the maid Cloelia
Selecting from the youthful hostages
Whom Porsenna will liberate. A piece
Noble and highly wrought, you will agree.
And by this vase, a terracotta plaque
Depicting in relief Da Vinci's great
'Battle of the Standard' – lavished round the rim
Oak leaves and acorns in the classic style.
This modelled wall-hanging won Second Prize
In 'Eighty-two at Braintree – Lucilus
Personates Brutus, an Old Master's work
Young Edward copied with a master's skill.
Glazed ornamental is our special pride,

Gem-ware encrusted, sprigged and polychrome –
But we love precedent in everything,
Old lessons handed on, the apostles' touch
Rendering all we make a sacrament
Blessed by the past – Egyptian, Roman, Greek,
Palissy plates and Babylonian shapes,
These ewers after Orazia Fontana's,
Tazzas adapted from Fijian ware
(Queen Emma of the Sandwich Isles came here,
And shook me by the hand, and bought a fine
Large model of our castle-keep, the source
Of so much inspiration – solid stuff,
Impregnable though ruined). Even these
Humbler creations have their ancestry:
Barm-pots and costrels, benisons and cloams,
Pottles and salt-kits, gallipots and tygs,
The rude plain earthenware, traditional instruments
Rustic amusement used, the puzzle-jugs,
The bird-whistles – I made them, one by one
And gross by gross, to stock the waggonloads
That left our workshop, sagging above wheels
Bedded in mud, for markets dwindling down
To half a dozen hawkers raucously
Shouting our old-style wares to new-style ears . . .

For that I fear's my story. What I put
In stone above the lintel is my text –
The psalmist's strong stern voice: 'Except the Lord
Do build the house, they labour in vain that build it' –
And vain the labour too. With sweating kilns
That marred whole bungs at firing, bubbles, bloats
Scarring the intricate sprays and sprigs and lugs,
Added to muddle casting-up accounts,
And sons who emigrated or who died,
And Fashion sniggering at our 'quaintnesses',
Grown fond of delicate mincing porcelain . . .
Fine feathering, tib-work, the antique ornate

Crossed with the sturdy native English style,
Slumped to mere jobbery, plain coarse flower-pots,
Nothings by anyone for anyone,
No individual stamp, no sense of that
Grandeur I gave a title to – 'Unique
Art Pottery Works of Castle Hedingham'
('The *Royal* Art', after Queen Emma's visit).
Zion bewails her pitiful estate,
'Esteemed as earthen pitchers' – meaning held
As low as dirt.

                    And yet our dirt is *clay*,
Grog, slurry to be fashioned into lives
As vivid as the mud our Infant Lord
Shaped into sparrows from the gutter-side . . .

                    *

The grunting drays convey the crocks away
Where they will gather dust in crumbling sheds,
Back-ends of warehouses, a bankrupt's stock.
Here in my cottage by the castle wall
I slowly foot the treadle of the wheel
That turns the last ceramic I shall make
Before the vessel's broken and the sherds
Are thrown on to the spoil-heap where we lie
Until the angels' golden trumpets sound,
The Master Potter works his mystery,
And every fragment to its fragment's joined.

A dozen dogs, poodles and nondescripts,
My darlings barking at the iron gate . . .
Who might it be? There's no one left to call,
And so I sit useless, the garden wall
High as my disappointment, sit and wait
For the moths to eat away the innocence,
The honesty, the decency, and then
The whole new wardrobe I could not afford
From Worth – the vanity, the vain expense,
The flirting with Marchese and with Lord,
The opinionated converse with true men.

Now Robert Lytton's dead – a heart attack –
And della Stufa – cancer of the throat –
And Mario, too, whose voice enslaved me once –
All loves, all friendships, straitened and remote
As former fame, and flower-filled hotel rooms,
The Langham thirty years ago . . . Look askance,
You moralists who jib at genius,
At the pert message posted in the hall –
'Leave morals and umbrellas at the door.'
No invitation to reception, dance,
Wine, *conversazione*, concert, play,
For – what? – a dozen years . . . A villa, dank
And crumbling among cypresses, four floors,
Twenty-five rooms – myself and Gori stay
When Bagni drifts with leaves, and all have left.
Condemned to solitude, in poverty,
Furniture seized by creditors, bereft
Even of letters bundled over years,
Manuscripts auctioned, each royalty and fee
Reduced to farthings . . . No, these are not tears
But the dulled liquids of blue eyes that saw
Irving perform my gestures and my words.
Out of the world, my world, perhaps so much

233

The better, walled up here midst dogs and trees –
I am old, pathetic, angry, out of touch.
The world takes its revenge on us, because
We once despised it. Play it as you please,
Rewards must dwindle, style must go awry,
Voluptuousness grow vile, and Europe learn
The rage for slaughter. Middle-class spirits crush
The rapture and the passion of the soul,
Making it mute: thus Browning, Tennyson,
George Eliot – in chains, or chanting odes,
Or hypocritical in homilies.
Our genius is our spur, our passion goads
The highest from the best. Even in the tomb
The lustre shines like gold from sepulchres
Of lost Etruscan kings, or on the breast
Of some fair living woman, undimmed by dust,
The length of ages, or men's pettiness.

*

My dogs bark on among the cypress gloom,
A dozen Cerberuses whose yelps press
Hotly against the neglected effigy –
My own – where like a Florentine princess
I lie in Bagni, dead, unread, my name
A half-romantic joke, something to see
If tourists can be bothered to search out
A deaf custodian with a rusty key.
No flowers, no candles, no *frisson*-laden words
Await you there: the candles have gone out,
The flowers have faded, and the words are dull
As out-of-fashion dusty ballroom clothes
Hanging in wardrobes in deserted rooms.
The iron bell-handle's broken: when you pull,
The dogs grow hoarse not at the sound of it
But at the unfamiliar, painful smell
Which men call Life. And I am out of it.

234

Notes to 'Victorian Voices'

Most of these poems draw on actual individuals. It would be very nearly impossible to establish all the sources I have used, or for me to make a firm line between transcription and invention, but what follows is a list of the 'subjects' of the poems and an acknowledgement of those sources of which I am most conscious:

'At Marychurch': Philip Henry Gosse (1810–1888). Gosse (the 'father' of Edmund Gosse's *Father and Son*) published his explanation of Creation, *Omphalos*, in 1857: Darwin, whom Gosse knew, published *The Origin of Species* in 1859. Marychurch, on the Devon coast, was where Gosse lived for over thirty years, and here he made many of his observations of marine biology.

'A Literary Life': John Churton Collins (1848–1908). Collins was an industrious literary journalist and freelance lecturer who eventually held the first chair in English at Birmingham University. His attack on his old friend Edmund Gosse's Clark Lectures in the *Quarterly* was controversial, and earned a famous rebuke from Tennyson. His son, L. C. Collins, published the *Life and Memoirs of John Churton Collins* in 1912.

'To a Girl of the Period': Eliza Lynn Linton (1822–1898). She married the engraver (and, in a mild way, bohemian social reformer) W. J. Linton, taking over his children by a former marriage, but was soon disillusioned and they separated. She was an indefatigable contributor to the periodicals, chiefly of essays on 'the new woman', and in particular of a group later collected and published as *The Girl of the Period and other Social Essays* (1883). George Somes Layard published *Mrs Lynn Linton: Her Life, Letters and Opinions* in 1901.

'Messages from Government House': James Ramsay, Marquess of Dalhousie (1812–1860). He became Governor-General of India in 1848, and left India in 1856 before the Mutiny the following year. The *Private Letters of the Marquess of Dalhousie* were edited by J. G. A. Bair in 1910.

'Parables from Nature': Margaret Gatty (1809–1873). A prolific writer for children, she was married to an Anglican clergyman, the Rev. Alfred Gatty. Her *Parables from Nature* appeared in 1896 with a memoir by her daughter, Juliana Horatia Ewing, also a notable children's writer.

'After High Table': an amalgam and/or invention, drawing on several hints in (among other places) Jan Morris's *Oxford Book of Oxford* (1978) and Mark Pattison's *Memoirs* (1885). I imagine an elderly don in the 1860s and 1870s, ordained, but in many ways a survival from a period less given to religious searching and debate.

'The Mentor': Horace Moule (1832–1873). Moule came from a family of respectable dons and clerics, and had hopes of becoming a scholar and literary man. In 1857 he befriended the young Thomas Hardy, who later made use of him in *Jude the Obscure* and several poems. Moule was said to have got a village girl pregnant: the son of this union was later hanged in Australia. Moule killed himself in his brother's rooms in Cambridge. See *Young Thomas Hardy* by Robert Gittings (1975).

'A Message from Her': Mary Ellen Meredith (1821–1861). She was the daughter of Thomas Love Peacock, and married George Meredith in 1849. After eight years of unhappiness, she left with the painter Henry Wallis, but died in 1861, alone and after much illness. Meredith's sequence of 16-line poems, *Modern Love*, is in part based on their marriage. A standard source for the story is Siegfried Sassoon's life of Meredith (1948); a much more biased account is Diane Johnson's *Lesser Lives* (1972), but it has the advantage of drawing on some hitherto unpublished material.

'Seventy Years a Beggar': see Henry Mayhew's *London Labour and the London Poor*, Volume Four, 1864. The beggar is based on one of the people interviewed by Mayhew for this pioneering work of sociology (or investigative journalism).

'The Studio': loosely based on Lawrence Alma-Tadema (1836–1912). Alma-Tadema's best-known paintings are neo-classical studies, such as *In the Tepidarium*. His work was technically adept, erotic in a subdued mode, and fashionable in its day.

'The Consul at Benghazi': George Dennis (1814–1898). Dennis combined civil service and consular duties with a passion for antiquarianism, first in Italy (where he made some considerable researches into the Etruscans), then in Benghazi between 1864 and 1868. D. E. Rhodes published *Dennis of Etruria* in 1973; in spite of its title, the book also covers the later period of Dennis's life, including the Benghazi years.

'On Horseback through Hokkaido': Isabella Bird (1831–1904). She was the delicate daughter of a Yorkshire clergyman, but in time became an intrepid traveller in many parts of the world. She published *Unbeaten Tracks in Japan* in 1880. Pat Barr published a delightful biography of her, *A Curious Life for a Lady*, in 1970.

'The Potter's Field': Edward Bingham (1829–190?). Bingham's father founded the Castle Hedingham Pottery in Essex in 1837. Edward Bingham specialized in extraordinarily fanciful – and frequently ugly – variations on medieval earthenware, mixed with a widely eclectic range of other styles. He was a devout and fervent Evangelical. The standard study is *The Story of Castle Hedingham Pottery* by R. J. Bradley (1968); in the same year Bevis Hillier published his *Pottery and Porcelain, 1700–1914*, which contains a good brief account of Bingham and his work.

'From the Villa Massoni': 'Ouida' (Louisa Ramé, 1839–1909). Between 1861 and 1867, Ouida published the astonishing number of forty-seven books, many of which (in particular *Under Two Flags*) were very successful. Exhausted by such productivity, she travelled to Florence to recuperate, and spent almost the whole of the rest of her life in Italy. In 1895 she moved with her faithful maid Gori to the Villa Massoni at Bagni di Lucca, by which time her literary reputation was in eclipse. Her effigy, deliberately imitating the style of della Quercia's statue of Ilaria del Carretto in the Duomo at Lucca, is in the Protestant Cemetery at Bagni. Ouida's *Views and Opinions* were published in 1895. Another useful source was *Paradise of Exiles* by Olive Hamilton (1974).

from *Poems 1953–1983* (1984)

180 *Fuel*

Damp logs, foul spitting planks,
A smoky pile of still unseasoned timbers –
The river sniffs and pushes at its banks,
Remembering the embers
We hauled from its turbulence and tried to burn.
Now it is our turn
To feel that loss, to be punished for our pains
As a stinging cloud billows out and stains
Ceiling and walls, prickling our eyes
With half-dead fumes, resinous memories.

These bits we cannot burn – lumber
Not to be consumed, reduced to ash –
Fill the shared room with odours, and encumber
Our lungs with dross, with trash.
What is combustible goes quite away
And will not stay
To simmer, splutter, blanketing the place
With reeking sullenness we cannot face.
Let them lie long, dry out, forget the river,
Ignite and flare and drop away forever.

181 *Observation in Winter*

The surfaces of earth – all rigid now
Wherever mud hardens or branches brace
Their strength against the hoar-frost as its lace
Drenches in stiffly whitened mists – show how
Things keep their postures as an accident,
Were never meant
To be seen *now* or *now*, a moment caught,
Frozen, recorded in an eyelid's shutter.
A pheasant rises, brilliant, in a flutter
Of skirling bronzes, noisily distraught,
Wrecking the field's composure.
Everything falls back startled, disarrayed,
Begins to flow again; after that brief exposure
Resumes a world that can't be stopped or stayed.

182 *The Stump*

The mower hits it, screeches, sheers away:
No more than half an inch of surfaced wood
Bedded in grass, each year seems to be dead,
Lopped with an axe by someone on some day
Before we bought the place. What sort of tree
I can't begin to guess, so little's left
As, year by year and cut by cut, the shaft
Prods up, is sliced, reduced, until I see
Nothing except a disc flush with the earth.
Dead, surely. Till in summer, mowing there,
The blade tears round it, screaming, giving birth
And being aborted, as the growing year
Refuses to forget what once grew there.

183 *What Animal*

What animal is this, so safe and cared for,
Cosseted even, with his mate and young
Trustingly by him, comfort and room to breathe,
Nourishment guaranteed, secure among
Refreshments such as spirit and body crave for –
Why, then, does he seethe
Resentfully, stare at the far horizon
As if bars blocked his way, making a cage
Where no cage is? What walls enclose his prison?
A futile aching rage
Seems to bow down his head and fix his teeth
Wretchedly in his own well pampered flesh,
Nuzzling to touch the bone buried beneath,
To start afresh
Wounds healed and mended, convalescent sores.
What animal? Such questioning ignores
The trail of trodden footprints to this place,
The old familiar smell, the placid stream
Running so clear and slow you see your face
Reflected, as with the sharpness of a dream
You know the creature, know the cage is yours

Though there is neither cage, nor walls, nor bars.

184 *The Bed*

Facing the head of the bed, a stranger would see
Always you on the right, me on the left:
Your pillow higher, softer, mine no more
Than a thin ridge tilting my sleeping head
Above the horizontal. Your body curled,
A question-mark, a foetus: mine hulled down
Prone, legs straddled, left hand flung above.

Habits of night, when bodies meet and touch.

Reach for the bedside lamp and put it out.
A hand exploring, two hands moving over
Familiar surfaces. The tender ache, the comfort.
Each knows the other's places like a face
Daily encountered in the bathroom mirror.

Also, at times, the tears, the silences,
Bad dreams before sleep comes, and absences
Waking to shrill alarms' routineless clamour,
With you alone, as I have been alone,
Elsewhere, waking to stare at shattered patterns,
Feeling the sun come up in other rooms.

The cold bit of the bed no bodies touch.

185   *Dream Time*

Waking from a bad dream, and thrashing out
So that you too woke, and I heard you say
'What is it, love?' – why, at my sudden shout,
Did I pretend more stirs, more mutterings,
A kind of baleful play,
And knew I left you with sad wonderings?

Was it because the dream that made me speak
Excluded you, close though you were to me
And are? For each one's dreaming is unique:
Rejected here and there we lie alone,
Separate, distinct, free,
Each one's heart as heavy as a stone.

186 *Waiting*

All day the telephone in silence sits.
We are forgotten. The whole sky is blank.

I read a Kurdish poem: 'Nothing sadder
In early morning than to see stooped workmen
Building prisons'.
      This is where we live,
Envied for what we have, for what they think we have.

Love isolates and binds, puts up its walls.
We are inviolate. The air is still.

From dawn till bedtime, nothing.
Jangle of keys beyond the outer gate.
Promises simmering, a lifetime's pause
High on the brink.
      Whatever lies below
Covers its wings, folds over, falls asleep.
The telephone in curtained darkness sits.

187 *Now and Then*

How difficult *now* is:
Then silts up, spills over
With unstoppable memories,
Or – if to come – is a hill
In the distance under a cover
Of cloud, unseeable
And yet predictable.

Now is the point of the pen
Making a single mark
And hurrying on, till *then*
Is the whole page covered,
Or the page covered tomorrow
After the passing dark,
The plough passing over the furrow.

188   *To a Manichee*

In a dozen different ways
All of them the same
You tell us life is terrible

You tell us with crushing of bones
You tell us with rending of sinews
You tell us with boiling of blood
With the man degutting the woman
With the woman decapitating the man
With the ant devouring leviathan
With the wren dissecting the octopus
With the wolf drooling over the lamb

And all this while
Someone called God is there
Doing nothing about it

So it goes on
So it goes on

Till another book hits the shelves
With a noise like thunder
With a sound like applause
With a high cry of approbation.

And life goes on just the same
Terrible terrible
The whisper of terrible despair
Comforting the comfortable.

189 *The Small Brown Nun*

The small brown nun in the corner seat
Smiles out of her wimple and out of her window
Through thick round glasses and through the glass,
And her wimple is white and her habit neat
And whatever she thinks she does not show
As the train jerks on and the low fields pass.

The beer is warm and the train is late
And smoke floats out of the carriage window.
Crosswords are puzzled and papers read,
But the nun, as smooth as a just-washed plate,
Does nothing at all but smile as we go,
As if she listened to something said,

Not here, or beyond, or out in the night,
A close old friend with a gentle joke
Telling her something through the window
Inside her head, all neat and right
And snug as the white bound round the yolk
Of a small brown egg in a nest in the snow.

Lutyens' red sandstone stands and lords it still
Over the laid-out placid capital,
Far from white oxen ploughing, where a boy
Follows behind to catch the falling dung,
To bake it dry for burning; far away
The poison lodged beneath the cobra's tongue,
The plaintive voice entreating you to stay.

Happy the dancing mango-breasted girls,
Happier the fondled gods embraced by them.
Clay on the potter's wheel spins out, unfurls,
And the black lingam, sticky at its stem,
Renews the fertile world; while down the road
A charpoy bears a shroud, no follower,
No family. At railway-halts, 'Stop Dead'.

Earth wears, and earthenwares – a child's whipped top
Slowing and tilting. In the barley-pot
A mongoose; on the slopes, Golconda's fall.
Red fort, white mausoleum, beautiful
The insolent vulture wheeling over all.
Insects' monotonous bleep; a steady flood
Blessing the roads with betel and the fields with blood.

191   *For Frank Coe*
      (1907–1980)

Drinking cold beer with my uncle in Peking
Night after night that cold and windy spring
(And he was dying then, and is dead now),
He told me in his pinched exhaustion how,
When the Red Guards went crazy, it was Mao
Held back the mob and let them live in peace:
The compound by the Drum Tower, the small trees
Ruth planted and watered, shelves of pots and scrolls,
All safe against the furious tide that rolls
Towards the things it envies.
                              You survived
Burnings, jail, purges. So the 'new age' thrived,
And in your lungs the cancer too. Your room
Stifled because your body froze. The bloom
Touched the first branches of the peach: out there
A million bicycles swerved and clanged, unaware
Of all your years in exile, renegade
And refugee, wry dignity that stayed
Even as in your pain you joked and drank.
Strange relic from my childhood, when I thank
Your kindness and your love, I must thank too
The inscrutable caprice that granted you
That end in your walled garden that cold spring
And the first peach buds blossomed in Peking.

The world exploded: ash and atoms both.
But it was not 'the world': only Japan,
And only part of that. It was a myth.
Under the myth, people once more began
To crawl through ashes, wreckage, poverty.
The fumes subsided. The volcano's breath
Exhaled on the horizon.
                              Stand here, see
This tiny spider chancing its puny death
On mud that bubbles half an inch below.
Coke-tins and plastic judder in the pool,
Boiling and rising.
                         Spring Festival; and so
The affluent crowds (young ones with *Cool, Man, Cool*
On sweatshirts) mill about, spill out from cars,
Enjoy the blossom, holiday, rich peace.
Try *Sexy Carnival*. There are no wars:
Only the TV Space War stuff. *The Police*
Throb from transistors, transliterated *Pax
Nipponica*. The red sun is unfurled.

Across the western sea, a billion backs
Bend to the four trends, lug the turning world.

193   *Neo-Gothic*

At the edge of the world is a very neat castle
In miniature, owned by the National Trust.
It is possible to rent it on a weekly basis,
Briefly enjoying neo-gothic illusions
As one gazes west through narrow-leaded windows
On terminal rocks assaulted by fierce seas.

Like a chess-piece isolated in an extreme situation,
This rented folly is a thing to play with.
Among simple and tasteful furnishings, a plain table
Carries a drawerful of journals with consecutive entries
By previous temporary tenants, praising the amenities,
Suggesting pubs, recommending itineraries.

But stranded awkwardly among all these pages
One entry is different: evidently by a woman,
Taking the place on her own, beginning like the others
With observations of birds, of walks, of weather,
It modulates gradually to tell of encounters
With a strange man polishing a scythe, of finding a stone

Inscribed with obscure words, of dreams about witches.
The handwriting degenerates, syntax goes incoherent,
Lurid obsessions spill over. Then, abruptly, it stops.
Perhaps she was playing at fiction, putting on a style
Suitable for a week in a neo-gothic folly.
But, having read it, my mind has not been easy

Here at the edge of the world in this very neat castle.

194   *At the Flood*

He comes by the window, or I think he does.
The river is up, the water close to the door.
Will he reach the field beyond us, and come back
Saying the bridge is dangerous? Will I go out
And guide him with a torch, trying myself
With careful footfalls, showing him it's safe?

He is at the door. It is dark, and the water laps
The fence a yard away. Will I ask him in,
Give him a bed, acknowledging the bridge
Is now one with the river, can't be crossed?
Will he take advice, or trust himself, or will
The river, rising, answer for us both?

He has knocked. I open to him, speak, and take
The torch out in the dark. We reach the bridge.
The water covers it: I show the way.
He goes across, the field is now a lake,
The far field takes him in. I turn and go
Back to the lit house. And the rain comes down.

195   *In the Gravel Pit*

In the steady rain, in June,
In the gravel pit by the pylon,
This empty afternoon
Walking there in a dead
Mood, I found one
Not caught inside my head.
Caught quite otherwise,
What was a rabbit, just,
Crouched with its blank eyes
In a sodden lump of fur
In grey indeterminate mist.
It did not even stir
As I stood there in the rain.
Mud-trickles down the bank
Oozed under its paws. What pain
It felt I do not know.
The gravel pit had the stink
Of wet silage, of the slow
Decay of thrown-out stuff.
And as I stood and watched

This end of a scrap of life,
I did what I had to do.
For the first time, it twitched
As I stooped and set my hand to
A broken plank in the mud.
I struck maybe seven times,
Till its eyes burst, and its blood
Covered its wretched fur,
And no sound, no whimpers or screams,
Only my own roar
Of misery, ignorance, pain,
Alone in the gravel pit
By the pylon in the rain,
And my hand with its own blood
Torn by a nail that bit
As I struck at a dead mood
And an animal dying there
Without meaning in the mud
In the warm summer air,
With the rain still soaking the earth,
And everywhere, in the blood,
The dying, the giving birth.

196   *Selling Them Off*

Profiles. Some sharp, some worn; some bright, some dull.
Coveted, shut away, now brought to light.
Forty-five years ago, trays heaped and full
Were spread for my inspection as I knelt
High on the Leeds shop stool and took my pick.
It was of history they felt and smelt:
I lingered over them.
                              Now, quick
And furtive, almost, as if fingering dirt,
I pluck them out, confront the expert's stare.

He squinnies at them, mutters, asks what's fair,
What I expected, what they'd fetch. So, hurt
Or just resigned, I let him name a price.

Forty-five years ago, each was a trophy, each
Saturday sixpence snared another catch –
A William or a Charles, farthing or groat,
Rubbed Roman bronze (silver was far too much),
Devices puzzled over, dates deciphered,
My father looking on, helping me read
Blunted inscriptions, emblematic coat,
Or lurking mint-mark.
                                        Later, shut away,
They waited to be sold off till today,
An attic windfall picked in middle age.
The cost of things, inflation rising fast,
And bills to pay and mouths to feed, or just
A weariness at so much bunged-up past . . .
I see his bits of paper, glad to have them.
(So much sour verdigris, corrosion, wear
Among the bright and sharp ones. So much dust
Gathering in attics, never put to use.
What would I want them for, why should I save them?)

'Thank you, in cash.' The past is an excuse.
Achievement; shame; blankness; relief; disgust.

197   *Death Assemblage*

Insect remains extracted from a sample
represent a 'death assemblage'; their
bodies have come to lie together in the
archaeological deposit, but there is no
proof that in life there was any connection
between the groups.

> From *The Analysis of Archaeological
> Insect Assemblages: A New Approach*,
> by H. K. Kenward.

They huddle together,
Heads, trunks, limbs – see,
Rigid in ashfall,
Blasted in fusion,
At the end of their tether,
Solid but flimsy.
At this long interval
In time's deposit
There must be confusion
Whether their exit
Brought them together,
In semblance of unity
Assembled, or whether
In life they were separate.

Disaster-theory,
Archaic but possible,
Assigns them a date
Which (in old reckoning)
Is quite conceivable
As late nineteen-hundreds.
But no true connecting
Of body with body
(And so many, so many)
Can ever be ventured.

198   *Afterwards*

Look at it now: a country drugged with language,
Familiar streets and houses with their posters
Stripped from the walls and windows, the dead echoes
Of rhetoric still lingering on the air,
Prolonged in chat-shows and in interviews.
Exhausted faces grey in newspapers,
Poets reading to embarrassed sniggers,
The sound turned down, the vision flickering.

So for the jeremiads, the post-mortems,
The letters-columns stiff with rectitudes.

I can't believe all this. I'm feigning anger,
Or disillusion, or the end of things.
My little world is not made cunningly,
And yet it's made, has lasted until now.

199   *At Evening*

They were always there, at the end of the garden or elsewhere
Talking unfathomably about whatever it was
In a way that even in childhood I could understand
Enough, at any rate, to feel frightened of.
And here they all are again, as I stoop to brush off
Four or five grey hairs from the arm of the chair – still talking,
Their heads close together, familiar faces in congress,
Knowing I'm there, not afraid to talk when I'm there,
But secret too, surreptitious. I wish I could hear.
The shadows move down the garden, the bonfire smoke
Drifts across hedges, the smell of the smoke pricks my nose,
The hairs on my arm stand up as evening comes on:
And still they are talking, talking, and I want to go in,
Into the house where I know I have always been.

from *Letter from Tokyo* (1987)

Part I

200   *Letter from Tokyo*

This season of spring/summer/autumn/winter is treacherous.
Please be vigilant of your fragile health throughout it.

My garden is only the size of a cat's forehead.
This is because my fees are a sparrow's tears.

You are welcome to visit me whenever you wish,
Though the squalor of my abode will shock your feet.

Your handsome frame undoubtedly will suffer
From submitting to the rabbit-hutch I inhabit.

Perhaps when spring/summer/autumn/winter succeed in their courses
I may trouble you with another communication.

My command of your language is, you will see, defective.
Can you understand my poor meaning? That is remarkable.

201   *A Word of Advice*

This is a holy place. It is not a hotel.
You are guests, true, but also pilgrims.

Here we eat no flesh or fish: it is well
Two of you already follow this rule.

You must follow our other rules, including the times
Baths must be taken, the dimming of lights,
And the extinguishing of talk.
Gongs will be sounded to let you know of these things.

We expect you to consume whatever you are given –
Give thanks for it, and always abhor waste.

The hangings on the walls, which you cannot read,
Are prayers and reminders of prayer.

You seem unenlightened. You will, I hope, not stay long.
Something about you disturbs the atmosphere:
I noticed you smiling as if in doubt
Whether this was quite the place the guidebook described.

I am the bride of the priest. I do not smile.

My manner may seem unfriendly. It is not so intended.
Simply, you must accept.
                        And remember
This is a holy place. It is not a hotel.

202 *Abroad Thoughts from Abroad*

Mozart on NHK, *The Messiah* in Shinjuku,
Cinzano cold in the hand, fragrant in the mouth:
I am a citizen of the world, and so are they.

On Wednesday we shall continue with Sylvia Plath,
On Thursday the undergraduates
Will attend my lecture on Hopkins and Kipling.

People in England send us Christmas cards
With jokes about holly festooning the 'crispy noodles'.
Daft. We can even buy Marmite quite easily.

In the street, I avoid the eyes of foreigners,
Who in any case are few and far between.
Being abroad, why should we mix together?

I am a citizen of the world, and so are they,
And so are the students drifting under the window
Giggling about something or other in Japanese.

This is an ironical poem about happiness.
I am as happy as I could ever be.
The Japanese say they do not understand irony.

203 *Kanji*

As I walk I notice the shapes of characters
Bold on shop-signs, on the indicators of buses,
On the covers of magazines, on the doorposts of houses.

Some I know, and say to myself quietly.
Others I recognise, understand, but can't remember
What sound they make. Many I recognise
But cannot understand. And many more
Always seem new, unknown.

Ya, valley, is like a little house
But often pronounced in quite another way.
I is a well, but looks like a word-game's grid.
Ishi is stone – a quarry-block, chisel above.
Kawa (or *gawa*) is easy – a river with banks.

But three horizontal strokes need puzzling out –
The numeral three, but spoken sometimes as *san*,
Sometimes as *mitsu*, and no indication which.

A rice-paddy, or a field, is a cross in a square,
Called *da* or *ta*: an entrance a different square,
Or it may be an exit.

So it goes on, as I walk. I am learning to read
Like a child, an illiterate, adding and adding
Here a new shape, and there a new sound, and sometimes
Shape, sound, and sense together.
                                        But it is too late.
I sit in the bus and watch a ten-year-old turning
Page after page of characters, reading them all,
Not noticing what he is doing, simply becoming
Someone who knows: leaving me learning, alone.

204   *Cicadas in Japan*

Hearn heard them, and thought them magical,
Tried to distinguish
The multiple trills and screechings, different
From decibels in Italy or Provence:
Shrill carapace of shellac, trembling membranes
Strumming glum cacophonies.

And they are indeed alien, their quavers
Underline again
And yet again how different they, and we, are –
Like the nightingale that is not a nightingale,
The crow that will never be a crow,
Though sweet, though raucous.

And yet, in the swelter of summer, in a thick sweat,
Why not different?
They go with the twilight, the night, the day, the dawn
Coming again in shrill loudspeaker vans
Announcing news I cannot understand,
Speaking in tongues, wheezing out miracles.

205 *Music to My Ears*

A language to be learned, like any other,
Absorbed in childhood without knowing how,
Simply exposed to it and beating time
Before we read it, if we ever read it.

But it has rarer forms, has dialects
Unheard until a samisen's nervous strum
Plucks at the ears' plectrum, or a missing thud
Expected on a drum tells us its rules
Are not our rules. A single quivering string
Excites the desert, or a quavering howl
Means long-lost beauty to another's ear:

Barbarian gibberish to an audience
That has never heard the other harmonies
Other feet tap to, deaf to other tunes.

206 *Shrine*

Postures that are not dances; chants
That weld together words that are not words;
Drum, flute and bells making a kind of music
That is not music – shuddering, then still,
Then moving at a steady rhythmic pace
Under an almost mindless tuneless tune.

These negatives betray their ignorance:
Things that are not imply that something is.
Beyond the postures, chants, drum, flute and bells,
Beyond the celebrants, behind a screen,
Something is hidden in the sanctuary
Locked in a box no one has ever seen.

207 *Shock*

An easing of walls,
A shuddering through soles:
A petal loosens, falls.

In the room, alone:
It begins, then it has gone.
Ripples outlast stone.

Rain-smell stirs the heart;
Nostrils flare. A breath. We wait
For something to start.

The flavour of fear,
Something fragile in the air.
Gone, it remains here.

208 *Dawn in Zempukuji*

Phlegmatic hawkings, stertorous plummetings –
Our Chinese neighbour through the bedroom wall
Reaches for virtue from her tubes and lungs,
And serenades each dawn and dusk, her call
Shaking the frail partition. Then there comes
A genuine tremor like a roll of drums.

Birdcalls begin, unrecognised. Soft rain
Sifting through leaves, tapping through guttering.
Clatter of wooden sandals. At the pane
A moth is trapped in mesh, is fluttering
Against my pillow. Up through jets of dreams
Another tremor, then another, comes.

Look for the radical. Establish context.
If necessary, magnify the sign.
Use of the syllabary script may help.
The homophone is frequent. Now read on.

A most decisive battle. Build a dam.
Lose by a whisker. Neptune's revel. Pink.
Man of profound learning. Budgerigar.
A cough. The spine. Dead silence. Barren land.
Wages of sin. Stone pillar. Wipe the slate.
One-eyed. Red Army. Rice steamed with red beans.
Impromptu drawing. Evil of long standing.
Here. Bygone days. Put out of countenance.
Stark naked. Snowdrifts. One-armed person. Load.
Responsibility. The best one can expect.

O interlocking mesh of stroke and brush –
A web of dew which no sun clarifies:
Thesaurus of small treasure-houses, locked
Against the outsider, the illiterate.

210 *Patterns*

There is a word for the pattern in things –
The grain in bamboo, the markings in jade,
The lie of an animal's fur, strands in a thread.
Each has its quiddity of patternings,
And none can fade.

There is an order. There is a fixed place
Established within the pattern. The prince
Speaks only within his rank. It is a dance
Where each must put a mask before his face.
We must convince

The gruff barbarian that he cannot play
This skilful game, or even learn the rules:
Our scholars know his blundering reason fails
Trapped in the torments of the only Way
Taught in our schools.

They cannot penetrate our subtleties,
Our precepts of the Gods and of the shapes
Taken by the divinity that slips
Between us; between our divinities
And theirs – mere tropes,

Approximate translations, figures flicked
Inaccurately on a counting-frame.
Ours is a pattern flowing down a stream,
Not to be caught, a language none inflect
And none can tame.

211 *The Court Examination*

In this time of lack of wisdom
When the turbulence of all things
Threatens harmony and order,
We shall now propose conundrums
To the Ministers and Princes,
And afterwards give prizes
To those who give wise answers.

In this year a serpent and a dog copulated. Presently they both died together.
If conception had occurred, what would have been the result?

The stinking leeks
In the fields of millet,
The roots and shoots of them
We shall strike down,
Sang the soldiers of Kumé,
The valiant soldiers.

Stones disappear beneath the surface of the earth, great trees wither away,
saplings take their place. Where are there trustworthy memorials of events a
millennium ago?

The pungent pepper
That grows in the hedges
Fire on our tongues,
We shall strike down,
Sang the soldiers of Kumé,
The valiant soldiers.

At the time when Heaven and Earth were not yet entirely separated, a
certain thing was produced between them. It was in form like a reed-shoot.
It became transformed into a god. What was the name of this deity?

And those who creep round
The sea-rock of Isé,
Creeping like sea-snails,
We shall strike down,
Sang the soldiers of Kumé,
The valiant soldiers.

The contest is now over,
The answers all examined.
It is clear that ancient wisdom
No longer dwells among you.
Let the Ministers and Princes
Be bound in hemp and rice-straw.
Let the soldiers have their way.

        at the Tori-no-Ichi

She is quite pretty, young, and she swallows fire.
Her kimono has a special bib to protect her.
She mops her mouth with tissues daintily
In preparation for the plume of flame.

After she has done the necessary – a conflagration
Sucked down her throat and belched with a roar upwards –
Our attention is drawn to a writhing sack of snakes.
She is handed one snake, which she smoothes like a length of string.

Then, with a steady hand, the snake's head is inserted
Between her lips; she inhales, and it disappears
Along with four inches of body. The drumming increases.
The body withdraws, headless. She frowns and chews,

Opens her mouth, allows a trickle of blood
To flow down her chin, and wipes it gently away.
She has swallowed the snake's head. She smiles at the joke.
She mops her mouth with tissues daintily.

*

She is three feet tall, her head and trunk are those
Of a woman of sixty; but her arms are short and muscled
Like an infant Hercules, and her legs are stumps
Wrapped in bright rags, taffeta sausages.

She plays with a saucer balanced on a stick
Which she twirls in time to the music. By her side
Is a life-sized head of a puppet. She puts her own head
On the floor, and raises her trunk with a flip of her wrists.

But something is wrong with the tape-recorder.
It should be giving her something to dance to,
With the puppet's head stuck in her crotch and her tiny stumps
Waving like arms though they are really legs.

An assistant is called for, a big young capable man
Who fiddles with switches and knobs. But the tape-recorder
Refuses to play the game. The crowd is waiting.
They have paid their money and are waiting for something to
    happen.

But nothing happens. Till the three-foot woman shrugs
With her massive shoulders, and begins to move,
Waving her ragged legs, jiggling the puppet's head
In time to nothing, in a silent dance.

213   *Osorezan*
(for Hisaaki Yamanouchi)

Hell's various images, each labelled, mapped.

Scurfed shed-skin puddles,
Blood-pools and litter mixed,
Beaches of leprous rock,
Contusions of sand stained blue with votive coins,
Sulphurous stink drifting across dunes,
Eroded Buddhas roguish in red bibs:
And everywhere the pebbles to the dead
Inscribed, heaped up forever, scattered, piled
High for the billion foetuses aborted,
Now lost in Hell, who cannot reach the bridge
So close, so crimson, that leads to Paradise.
Frantic toy plastic windmills whirr above the cairns,
Rasping against the rooks' raw sniggering,
Chanting their sutras to the sanctuary
Here where we kneel and catch the priest's response,

Dead faded photographs, old cast-off clothes
Cluttering the beams with passed-on images
Of the known dead, those who were born and died,
A thousand years of shrined and shriving guilt,
Precise, clear, poignant, terrible, banal.

Hell is well mapped, but Paradise is not.

214   *Hiroshima: August 1985*

No way to deal with it, no way at all.
We did not have to come, and yet we came.
The things we saw were all the very same
As we expected. We had seen them all:
The fabric pattern printed on the skin,
The shadow of a body on a wall.
What wrapped our bodies round was much too thin.

Voyeurs, but sensitive not to display
Unseemly horror; yet sensing that we felt
Horror was here, and everywhere was shown.
We knew the arguments the other way –
If they had had the thing, it would have blown
Some other city, one of ours, away.
Was it guilt, shame, fear, nausea that we smelt?

Self-accusations, bewilderment, disgust:
Those dripping rags of flesh, that faceless head,
The sky wiped black, the air crammed black with dust,
City of ghosts, museum of the dead.
No way to deal with it, no way at all.
We did not have to come, and yet we came.
The things we saw were all the very same
As we expected. We had seen them all.

215 *Joshidaimae*

That thin, sweet, pure cry
Like a hymn to the lost gods
Echoing over the traffic

At last comes into view:
A battered truck, its back
A banged-together oven,

Jerking between the gleaming
Nissans and Toyotas.
On this cold, brilliant day,

Crisp leaves falling like money,
The smell of roast sweet potatoes
Wafts from the glowing embers.

No one seems to want them.
Over the fortunate city
The January sun

Hands down magnificence
To the traffic-jams and the truck
And that thin, sweet, pure cry.

216 *At the Fox Shrine*

On the last day of the year at the fox shrine
I lit a candle. It blew out
Among the red banners and broken figurines
In a rubble of leaves and votives by a tree root.

I had found the candle, unlit, in all that mess,
Put my lighter to it, set it in a dish
Before the kitsch foxes. The first breeze
Extinguished the flame, before I could even wish –

Whatever it was I wished. Today was the wrong day
To come to the shrine: tomorrow the new year
Would bring out the crowds to scatter their coins and pray.
Today there was no one else there.

The hill path, the tall midwinter trees
Holding on to themselves, the late sun,
Were all indifferent to calendars,
To choosing a day for faith or superstition.

Whatever whim or instinct made me light
The candle at the tree root by the shrine,
The night ahead would blow the old year out,
Wind rising through deserted cypress and pine.

Sasuke no Inari, Kamakura

Part II

'Voices Through Clouds'

217　*Kirishitan Monogatari*
　　　Three Last Words

I

1620

Even my name is doubtful – Fabian,
Fabian Fukansai, Fukansai Habian,
Fabian Fucan, Fabian Unguio . . .
A Japanese chameleon, on whose skin
All patterns slide in reformation; judged
Most promising of novices, apt
Pupil, master of tongues and argument,
Worst of inquisitors. In sophistry
You will not find my equal: I am there
With scruple, nicety, and forked contempt,
With casuistry, logic, and the knife
That lets just blood enough to keep you hale
But not enough to kill you. I am there
Above you in the pit, or battened down
Mired in your crouching cage, or in the fire,
Or on the cross. And, last, I am still there
When you cry out in your apostacy,
My mirror-image, Father Christopher,
Whose name blurs also as my name is blurred:
Henceforth *Sawano Chuan*, held in thrall,
Fellow-inquisitor, balked of martyrdom.

II

1636

Behind this mask I hear you, Fabian:
Twenty years fruitlessly, barbarian
Reformed in religion, I staggered in the faith.
Now, in the thirteenth year of Kan'ei,
Transmuted, purged, pure adherent of Zen,
With the Dragon constellations set in heaven,

I embrace my death. I hear the sentences
Read out from chronicles that will banish me.

'He was three days in the pit, and died a martyr.'

'As one falls, another rises:
As one deserts, another bears the Crown.'

In seething waters, above bubbling turds
Suspended, O my God: trussed, should I trust
That crookéd path, perverse and curséd faith,
Those cross-yoked words –
Deceit Disclosed, Deus Destroyed, my God?
Out of the pit I cried, out of the dust,
Thy barbarous martyr, pleading for his death,
Printed in tears, gasped out with strangled breath.

'He bore a heavy cross, and down his back streamed blood.'

'The blood of the martyrs is the seed of the Church.'

Bateren Christopher, *Sawano Chuan,*
Superior turned renegade and spy,
I, the Apostate, knew three properties –
Of Man to sin, of Christian to repent,
Of Devil to perform the crime again
And yet again. This was my Trinity.
But these three now – blood, brocade, and gold,
The Cross, Christ's uniform, the weight of wealth,
The dazzling finery whose fruit is death –
I cast them off, and am come back to life,
Parodic resurrection, purged and shriven,
My eyes turned stalwartly away from Heaven.

III
1639

In the days of the Emperor Go-Nara, long ago,
The conch-nosed giant, eyes as big as saucers,
Stepped from the ship of Namban, screeched like an owl –
The long-clawed *Bateren*, the goblin breed.

At Sumiyoshi, by the sacred shrine,
There fell down at that footfall, in a flash,
Sixty-six pine trees, prophecy that all
Our provinces would topple at this tread,
This mouse-grey monster, wings spread like a bat.

Into our lord's presence came, bearing gifts:
Ten muskets, spectacles for near-and-far,
An insect-net fanned out huge as a hall
(Yet, folded, snug to fit a perfume-flask),
Picture-scrolls, medicines, goats, Cathay dogs,
Bolt after bolt of tawny russet cloth
(Pelts of orangoutang) – all bribes, all beads
Spangled with secrecies, with cruciforms –
Image of Deus hanging on the cross,
Virgin and Mother, womb besmirched with blood.

Thus the old stories . . . After *Bateren*
Came many *Furaten*, still goblin breed,
Still loaded with their baubled bric-à-brac,
But these wandered the streets enticingly
Curing the lepers, wretches poxed with boils,
Carbuncles, mange; beggars harelipped and lame,
Morons and menials, misfits and good-for-naughts.
These *Furaten*, too, concocted plots,
Pernicious mischief-work, deluded news,
Until our lord the Taiko took his stand –
Purged them, expelled them, drove them from our land.

Twenty-six criminals, their noses slit,
Dragged through the city streets: along the way
Gazed at the sky, looked for a miracle
Across the mountains – but no drop of dew
Succoured them then, or ever.

    By the shore
In Nagasaki they were crucified,
Joining their Jesu (Jizo mockery).
Their bodies rotted on the crosses, both
Bodies and crosses pilfered secretly –
Believers' trophies, crosses and bones and skulls,
Each scrap of bone, each toothpick stick of wood
Traded as relics, holy amulets.

But we had let the sawdust out of them,
Weevils and termites, filthy predators,
Stews of unheard-of things from barbarous lands,
The flowered words that strew the Devil's path.

This is the Land of Gods, a tripod based
Sturdily on three legs: the Royal Sway,
The Way of the Gods, the Buddha's Path – let one
Be broken off, then sun and moon fall down,
The lantern lost which lights the gloomy night.

The Empire is at peace, tranquil the land:
A sainted reign, a golden age indeed.

Completed here
on a propitious day:
eighth month of Kan'ei 16

Morning in spring, the fourth month:
But here are no spring flowers.
Nothing the same here
Except for sunlight and moonlight.
O how I miss Japan –
If I could but see it again!

So far, by so many leagues
Of ocean, it keeps its distance –
Yamato, out of my mind
Never, sleeves wet with my tears.
Why was my father foreign?
How long since I left my home?

As you know, every year (thanks to the benevolence of the magistrates
of Nagasaki) I have been able to receive letters and gifts. Last year
(owing to the fortunate opportunities offered by a Dutch 'black ship'
and the Chinese vessel) I have, as I confirm here, received letters and
gifts twice. I am very grateful for all this . . .

Exiled when just fourteen,
Yet it seems yesterday
When I hastily packed a few clothes,
Went weeping, bewildered, on board,
Took leave of my nurse, my friends,
Saw the coastline ebb away.

Now I entrust the following gifts of my own to you, through the good
offices of the foreign captain. You will find them thus: 94 rolls of undyed
cotton cloth, all rolled in one. One chest containing: three pounds of
carrots (finest quality); two rolls of satin in light indigo; six rolls of
calico; three rolls of deep green cloth tinted with yellow . . .

Writing like this, the ink
Is blurred and runs with my tears.
How you will think I have changed!
Dear one, please send me some seeds
Of oak and cedar and broom,
Some pine-cones, and incense-sticks –

Things to remind me of home,
Unchanging if I have changed.
All I can send you myself
Is this sash embroidered with flowers –
But they are the wrong flowers:
The home ones I have forgotten.

. . . a measure of woollen cloth better than any imported by the Dutch;
four rolls of printed cotton; a single roll of twilled silk in black; a single
roll of figured satin in black; a small assortment of sewing needles. All
these for Kifu, wife of Shichiroemon, in Shimabara: she waited on me
ever since she was a child, and I feel sorry for her in many ways.

Please do not laugh at me;
And if others do, you must tell them
The pattern is fanciful.
How could I ever forget,
As I have, those colours and shapes . . .
The years, the distance, the years.

As for the saké I have ordered this time, please deliver it to a man called
Karu, in Dejima, in a double-barrelled cask, just in time for sailing.
Unless this is done just in time, the saké might be stolen by the casual
dock-workers.

Lonely, my life, and sad.
My inkstone overbrims
As I think of the yellow rose
You gave me in full bloom.
Now it has long withered.
Like dew, I must go too.

Though I live in this far land,
I pray that you won't forget me:
For even the briefest moment –
Like a flash of lightning over
The full-eared rice-fields of autumn –
I shall never forget you.

If I want anything, I shall let you know. Unless I ask for something, it is unnecessary. I only want chrysanthemums. The plants you sent me last year have all died, probably because I made too much fuss over them. Tender shoots and grafted scions would root here: say, one of crimson and the other variegated.

O how I miss Japan –
If I could but see it again!

Last year you tried sending me some potted Japanese radishes, but they seem to have got lost, either on board the ship or after they were landed. But in any case all such vegetables are easily available here at any time of the year. As for fruit, we lack nothing. The *Capitão* in Dejima is someone whom we have always looked upon as if he had been our own relative. I entrust everything, including this message, to him.

O how I miss . . .
Very sincerely yours,
Oharu (widow of Shinmosu)

A turn around the yard, then back again:
A pint of gin, a game of dice, to bed

Knocked out, locked in. Twenty-two exiled men
Marooned like ghosts who do not know they're dead.

Krieger talks rubbish. Blomhoff wants a whore
And says so, endlessly. Van Puyck adds up

Consignment figures for the umpteenth time.
Wail of a shakuhachi from the shore.

Tomorrow night, some fiefling in to sup:
Adam the cook prepares a fishy slime

Fit for outlandish palates, and sweet wine
To tilt his brains indulgently our way

('Your eminence, do take another cup') –
Turn a blind eye to Rahder's escapade

Last week (a scuffle on the landward side,
A bloody nose or two): we cover up

For one another like a gang of boys,
Distrust and honour shiftily in turn

Keeping the balance. Distantly, a noise
Of drum and cymbals marking out some rite

Pickled in superstition. Candles burn
Down to each dish, spit smoke, and then go out.

The hills of Nagasaki ring the night,
Our dark horizon where we cannot go.

Each day creeps by, each minute labours slow.
A hundred years from now, perhaps some light

Will fall upon this heathen harbour town –
But let the gin take over, let me row

My numbed, thick, sleepy body out to sea.
Let me go easy. Let me sink and drown

Far from this fan-shaped offshore prison where
Seabirds screech alien words in alien air.

220   *The Envoys: 1860*

Over the Western sea hither from Niphon come,
Courteous, the swart-cheek'd two-sworded envoys,
Leaning back in their open barouches, bare-headed, impassive . . .
Florid with blood, pensive, rapt with musings, hot with passion,
Sultry with perfume, with ample and flowing garments,
With sunburnt visage, with intense soul and glittering eyes.

WALT WHITMAN

Grey-pink and shining flowers look down on us –
Thousands of faces peering from high windows.
The faces become flowers, we are showered with them,
The horses and the carriages strewn with blossoms
As we go on down valleys of tall buildings
To such wild shouts, to such wild thundering music!

Dismounting from our carriages, we step
Into the Congress, watch from a balcony
Members brandishing their fists as if in temper –
Speeches at tops of voices, all excited, unexplained.
Then the Smithsonian, pickled snakes, men's bodies
Pickled also, a vast display of hair-specimens
Cut from successive Presidents – disgusting to exhibit
The hair of dead men in a public place. But worse

That evening – men and bareshouldered women glued together
Hop round the floor to music: we are told
This is a 'dance', and that all classes (rich, poor, young, old)
Enjoy this pastime – the women's waists encircled
As if in copulation. Exploding liquors – champagne –
Then, arm in arm, each of us takes a lady
To face a banquet . . . Rice fried in butter, rice
Sprinkled with sugar, emetic dishes spread on tablecloths
White as a field of snow. And Morita
Drinks from his fingerbowl in ignorance . . .

We are the first Ambassadors, our Government
And people anxiously await our safe return.
We came to secure the Treaty, not for pleasure
(Though pleasure may be had from careful inspection
Of certain instruments, engines, maps, machines,
Rifles and pistols of the latest make).
Kindnesses shown are but seldom pleasures:
How often, to our shame, we bow, refuse, parrot the phrase
'Excuse us – it is not our country's custom'!

Washington, Philadelphia, New York –
We droop from so much travel, so much boisterousness
Battering our ears with unintelligible whoops,
Such heat weighing us down in robes designed
For simpler, gentler ways – for dignity
Hard to adhere to in such rough-and-tumble.
Democracy – Liberty – The Open Door –
A barrier without ceremony through which
Millions as yet unborn must push and jostle
Because of what we were sent to do, have done,
Cordial with gifts, received with gratitude,
Uncertain as the blossom that looks down
Poised for a moment, whether to stay or fall,
Destined to fall, now looking down on us,
Dissolving into faces, grey-pink, shining,
That stare at us in dreams that do not fade.

284

221 *Of Japan at Ten Hours' Sight: 1889*

– Whence the camphor and the lacquer and the shark-skin swords all
    come:
We shall stop at Nagasaki; on to Kobé northwards; then
By clockwork engine ticking by paddies, mountains, shrines,
To the Emperor's new capital spread out around the bay.

*

A tea-girl in fawn-coloured crêpe under a cherry tree:
Behind, green pines, two babies, and a hog-backed bridge that spans
A river (coloured bottle-green) and boulders (coloured blue);
In front, a little policeman in a badly-fitting suit.

Their language is a patter of no tone or weight or stress,
Their poetry is syllables on the fingers of one hand,
Without rhythm, with no rhymes at all – and what it seems to say
Is that seasons change and blossoms fall and nothing stays the same.

Their music is a squawk of strings and a rumble on a drum,
Their songs a caterwauling through a set of blackened teeth,
Their plays are Henry Irving guyed by drunken undergrads –
The howls and jerks and colours of a puppet on a string.

*

In a workshop like a fairy's house sit men and girls and boys,
Neat and proper in surroundings, with an iris by the pond:
They lift their eyes from painting on Satsuma with a brush
To gaze at sprigs of cherry or a pine against the sky.

We, the nation of glass flower-shades and the pink-puce worsted mat,
Red-green puppy-dogs in china, poisonous Brussels carpet-lengths,
Now presume to lecture haughtily on Art and Craft and Taste
To the humble yellow people of the Islands of the Dawn.

Bog-trotting Briton, blundering in among the porcelain,
New York Professor, blathering sententiousness through cigars –
Have you noticed (as you duck your head to go into a room)
What has happened, and is happening, and will happen ere you rise?

All the skittles we have played with for six hundred years and more
They have picked up in an instant, they have learned the Book of
    Rules,
They listen when we tell them things they've known since Time
    began,
But patiently, so patiently, they wait for what they don't.

We taught them engineering, we sold them lovely guns,
We gave them fine roast-beef to eat, and whisky by the quart,
The civilized black bowler, the most advanced white spats,
Corkscrews, penknives, stucco, Worcester Sauce – a Constitution, too.

Their women are like little dolls, their children dolls of dolls,
Their laughter is the tinkle of a thousand tiny bells.
Their cavalry is comic, their infantry a joke . . .
But they waited till they wanted us; and what they want is All.

*

This people is a question-mark, and a puzzle to the head:
Such babu-ways, such stick-at-it, such comic-tragic squints . . .
Yet they know what they are after, and they'll drop us smartly when
The tooth of their desire picks clean the bone of ignorance.

I have dreamed of foreign monsters come to life in fairyland.
I have seen the writing on the wall, scratched on the panelled gold:
Madame Blavatsky smoking 'neath the Nikko ginkgo trees,
And Mister Caine, MP, denouncing saké as a sin.

The Jap is not a native, nor a sahib, but an odd
Sort of hybrid of the species – Chink, French, German, Hottentot,
With a dash of Yank and Redskin – but under all the lot
He's a warrior, and an artist, and a Jappo through and through.

286

I weep to see the hybrid, I anticipate the man
Who in time will whip the Chinaman, the Muscovite, and all;
For the day is fast approaching when the Rising Sun will fly
Over Manchu Palace, Onion-Dome – and maybe on Big Ben.

*

We are sailing out from Tokyo, from the edge of fairyland:
I can hear the baby bugles blowing bravely in my head,
I can see the tiny horses with their midgets on the strand –
And no one now can tuck the toys back in their tiny bed.

222   *Soseki*
        (London: December 1902)

A lost dog slinking through a pack of wolves.

Sour yellow droplets frozen on each branch,
The tainted breath of winter in the fog:
Coal-smells, and cooking-smells (meat-fat, stewed-fish),
And smells of horse-dung steaming in the streets:
Smoke groping at the windowpanes, a stain
Left hanging by the mean lamp where I trace
Page after page of Craig's distempered notes . . .

        Winter withering
        Autumn's last scattering leaves:
        London is falling.

I want a theory, a science with firm rules
Plotting the truth objectively through all these infinite spaces.
I look out of the window over the whitened blankness,
And from the East the moon lights up half the river.

But it is hallucination: cab-lights from Clapham Common
Flash at the pane, my head throbs over the little fire,
I am crying in the darkness, my cheeks sticky with tears.
Far, far beyond the heavens the forms of departing clouds . . .

Downstairs, those sisters plot and scheme together –
I found the penny on the windowsill,
The one I gave the beggar yesterday. Ridiculous pity,
Sly instruments of torture!
                        'Natsume's mad' –
That telegram sent home by Okakura –
Will they believe it? Is it so? Is he my friend?
I have no friends. By the light of the dying fire
I underscore these lines, and more, and more . . .

        December evening.
        Light at the window shining.
        Something in hiding.

London is districts learned from Baedeker
And learned on foot. England is somewhere else.
A day in Cambridge seeing Doctor Andrews,
The Dean of Pembroke, offering me sherry.
Too many 'gentlemen' – at Oxford too.
Someone said *Edinburgh*, but the speech up there
Is northern dialect, *Tohōku*-style.
So London it must be – the Tower, its walls
Scrawled with the dying words of men condemned:
Lodgings in Gower Street with Mrs Knot;
That vast Museum piled with pallid Greeks;
West Hampstead, and then Camberwell New Road . . .
I measure out the metres as I walk,
Finding sad poetry in the names of places.

Sometimes, walking the streets thronged with such tall and handsome
    ones,
I see a dwarf approaching, his face sweaty – and then
I know it for my own reflection, cast back from a shop-window.
I laugh, it laughs. 'Yellow races' – how appropriate.

'Least poor Chinese' – I think I hear – or 'Handsome Jap'. . .
Sneers of a group of labourers, seeing me go by
In frock-coat, top-hat, parody of 'English gentleman'
Sauntering down King's Parade or in the High . . .
I walk to Bloomsbury, walk back to Clapham,
Carry my Meredith or Carlyle through the drizzle,
Munching with difficulty a 'sandwich' on a bench in the park
Soaked by the rain, buffeted by the wind . . .

Far, far beyond the heavens the forms of departing clouds,
And in the wind the sound of falling leaves.

It is time to be deliberate, to use
Such gifts as I am given, to escape
The traveller's to-and-fro, the flow of facts
Unchecked, to make a system that will join
Blossom to branch, reason to intuition,
Wave after wave uniting as each falls
Under the next that follows up the beach . . .

> A cry outside shakes
> The tangle of waterpipes:
> Midnight: a mouse squeaks.

A frightened mouse in a cell facing north,
I have almost forgotten what brought me here
Or what I do from day to day.
                    I know
I sat with Craig for an hour this morning,
Hearing him mumbling Shakespeare through his beard,
Gave him my shillings in an envelope

Bound round with ribbon which he plucked away
Impatiently and mannerless – due fee
For pedagogic drudgery. So walked back,
Wondering could I afford a mess of eggs
In the cabby-shelter out in Battersea,
And settled for a farthing bun and 'tea'
Scabby with milk served in a cracked white mug
At the stall by Wandsworth Bridge. Such humdrum things
To maze the mind and clog the intellect. . .

By the old castle at Komoro
The clouds are white and the wanderer grieves.

Impenetrable people, country bumpkins,
Nincompoop monkeys, good-for-nothing
Ashen-faced puppets – yes, it's natural
Westerners should despise us. They don't know
Japan, nor are they interested. Even if
We should deserve their knowledge and respect,
There would be neither – because they have no time
To know us, eyes to see us . . . Lesser breeds:
We need *improvement* (Brett has told me so),
And Western intermarriage would improve us.
We are the end of something, on the edge.

       The loneliness, the grieving heart of things,
       The emptiness, the solving fate that brings
       An answer to the question all men ask,
       Solution to the twister and the task.

  'Tears welling up in a strange land,
    I watch the sun set in the sea':
Yes, true, but for the sun, which once a week
May sidle itself weakly through pale clouds,
And for the sea, which somewhere – south or east –
Lies far beyond me, and is not my sea.
But tears well up, indeed, in a strange land

And speak of nothing but my lack of speech.
Curt monosyllables jab and jabber on,
Perverted versions of the tongue I know
Or thought I knew – the language Shakespeare spoke,
And Lemuel Gulliver's pure dictions mouthed
By me, alone, in Kanda, Matsuyama,
In Kumamoto . . . sailing through such seas
And on such seas of rhetoric and doubt
Towards these other islands where the sun
Has set before it rises, Ultima Thule,
Where tears well up and freeze on every branch.

I creep into my bed. I hear the wolves.

223   *Remembering Herun-san: 1931*

Half-blind, the other eye a livid bulb
Lighting the great beak of his *gaijin* nose
(Even when young, before the Oedipal wound,
'The large alarming eyes of myope') –
And tiny, too, 'mere mite of literature',
Fey Graeco-Irish wanderer in torment
Flinching away from fancied slights and jeers.

His introduction – by-ways of scholarship,
Martinique grammars, Creole dialects,
Mixed with 'artistic labours', Chinese ghosts . . .
His mind inflamed with all things Japanese,
So new, so ancient, fairy-folk who achieve
Delicate miracles on a bowl of rice.
He would live here, record the miracles –
'All the sweet glamours, translucent, milky, soft' –
But needed help, my help: poor amateur,
Keen to impress with learning; doubting; abject.
We found the post in Matsué. He went.

Letter upon letter, following a graph
Of ecstasy, dejection, blankness, rage –
Against 'the shallow-pated missionaries',
Against frock-coated fairy-folk who ape them –
Then soaring up to map his destiny:
'To set minds dreaming, or darkling in new dreams'.

We seldom met; but then, that one 'good' eye
Roved like a moth round everything it saw,
Details distinct, groped-round: the wallpaper,
The backs of books, ornaments, pictures, pots –
He could have made a catalogue of these.
Yet as for the horizon and the stars –
He had never seen them, could not understand
The whole of things, but only part with part.
He lived in books, worshipped the makers of them –
Gautier, Tolstoi, Swinburne, Loti, Kipling,
Joaquin Miller, Sacher-Masoch . . . Then
Feared he knew nothing, ought to curb himself
To birds, cats, insects, flowers, 'queer small things'
(Perhaps himself), leaving the larger themes
To 'men of brains' (myself?). Anxious, inflamed,
Pain working within him, filling his mouth with blood,
Wooing that mighty image-maker, Death,
Seeking its great, sweet, passionless unity.

*

Shy moth, perpetual foreigner, that night
We sat among the hotel's shrubbery shadows
At Miyanoshita, I saw your wings
Flutter and graze the objects you desired
And veered away from: seductive Western things –
Good wine, cigars, deep armchairs, play of mind
Following logic, wit, urbanity,
All that opposes those blind tendencies
You nurtured, desired, feared, subliminal
And startling outward consciousness. . . Romance

Stifled your disappointments, and renewed them;
Faced you with heavenly magic, then withdrew,
Faced you with ignorance – 'to have learned about Japan
Only enough to know . . .' *that you knew nothing;*
Stumbling through language you could but 'pidgin' in
To 'Little Wife', to 'Mamma-San', your toy,
Your shy interpreter of all you knew.
She was your voice, your ears, your oracle
Telling you ghostly stories in a tongue
Invented by the two of you – 'heart-things'.

Eternal restlessness, and joy, and rage –
Japanese angels devils in a wink,
And back again to angels. 'Enemies'
On every side, invented persecutions,
The stridulous telegraphy of critics
Buzzing behind your blinded forehead's dome.
Your 'Mamma-San' recorded what you said
On that September day when your frail heat
Burned itself out at last:
                                        'Never weep
If I should die. Buy for a few sen
A little earthen pot, and bury me
In some small temple yard in some dim place.
Never be sorry'.

Strange impulses, desires, and memories,
Inventing old romance, while all around
The red sun rose, presaging fire and sword,
And fairy-folk went burning through the world . . .

'And I have more, so much much more, to say'.

GFW: I am most honoured
to be received here
this afternoon.

VA: We are very glad
that you came
despite the heat.

GFW: I hear there are
many National Treasures
in this temple.

VA: This building is itself
a National Treasure,
as is the Buddha
deified inside it.

GFW: May I ask
how old
the temple is?

VA: This temple
is one thousand four hundred
years old. I am the one hundred
and nineteenth abbess.

GFW: In what dynasty
was the temple founded?

VA: In the era
of the Emperor Kinmei,
when the Buddha came
to Japan . . . May I ask

| | your purpose in coming |
| | to Japan? |

GFW: I came to Japan
to know more about
the Japanese people
and Japanese culture,
of which we know something
in my country, and admire.

VA: And may I ask how long
you intend to stay?

GFW: Three weeks.

VA: In regard to religion,
are you studying Christianity
or Buddhism primarily?

GFW: I am interested in all religions
as a form of man's behaviour.

VA: Is this your first
visit to Japan?

GFW: Yes, but I have known
Japanese history
Japanese art
and Japanese literature
a long time.

VA: I feel very much assured
that you have so much understanding
towards these things.

GFW: Thank you very much.
I wish more people from my country

could know your people
and your country.

VA: Can you eat
this kind of
Japanese cake?

GFW: I am sure I can
because I like
all Japanese food.

VA: Are you giving a lecture
or something?

GFW: I am attending a seminar
on our country's literature.

VA: It must be very trying
in this hot season.

GFW: No, this season
is like the season at my home –
very pleasant.

VA: Have you a message
for our youth? For the world?
What is your impression
of our women? Of God?
May I ask
what tobacco you smoke?

GFW: To thine own self be true.
May peace prevail.
Very beautiful.
The same to all but
called by different names.
A blend I have made up.

VA: Thank you very much for coming.

GFW: Thank you for all your trouble.

Together: Thank you. Thank you. Thank you.

GFW: *Arigato* . . .
(Did I get that right?)

Notes to 'Voices Through Clouds'

Kirishitan Monogatari
Three Last Words: 1620, 1636, 1639
I: Fucan Fabian (also variously known as Fukansai Habian, Fabian Unguio, etc. 1565?–after 1620): the chief Japanese intellectual of the so-called 'Christian Century' (1549–1650), he was converted to Christianity about 1583, admitted to the Society of Jesus as lay brother in 1586, rose as teacher in the Jesuit *collegio* in Amakusa, and achieved notoriety as preacher and as polemicist against Buddhism, Confucianism and Shinto. He abandoned the Jesuits about 1608, and by 1618 was actively engaged in the persecution of Christians in Nagasaki. In 1620 he wrote *Ha Daisu* ('Deus Destroyed'), a refutation of Christianity which mirrors and perverts many of the intellectual objections he had earlier made to the accepted faiths of Japan.

II: Among Fabian's chief victims was Fr. Christovão Ferreira, a Portuguese Jesuit who, after prolonged interrogation and torture, apostasised. He became a Zen Buddhist, adopted a Japanese name, Sawano Chuan, and himself became a persecutor of the Christians. However, it is said that later, in the extremity of illness, he renounced his apostasy and died a martyr.

III: *Kirishitan Monogatari* ('Tales of the Christians') is the title of an anonymous chapbook dated 1639, the first of many popular fictional narratives published in the 17th and 18th centuries dealing with early Japanese Christianity. The villains were in general the *Namban* ('Southern Barbarians', i.e. Portuguese and Spanish), and in particular the *Bateren* (Jesuits) and *Furaten* (Franciscan friars).

The poem draws on much material. I must acknowledge many debts to *The Christian Century in Japan* by C. R. Boxer (Stanford, 1951) and to *Deus Destroyed* by George Elison (Harvard, 1973).

Letters from Jakarta: 1641 and 1680

Much the most famous of the *Jagatara-bumi* ('Letters from Jakarta') is in fact a fabrication by a Nagasaki scholar, Joken Nishikawa (1648–1724), drawing on the story of Oharu (1624–1697), a girl of mixed Dutch-Japanese parentage who was exiled from Nagasaki to the Dutch colony of Java by the Tokugawa shogunate's expulsion act of 1639. This poetic lament had wide circulation, is still well known, and is often accepted as authentic. However, some genuine Oharu letters survive, full of prosaic detail, from the years 1672–92. I am indebted to Reiko Yamanouchi for a version of the Nishikawa piece, and to Yoko Okuda and Tomoko Nakagawa for their work on a genuine late letter. The poem draws on both.

On Dejima: 1845

Dejima was the name of the artificial island constructed in Nagasaki harbour by the Tokugawa shogunate between 1634 and 1636. Its 1.30 acres was the only place in Japan where Westerners, first the Portuguese and then the Dutch, were allowed to live from the 1630s until 1856. A short bridge to the north was its sole link with the rest of Japan, and comings and goings were rigidly restricted. In the Dutch period, drawn on here, its inhabitants were mainly the trading-company director, his employees, and some sailors. It is now part of the mainland, but its dimensions and some traces of its buildings can still be seen.

The Envoys: 1860

In 1860, a delegation of 77 officials was sent to the United States by the Tokugawa shogunate, the first of a number of such embassies sent abroad. A diary was kept by one of the envoys, Norimasa Muragaki. This was later published as part of *The First Japanese Embassy to the United States* (The America-Japan Society, Tokyo, 1920). Walt Whitman saw the envoys' arrival in New York: see 'A Broadway Pageant'.

Of Japan at Ten Hours' Sight: 1889

Rudyard Kipling visited Japan in March–September 1889. He published an account in *From Sea to Sea: Letters of Travel*, Pt. I (New York, 1900).

Soseki: December 1902

Natsume Soseki (1867–1916), by general consent the leading Japanese novelist of the modern period, began as a scholar of foreign, and in particular English, literature. In 1900 he was sent by the Japanese Ministry of

Education to study in England, where he remained until early in 1903. He worked privately in London, taking some tutorials from the Shakespeare scholar W. J. Craig. Towards the end of his time in England, a colleague reported to the Ministry of Education in Tokyo that Soseki was suffering from a nervous breakdown. I am indebted for several details to the curators of the Soseki Collection in the library of Tohoku University, Sendai, and to Hisaaki Yamanouchi. Two lines have been taken from Shimazaki Toson (1872–1943). The poem was first published in *The Times Literary Supplement*, and later in my *Poems 1953–1983*. The present version contains some revisions, in the interests of accuracy, mainly prompted by Kei Koike.

Remembering Herun-san: 1931
Basil Hall Chamberlain (1850–1935), born in England but largely educated in France and Switzerland, first came to Japan in 1873, taught at the Imperial Naval School in Tokyo 1874–82, and became so proficient in the language that he was appointed Professor of Japanese at the Imperial University (later the University of Tokyo) in 1886. He first met Lafcadio Hearn (1850–1904) soon after Hearn's arrival in Japan in 1890: they met several times, in Tokyo and in Miyanoshita, but their friendship is largely recorded in letters (see *The Japanese Letters of Lafcadio Hearn*, edited by Elizabeth Bisland, Boston, 1922; *Letters from Basil Hall Chamberlain to Lafcadio Hearn* and *More Letters from Basil Hall Chamberlain*, edited by Kazuo Koizumi, Tokyo, 1936 and 1937). Chamberlain retired to Geneva in 1911, and died there. 1931 was the year of the so-called 'Manchurian Incident', which eventually led to full-scale war with China, and then Pearl Harbor.

Great Foreign Writer Visits Age-Old Temple,
Greeted by Venerable Abbess: 1955
Based on a transcript, 'Interview at Zenkoji Temple', from *Faulkner in Nagano* (Tokyo, 1956).

Part III

225 *Imagine a City*

Imagine a city. It is not a city you know.
You approach it either by river or by one of four roads,
Never by air. The river runs through the city.
The roads enter at the four points of the compass.
There are city walls, old ones, now long decayed
But they are still there, bits of a past it once had.

Approach it now (shall we say) by the road from the east.
You can see the ruined gate from a mile away,
And, beyond the gate, towers that may be temples or tombs.
It is evening, and smoke here and there is rising in drifts,
So meals are being prepared, you suppose, in thousands of houses.
There is a smell of roast meat, a succulent odour.

Now enter the city, go through the eastern gate.
Great birds, like vultures, shift on its broken tiles.
The street in front of you is obscured by the setting sun,
A yellow-red ball in a dazzling haze of brilliance.
The paving under your feet is uneven. You stumble,
Clutching a door that leans to your hand as you take it.

And now for the first time you are uneasy.
No one is in the street, or in the side-turnings,
Or leaning out from the windows, or standing in doorways.
The fading sunlight conspires with the drifting smoke,
Yet if there were people here surely you'd see them,
Or, at the least, hear them. But there is silence.

Yet you go on, if only because to go back now
Seems worse – worse (shall we say) than whatever
Might meet you ahead, as the street narrows, and alleys
Flow in hither and thither, a dead-end of tangles
Looping forwards and sideways, neither here nor there, but somehow
Changing direction like water wind-caught abruptly.

303

And there you are, now. You may find the western gate.
It must lie straight ahead, the north to your right,
The south to your left. But where is the river
You heard about (you say) at the beginning?
That is for you to find out, or not to find out.
It may not, in any case, serve as a way of escape.

You imagined a city. It is not a city you know.

226 *Cairo*

Sleepless in Cairo, nine floors above the Nile,
The air-conditioning playing castanets,
The caffeine twitching at the ends of nerves.
Shrouded in fumes the city roars below.

And at its edge burnt Fustat chokes with dust:
Each footfall, treading, sinks and puffs up dust,
Cones of smashed brick, an avalanche of sherds,
Greased smoke from kilns, dismembered pyramids.

A dead dog fans up fast a wedge of stink
That hangs in heat, then falls to a rushed breeze.

Ancestral dregs: such fear encased in power,
Layer upon layer, ebony, silver, gold,
Chariots, sandals, incense, sweetmeats, toys.

The Rameses Hilton rises, catafalque
Above successive cities, holds us here
Shrunk Mamelukes and Pharaohs, side by side –

That frozen mask, magnificent, awake
Night after night, staring at no sky,
Airless in luxury, at its wits' end.

227 *On Alderney*

Under the stars' fixed, distant, cold regard,
The lighthouse beams are pulsing, nervous, hard.

Islands are prisons: so are metaphors.
Walk inland from this beach, beyond the shore's
Display of *son et lumière*, and find
A darkness visible, an age defined
In bunkers, towers, concrete under gorse,
Snarls of barbed wire bunched in a fist whose force
Rises through scrub to trip you. All round,
Beneath it all, exiles lie underground:
Thousands of bodies, tortured, starved, hanged, shot,
'The scum of Eastern Europe'. There is not
A beam to light them there. But by the sea
Their ghosts walk through the pulsing flashes, free:

Though light-years of the stars can't drown their agony.

228 *Dredging*

They are dredging the stream: the praying-mantis face
Of the nudging shovel goes in, its teeth on edge.
Mud seethes and settles, settles and seeps back.

Tangle of juicy stems, strewn, cut and bleeding:
Their moistures are at one with the cleared stream,
Drop down, uprooted, yellow-petalled, melt.

Jaws grunt and champ, wisps dripping at the mouth,
Fetch up smashed crocks, slashed tyres, knobs of barbed wire
Under the strewn weeds and the welted clods.

305

And the thunder thuds, the swollen clouds disgorge,
Swelling the channel, neatly grooved, with flood
Superbly tamed, as accurate as rain.

229   *The Dancing Foxes*

An early morning walk in Gloucestershire
Twenty-five years ago: the borrowed cottage, then
A rutted track, a gate, a rising copse,
The wind blowing against me, when
Among the trees I reached another gate.

Leaning, at first I saw the distance rather
Than what the morning gave me . . . Straight
In front of me, six feet away, a vixen
Lay in a couch of bracken, muzzle raised
At her two cubs, dancing on their hind paws,
Rapt as their mother's gaze.
Nimbly they moved. Moved and unmoving, we
Watched as they danced, vixen and man content
In what we saw, separately and together.

Until the wind turned suddenly, to scatter
Vixen and cubs across those distances,
Leaving me at the gate among the trees.

The making of memory – how it tests and twists,
Delving, arranging, covering things over
Till what was so is not, what was is never,
And the seven-year-old bully who gripped you by the wrists,
Burning them Chinese-fashion, is overlaid
With made-up stories, or pretended nightmares:
Or a half-remembered face stares and stares
Riddling your trite account of what you said
Better in the retelling, an audience
Quite taken in by what you chose to say.
No, it was not like that, was not the way
Things happened to fall out. Yet to make sense
You make a fiction, shut the truth away,
And put it all down to experience.

231   *The Bumps*

Nettles and hollows, at the end of the Terrace:
'The Bumps', we called it, and it's now I see
It was a waste land. But not waste to me
Then, five or six years old, who found a space
For things to be imagined in. I went
Day after day in search of butterflies,
For grass-snakes, newts, the bones of dinosaurs,
Whatever dreamed-of currency could be spent
On trove of any sort. And ever since
That place was what I wanted, looked for, found
In wastelands here and there, the cast-off dumps
Where things were to be found which no one found
Except myself, focused too narrowly,
Too innocent to know how memory's tricks
Would play a good half-century later on,
Confusing what's been spent, and dead and gone.

232   Cousin Anne

Did people live like this – stone floors, no books,
A smelly place out back? Not only that –
Was she our cousin, in the family . . . ?
It was a slum. I knew slums were in books,
But they were all in cities, not the Dales,
And not our family. How did they live,
Living like this, with chilly stone, and smells,
And dirty-looking children, and no books?
I didn't ask while I was there: I knew
They wouldn't want me to. But back at home
I asked, 'Does Cousin Anne live in a slum?'
And heard the embarrassed laughter. What was said
To explain it all I can't remember now,
Nor can I now remember why I asked.

233   *A Set of Metaphors*

This frame that feels itself, without desire;
This jointed bonework aching at its joints;
This cavity catching the touch of fire;
This skin a brick wall crumbling, lacking points.

The propped-up dwelling poised to hit the ground;
The vehicle abandoned, obsolete;
The temporary structure, now unsound;
The scaffolding collapsing in the street.

An amplitude that stirs, slow with disuse;
A withering of the thin contagious breath;
A drying wind; a slackening of juice;
A portioning-out of rations against death.

And so much more than each sly metaphor
And so much less to come than went before.

234 *Forgetting*

The glasses left at last night's restaurant.
The raincoat in the alcove where you hung it.
The bag you knew you had when you reached London.
The muddle about the name of the booked garage.
The confusion over a number, an address.

What you perhaps said, or might have said.
What comes back later, laughed at by a friend.
What's scribbled in the last page of your diary.
What surfaces next day at 5.0 p.m.
What wakes you from a dream, and is still bad.

Missing, as the ratchet slips on the motor-mower.
Missing, like a tooth the tongue can't leave alone.
Missing, a gap between familiar houses.
Missing, a beat of the heart in fear or exhaustion.
Missing, as in a battle, but not presumed dead.

235 *Worried*

One about liver condition, noted by doctors
Giving him four or five months, possibly longer.
One about mortgage-repayments; one about body-smell;
Another who wakes at dawn drugged with psephology,
Recking boundary-changes.

Some with the death of the elm, or the whale, or the planet;
Those who go out with petitions, long-time committee-sitters.
Dreaders of final exams or boards of selection,
Of being found out in adultery, or peculation,
Or organ deficiency.

Others with mothers, too old to be told what is proper,
Or with children who, now far away, are bad correspondents,
Or with colleagues who chatter too much, or too little, or dreamers
Who find their dreams true too often, disaster-prophets,
Hoarders of omens.

All of them gripped by pain, boding, guilt, the inferior furies,
All of them monomaniac in ailment,
All unhelped by spilling the beans, in surgery or confessional,
All obsessed with a thing that is possibly nameless
Or, if named, incurable.

236   Two Poets*

One is asleep, one dead. Both lie inclined
Towards us, who are awake and still alive.
One's work is over, torn and discarded scraps
Strewn by his elbow. One's is yet to come,
A childlike promise hovering in the trees.

An attic above London, where the dawn
Peers at the burnt-out candle and the boy,
Finished with faking, stretched out on the bed.
A rural toyset static as a dream,
Where horse and pig and poet share the green.

The trees come closer. London vanishes.
The dream is taking over from the toys,
Breaking the promises, poised now to invade
That farmyard round which Russia stretches out
Endlessly, beyond livid smoky clouds.

* *Chatterton* (Henry Wallis, 1855–56)
The Poet Reclining (Marc Chagall, 1915)

237 'The anaesthetic from which none come round'

Now what you feared so long has got you too.
The blankness has descended where you lie
Deep in that building you already knew,
And nothing reaches you in vacancy.
Toads and hired boxes all pushed to one side,
Lugubrious jokes made serious at last
There in the loneliest, cruellest, final place,
Your turning over of the wasted past
Has stopped forever. And you meet full-face
The shot that's never missed or fallen wide.

238 The Mole at Kilpeck Church
(for Geoffrey Grigson)

Fierce kicks and thrustings under turf and leaf
Reveal you, revenant,
Still lively under so much buried grief,
So ready to be quick when all are dead,
So plucky in extending your dark head
Among the carvings of the lost and spent.

Even that famous randy lady who,
Spreading her swollen thighs,
Enacts in stone the acts that we would do,
Seems nothing to your rushing push, your flair
For room to breathe when all the churchyard air
Shrinks to a mere frame for your energies.

239 *Second After Trinity*
(for Norman Nicholson)

Nine in the congregation. A clergyman
Who's filling in this Sunday: Austrian, Pole,
Some accent I can't place. Why is he here
(Our usual's off, I know: he told us last
Sunday – trivial details lost in church),
But why this foreigner, whose voice is stranger
Even than 1662? But then, there follows
The question, *Why are we here?*, who duly follow
This staid, familiar, dignified, dead rite.
The ritual itself takes over, just;
And unaccompanied (the organ's off)
We sing two hymns we know but don't quite know,
And speak the words, and slowly up the aisle
Follow the other seven who have come,
Knowing they must, with questions of their own.

240 *Cold Comforts*
(for John Betjeman)

What is it to grow old? *Matthew Arnold*

It is to know that what may just survive
Is nothing but a footnote in a vast
Compendium in 2005,
Bought by five libraries which keep the Past
Locked in a cellar for the literate.

It is to see one's face familiar, but
Changed in a way one did not hope to see:
The eyes too shifty, and the mouth too slack.
It is to alter into vacancy,
Not looking forward, frightened to look back.

It is to wander down that much-trod track
Which leads to private groans and oaths and sighs,
Muttering to oneself a name or two,
Remembering a face, or breasts, or thighs,
How many of them, and yet now how few.

And all of these are known, and all are true,
And none of them gives comfort or relief.
If we could try the whole thing once again,
Would they be different? O the blank belief
That everything is so, and all things vain.

241 *For Roy Fuller at Seventy*

A Fuller on the shelf: 'the image noted',
Though whether Roy or John I cannot say
Until I put my specs on. What I've quoted
Is Roy's, of course, and the three words convey

The antiseptic note I find so cheering
Among the dank piles of the verse that comes
(With truculent letters, or, much worse, the leering
Bonhomous scrawls accompanying the Glums)

Onto my desk, or thumping on the mat
Here at the Mill House. You keep up the standards
Old X, young Y, have trampled till they're flat –
Ungolden Oldies or sleek Standard Vanguards

Praised by the ignorant or the tin-eared trendies
Who tell us what is what, and week by week
Build their snug houses frail as Barrie's Wendy's –
The vain, the mad, the stupid, and the chic.

Dear Roy, these quatrains are, I know, splenetic,
Not quite the thing to send on Feb 11.
Past fifty, is the New always emetic?
At seventy, perhaps one thinks of Heaven –

A polished harp, a due reward, a choir
Singing in harmony one's better lines . . .
Below, the ceaseless unremitting fire
Consuming all the others' dim designs.

You will go on for twenty years or longer,
Giving us more of what we seek from you,
Neater and sweeter, crisper, darker, stronger;
Here's to *Collected*, 2002.

242   *A Sort of Ballade for a Sort of New Hero*
(for Craig Raine)

Who speaks of Foxall now? In what dark grove
Sits Ketton-Cremer plucking at his lyre?
Where are the followers of Titterton
William Kean Seymour put among the choir
Of heavenly minstrels? And where Fredegond Shove?
Their reputations shrouded, vanished, gone.
There is but one now whom the Muses deign
To set within the pantheon: Craig Raine.

The harp of Humbert Wolfe is quite unstrung,
And Stephen Phillips – that almighty voice –
Is heard no more. The elegiac Rook
Whose Dunkirk verses once resolved our choice
To stand firm on the brink when we were young –
No longer mentioned; he whose metres shook
The heavens, William Watson – sought in vain.
Our single talent's well employed with Raine.

314

Ask you for Gerald Gould? His tongue is mute,
Like that of Redwood Anderson and Trench,
Fine bards whose promise burst upon the world
But yesterday. The fire that none could quench –
Theodore Maynard – has mislaid his lute.
J. D. C. Pellow, whose great stanzas hurled
Defiance at the night, won't come again.
Our only hope lies now with one: Craig Raine.

Prince, when the slughorn trembles at your lips
Calling disconsolate for Carman, Shanks,
Snaith, Kirke White, Luce, at that apocalypse
When for forgotten poets we give thanks,
Hold firm the note, prolong the dying strain,
Yet is there bounty: we still have Craig Raine.

Poems 1986–1988

243   *The Return*

I picked her up that hot sand-blasted day
In Euhesperides – a rubbish tip
Where all Benghazi's refuse piled across
Scatterings of a millennium of mess:
A broken head of earthenware, a face
Staring out silently, wreathed in her dress
Of fragile terracotta. Picked her up
And brought her home, and meant to let her stay.
She lodged there in a cabinet, and moved
As we moved, to this other place, and lay
For twenty years in England.
                               Till today
I looked inside the cabinet, observed
The spilth of dust and splinters at her neck,
A fallen garment. As I gently took
Her head within my hands, she split and broke,
Her chaplet and her vestiges of dress
Shivering to sand.
                    I threw her all away
Onto the flowerbed: all of her except
The one remaining scrap, her oval face
Lying within my palm. I have it here,
This small masked relic. In this chilly year
The northern damps had killed her where she slept –

The last frail remnant of Persephone,
Whose head it was, whom I picked up that day
After so many broken centuries,
Miraculous and lasting testimony
Among the camel corpses, salt, tins, glass,
And brought her home to live here, till today
She went back to the underworld, as dust.

Her tiny face looks up, and will not last.

I

A plastic bag of everything and nothing,
Bulged earth, damp clay, spiked twigs, charcoal, sogged ash.
Lump heavy as a body. Tip it out,
Let it resolve itself to what it is,
A shovelful of everything and nothing

Crammed where it silted up through centuries,
Now loosed and prised apart and spilt, rinsed out
In washing-up bowls, stacked and left to dry.
Distinguish it, so each becomes a thing,
Each from its separate silt of centuries:

Here sherds, there glass, here iron, flint, wood, bone,
Waste lead, worked stone. The property of each
Begins to show, comes clear, fit to be named,
Then to be labelled, given provenance:
Thetford or Pingsdorf; tibia, cranium, rib –

Each speaks itself, identified, distinct,
Datable, namable, however smashed,
However humbled to a rim, a scrap,
Discrete in fragments, now assembled here,
Articulates itself, and everything.

II

Deposit, anaerobic: waterlogged,
Free from bacteria, it seems unchanged
Since left there in its burial, prolonged.

Roots absent, but some root-marks visible
On flakings, fissures. Delicate, requires
Careful handling, soft to finger pressures.

Organic, not an artefact. Suggest
Submit to conservation. Drawing shows
Trace-marks recorded. Condition varies.

Age and description multiple, repeated
Within parameters. Volatile condition
Makes difficult a certain recognition.

Retrieved from damp environment, encrusted
In find-spot, still unfractured, held in storage,
This layered thing, or object, defies knowledge.

Put it down, then, *Unrecognisable*:
This is the word usually applicable.

245 *Nevertheless*

Nevertheless, if all things fell away
And nothing else was left, what would you do?
You cannot say.
If you could say it, it would not be true.
You have embarked already, Pascal said:
You cannot stay,
You move, not knowing it, to join the dead.

And yet you know it, travelling a route
Marked with such signposts as you recognise:
Not absolute,
Provisional rather, but clear to eyes
Trained in the sign-language of mortal speech,
Grave or acute,
Place-names or common names, each linked with each.

Not knowing or knowing, asleep, awake,
You journey on, as some things fall away,
Dry up, or break,
Explode or wither, burn down, or decay;
And what remains, next year, or month, or week,
Even today
Is what you cannot write, or even speak.

246   *Duet*

The cellist groans behind his instrument.
The listening microphone once picked it up,
Now cut in disc and looped in tape forever.

Was it the effort, was it ecstasy,
Or the relief after each burdened stave,
That made him groan behind the trembling bow?

Such human noise disturbs the dream of art
But makes it human too. Each panting breath
Reminds the instrument what made it weep.

247   *Mother and Child*

Big-headed, tidy, about my own age,
He stands attentively beside a woman
I take to be his mother, small and frail.

Then suddenly he blurts some words out, child
Wanting a sweet, clamouring noisily.
Something is wrong with him. I look away.

His mother calms him quietly. He nods
But lets his lower lip tremble, a tear
Roll down his cheek in dumb resentfulness.

322

How many years they must have lived like this,
Since over half a century ago
She felt the leap of something deep within,

Not knowing what it promised was this child
Who now stands by the counter neatly dressed
In a man's clothes, weeping not like a man.

248   *Undreamt of*

How do I know I spend the whole night
      dreaming,
As I do know, yet never can recall
More than a moment of what happened, seeming
To blank out images I don't need at all?
A third of life spent sleeping, dreaming – then
Immediately cancelled. So many folk
Remember every detail, tell you when
It's boring as some long elaborate joke,
Or plots of novels, or films you've never seen.
Why do theirs stay and mine all slip away?
Is there some censor crouched in my machine
Who puts the scrambler on, from night to day?
Nightmares and fantasies and Jung and Freud
For me are long white banners in a void.

249   *Civil Service*

The government department is deserted
But all the lights are on. It lies below
The pavement, rises up, a stump of glass,
And all the lights are on, and no one there.
It's Friday night, at nine. And why indeed
Should anyone be there? But all the lights are on.

Banks of computers sit there, room on room
Frozen in rectangles of green on black;
And here's an office where two chairs exchange
A dialogue which must have finished when
They left at half-past five. Beyond that door
A drinks-machine winks to itself, alone.

The filing-cabinets are shut. A desk-top
Opens itself to any passing eye
But keeps its drawers locked. Hunched, apart,
A word-processor has run out of words.
Round it, the streets are screaming, siren-rent.
The government department is deserted.

250   *Tested*

The test we do is simple. It was tested
In the laboratories where such tests take place.
Reactions have been measured, noted, tested.

The aperture is touched. We do the touching.
Dilation follows from the touch we give.
What follows is so simple that it's touching.

Arousal as reaction is what's normal
And that reaction is the one we want.
Once that is known, the whole thing is quite normal.

Even the youngest show the same reaction
As older ones who recognise the sign.
Our touch expects a uniform reaction.

And so our tests have proved how very simple
The mechanism is that proves the crime.
What follows may be hard. But this is simple.

251 *Beginning Again*

On the first day of spring
They begin again,
Riddling and twisting
In the lath walls,
Or ticking in timbers,
Or scrawling through beams:
Message we dreaded
Threading the house.

Trying to track them,
Warmed by the fireside
We share, we can hear them.
It seems that the season –
Outside and inside –
Has coaxed them to signal
Life is returning
In these dots and dashes.

So now at nightfall,
Sudden in springtime
Spilling into our lives,
They prattle and smirk at
Warrants and pestilents,
Tell us again that
No matter what action
They will prevail.

He's gone with her, and she has gone with him,
And two are left behind; and there's four more –
The children, two of each; grandparents, still
Alive and well, till now, and taking sides;
And neighbours, six close by, and more besides
In half a dozen villages . . . Until
The whole thing multiplies by seven score –
Why he went off with her, and she with him.

One, left behind, has changed the locks and keys:
The other keeps inside and draws the blinds.
The ones who went have rented somewhere near,
But no one's seen them yet. The children play
With neighbours' children. Those who've gone away
Will haggle over them, and fret in fear
Absence will blank them out. What clasps and binds
Shreds down to lawyers, judgements, mortgages.

So what began in two especial lives,
Involving many more in church and bank,
Florist, wine-merchant, dressmaker, Moss Bros.,
A regiment of relatives, a ring,
Has now become this other tangled thing:
Two grew to eight, with dozens at a loss
To know whom they should blame or love or thank.

So many husbands gone, so many wives.

253 *Sigma*

Unable to get on with anything,
Throwing out papers, fiddling with piled mess,
I pull a box of sherds out, stacked up here
Among the whole accumulation, less
Because I want to but because it's there –
A scattering of pottery I picked up
Among the Libyan middens I knew once,
And rake it over, chucking out here a cup-
handle, broken, and a flaking rim:
And, in among it all, there's suddenly
This scrap that carries a graffito – Σ,
A sigma, a scratched *ess*; and try to tell
Where it once fitted – as beginning or end,
As some abbreviated syllable,
Or sign of ownership, or just a scribble
Made on a day in 450 BC
By someone else who messed about like this,
Unable to get on with anything,
But made his mark for someone else to see.

from *The Dust of the World* (1994)

'The reason for a cockroach in a story must differ from the reason for a cockroach in a kitchen.'

Leon Wieseltier, TLS

It was not home. It was in Tokyo
At half-past ten at night or thereabouts.
I went into the kitchen, flicked the switch,
And saw him crouching on the table's edge.

He was enormous, brown, and very still.
His feathery branches waited, so it seemed,
For further movement, and for me to move.
We looked at one another very hard.

He did not move, nor did I, watching him.
The jet-lag left me drowsy still, though sleep
Seemed far away, as I was far away.
I studied him as if in Japanese.

Aburamushi is the name for him
I suddenly remembered, wondering
What *abura* means: *mushi* is 'insect' or
A dozen other things in Japanese,

Such as a kind of soup, both clear and poached.
This cockroach, though, was more a samurai,
Plated and helmeted and plumed and proud.
I faced him as a common yokel might,

Lest he should shove me sideways with his sword,
Or leap across the tabletop and land
Bristling with fury in my sweating hair.
It was a hot September night, and I

Was tired of travel. 'I'll get it over with –
This stinker from the floorboards makes me sick,'
I thought, 'and I am sick of fantasy.'
I took one slipper off and lunged at him.

He skidded off the table, hit the floor
With a soft slushy plop, and sidestepped back
Towards the sink. I threw myself full-length
And smashed him with the slipper, and crouched down.

His scales fanned out. He bled onto the boards,
Gave half a shrug, and then lay still and dead.
I wiped the slipper with a newspaper,
Rinsed both my hands, and groped my way to bed.

That is the story. This is the poem, told
In metre, with a rhyme to end it all.
The reasons for the cockroach, or the poem,
Or why I've told the story – who can tell?

A cockroach in a kitchen is the truth.
A cockroach in a story may be lies.
The insect was both noble and uncouth.
The writer makes a life from mysteries.

255 *Butō*

A stick; a stone; a shape with arms and legs.
The background, blank; the foreground, faces turned
Towards this stick, this stone, this shape – which then
Begins to move. Its robe is stained
(If it is called a robe). A man
Moves under it (if it is called a man).

And all so slowly, with such sense of pain:
The stick picked up, and then the stone, and both
Heavy as forests, heavy as boulders, each breath
Laboured, though silent. The robe, a rag
Torn between unseen hands. Again
The thing under it all reveals a man.

And this is art, for which you have to pay
To see a man bowed down by sticks and stones
And his own pain, against a wall which may
Be nothing but a rag, a trick
Along with all the pain and strain and stains
Enacted by a man, a stone, a stick.

256   The Last Byakkotai

I was the one who did not die.
Of course I died at last, but do not lie
With all the others, nineteen shafts of stone:
I, the one failure, lie alone
And nothing indicates the way I failed,
Evading suicide. My botched wounds trailed
Year after useless year, from youth to age,
While worshippers who come on pilgrimage
Remember my companions in their youth,
Eternal witnesses to blood and truth.

What was the glory that I did not earn?
This kind of truth is difficult to learn:
To reach sixteen, and fail, and spill your blood,
And so to be symbolic of some good
For which successive pilgrims will come far,
Light incense-sticks, and smell the smoke of war
Long vanished but still strong – or not succeed
And become infamous as one who tried to bleed
But did not bleed enough. No twentieth stone
Marks out the place I suffer in, alone.

257   *Changes*

After a day of cloud, a bright morning.
Sun prints a firm shadow on the screen.
Outside, green leaves are brilliant on a branch.

The abacus becomes a cash register
Reading the prices electronically.
Sony Walkmen walk the streets alone.

Cicadas, dying, slur their final notes
Before the evening crickets endlessly
Repeat their scales they say we cannot hear.

Night in the metropolis is a rainbow
Of distant neon, and my glaring lamp
Winks with a tremulous and silent shock.

Time is a moss, a river, and a stone.
Today grew cloudy as the Asian winds
Blew into the Pacific. Tomorrow lies

Pinned to the television screen's bright charts,
Clearer than weather, predicted in chirrupings
Spoken by girls who smile, and bow, and fade.

Shadows at the door, through the door.
No one comes in. The television screen
Flickers news from Panama, ads for tampons.

Slurping of noodles, sucking of plenitude.
We eat alone, polite and separate:
Three Japanese, one foreigner. And then

The screen reveals a slaughtered chimpanzee
Which (if I understand the bulletin)
In Kyoto managed to pick up a key,

Unlocked his cage, and rampaged through the lab,
So had to be shot. We see his body, flat
Down in some other monkey's cage; we all

Look up from eels or noodles to take stock
Of something not like news, so singular
We look at one another in surprise

And murmur common nothings, and shake heads
In shared amazement that such things should be
Here in our little world of food and drink.

It doesn't last long. Apes are animals,
And we are human, though we're different,
Polite, and separate, beyond the shadows.

259 *Festival*

Autumn equinox: pink and white
The lanterns wave above the narrow street,
Swayed by a casual light September breeze.

Some lanterns lit, some dark: they'll soon come down,
After the families have visited
The shrines of all their dead, and brought their flowers,

And lit their sticks of incense, put to rights
The crowded little plots of earth and stone.
Look, they're already coming down: four men

Nimbly unstring them, take in loop by loop,
And concertina them to plattered disks,
Stack them in rows.

                   Much like the ordered dead
Under the lettered stones and staves and flowers,
The lanterns are put tidily away.

A whole year passes marked by rituals,
As if some punctuation must be here
To say what day or season has arrived

Again and yet again, in wind or rain,
Or simply by the calendar to prove
Things happened then, and now, and will again.

260 *In Nara Park*

The light goes in the deer park, and the deer are crying.
A young doe reaches for a lower branch
And plucks the paper prayer. Her soft lips munch
Somebody's wish for luck, or love. The leaves are dying,
Red, gold, and blackened on the shrine's dark path.

The old bucks cry and stumble, their moist breath
Poised in the cold air of this late afternoon.
The lanterns are unlit, and each white screen
Shows blind and still as a face set in death,
Fixed in its frame of carved and weathered stone.

The schoolchildren and tourists leave the park,
Letting these deer, these holy messengers,
Cry through the shadowy trees and gently browse
Where trees and lanterns merge into the dark,
Prayers hanging where the last light faintly shines.

261   *Together, Apart*

Too much together, or too much apart:
This is one problem of the human heart.

Thirty-five years of sharing day by day
With so much shared there is no need to say

So many things: we know instinctively
The common words of our proximity.

Not here, you're missed; now here, I need to get away,
To make some portion separate in the day.

And not belonging here, I feel content
When brooding on the portion that is spent.

Where everything is strange, and yet is known,
I sit under the trees and am alone,

Until there is an emptiness all round,
Missing your voice, the sweet habitual sound

Of our own language. I walk back to our room
Through the great park's descending evening gloom,

And find you there, after these hours apart,
Not having solved this question of the heart.

262   *Terminal Happiness*

To be conspicuous for complexion,
Length of nose, texture of hair,
Colour of eyes, cut of clothes,
Growth of facial stubble,
And posture of displacement.

To wait on Platform Zero
For a destination on the board
Indicated in characters
Capable of two readings
And in opposite directions.

To spend the blank interval
Rehearsing the simple numerals,
Copying the place-names,
Overhearing conversations
Punctuated with paranoia.

To board the train at last
Having checked with embarrassment
And for the third time
That it is indeed the right one
And not the non-stop express.

And finally to alight
At the station one intended
With no more luggage than necessary
And money for the next journey
On a bright October morning.

263　*Sado*

I

In the old port
between the lake and the sea,
a man plaiting fish-baskets,
fish-hawks crying,
hills soused in clouds.

Roofed trays of squid drying,
rain gathering in sheets
above collapsed huts.
Timelessly out-of-date,
a few faded words.

II

Jags of steep rocks, dragged cliffs
sifting down sand, crowned
with wind-spun pines, drowned
figurines in soft stone.

Villages straggling under
heaped maple hills, ridge-beams
heavy with hung persimmons
fronting the netted sea.

Bowed stunted women
pushing loaded carts
along narrow winding roads,
straws caught in the wind.

264   *Above Ryotsu*

Come here in the rain, under the dark pines,
Late afternoon in mid-November.
The steady rain drips from your umbrella.
No one visits the shrine above the little port.
It is not a famous place, this temple,
Unmentioned in the guidebooks. The stone lions
Grimace with ordinary rage, stare down
The avenue towards the new hotel.
Below, the ferry's foghorn blares twice, stops.

What strange needs made them build it here, and when,
Seems beyond explanation. Standing here
Under the rain, with nowhere to go
Except back to the hotel, is a banality
Equally inexplicable. This holiday
Comes at the wrong end of the year, away
From all the urgencies you've vanished from,
But satisfies another need, somehow:
To be foreign, tied to nothing, and yet happy.

No one will watch you, alone here in the rain:
Even the straggling schoolboys, going home,
Won't notice you, another dark dim shape
Beyond the torii, hidden in the mist.
Tomorrow you will take the ferry back,
Leaving the little port, the new hotel,
The temple with its lions, the wet pines;
And no one will have noticed anything,
Even your absence unremarked, at peace.

265 *In the Missionary's House*

After the persecutions and apostasies,
The tortures, crucifixions, secrecies,
The foreign fathers landed here again:
Two and a half centuries, and then
Came back to preach, to teach, and so to build.

And built this house. It is not an old house,
But even here, where few houses are old,
There are sounds: strains of something, not
Just earth tremors, come suddenly
At moments you don't expect –

Abrupt small punctuations, the dark wood
In beams and posts and floorboards snapping out
Orders or reactions, sometimes like a drum,
Sometimes a cry. In the missionary's house
They are like the sounds of something driven down,

Something suppressed, in pain, or leaping up
In joy to be back again, or murmurings,
Or prayers, or chants transformed to fossil wood
Yet capable of such articulation,
Such firm insistence in this foreign place,

Night in the missionary's house can be
A deep uneasiness at what has happened
Between the ceaseless crickets, and the drums
Come from the far temple, and the hush
Of wind and rain against the insect screens:

Until the dawn, when the birds start again,
Cicadas chatter in a different key,
The trucks and cars hurry familiarly,
And the missionary's house stands square and clear
In its old place, though not so very old.

266 *Potter*

He took a lump of clay,
Squatted above his wheel,
Threw it a certain way,
Spun it till you could feel
His thumbs splay out the rim
And spin and spin and spin,
Then pulled, and pressed, and let
The clay become a jet
Rising, controlled by air,
Then let it go; and there,
Below the plume of clay,
Cut it and made it stay
Perfect, a moulded bowl.
Three more grew from the whole
Pillar of clay, and lay –
Accomplishments, and final.
                              Till he took
These four perfections like a finished book
And closed the pages with his open hands,
Collapsing clay back into clay. His smile
Mocked at the skill he nullified, while
Only the shapeless lump remains and stands.

267 *After the Japanese*

I

If only, when the news came through
Old Age was on the way,
One shut the door, said 'Not at home',
And turned the bore away.

Though I had always known it was the way
I had to follow at the very end,
I never thought as yesterday went by
That it would be the road I walk today.

268 *Legend*

The superstitious Japanese
Are an inevitable prey
To devils, goblins, sprites; and these
Can be invoked, they say.

So thought U.S. Intelligence,
With forces poised to invade Japan.
It made a certain sort of sense
To an American

Who, studying stories soaked in age,
Myths stretching back to fabled days,
Pondering legends page by page,
Found one which would amaze

The credulous little men who hid
In the last island on the way.
This ploy was an impressive bid
To bring the end of play.

Foxes, caught wild and dipped in bleach
And trapped in waiting landing-craft,
To swim ashore, where they would reach
The Japs . . . The experts laughed,

And saw, already, terrified
Soldiers throw down their limbs and arms.
The fox is almost deified
By Japanese, and charms

Are sold at shrines to ward them off –
And yet they're very holy too:
A mixture at which none could scoff –
Bad news, half-gods, and *true* . . .

The trouble was the sea, which bore
Most of the ghostly white away.
Some forty foxes swam ashore
And scampered round the bay.

These sodden creatures, scared and tamed
And stripped of all their ghostliness,
Looked humbled, miserable, ashamed,
Shrunk to a nothingness.

And then it was the Japanese
Who laughed, and sighed, and primed their guns.
Cultural errors such as these,
Indeed, are anyone's.

I am very nervous. You can tell I am very nervous.
The moment I greet you, I begin talking too much
And the words are not right, I know they are not right.
Anyway . . . They have asked me to do this job
Which means speaking your words in my words
And their words in your words, and so I begin
Talking too much before you have even begun
Using many words at all. In fact, as I say . . .
Anyway . . . I wish I could keep calm, and listen, and say
Exactly the words that they speak and you speak, and begin
To know what you want to know about what that is
Over there (I'm not sure – I think it historical).
Anyway . . . But now I begin to tell you about my life
Since you kindly asked a question, and so I go on –
Too much, too much – about father who passed away, and
      mother ill,
And how I was ill too, often, when young, and how
I never became married, because my fiancé
Disappeared – no, not exactly, he just stopped coming, and . . .
Anyway . . . That was a famous temple, I forget the name.
And I am a Latter Day Saint, which is very strange,
I know, in this country, but I know it is true for me,
And could be for you – but you are a Protestant,
Have I got the word right? And I have my faith, yes I do,
And though I am nervous I know it is true for me,
Though my colleagues despise me, and whisper about me, and
      are rude
In front of my face and behind my back, and I . . . Anyway . . .
Yes, I think we are stopping a moment to see this famous
Historical place, I forget the name, I don't know the words,
And believe me, believe me, believe me, dear foreign guest
(So kind in your questions, so gentle, so worried – I see)
You are welcome here, very welcome. Anyway . . .
Please excuse how nervous I am. I think I shall die.

270 *Gairaigo**

Sitting in apāto
Quiet in my manshon
I write this in my nōto,
Lacking a wāpuro.

I am on a tsuā
From faraway Yōroppa
Where I wear a toppā
Or ōbā in the winter.

Terebi and rajio
Speak to me Nihon-go.
Tabako, arukōru
Help my arubaito.

Invite me to a konpa,
Give me a haibōru,
I have no abekku . . .
Show me please the toiré.

Better fetch shaberu.
Now I need a beddo,
Feeling pretty ierō . . .
Ga-gi-gu-ge-go.

*Japanese 'words that come from outside'

apartment; mansion (block of flats); notebook; word-processor; tour; Europe; topcoat; overcoat; television; radio; cigarettes; alcohol; work (from Ger. *arbeit*); party; highball; girl-/boyfriend (from Fr. *avec*); toilet; shovel; bed; yellow.

271 *Alms*

Two things the size of whittled pencil stubs
Poke through the taxi window, pink streaked black.
And through the window drifts a plaintive voice
Spun from a mouth that's also pink and black.

Leper, or thalidomide, or maimed –
What's diagnosed at this brief traffic halt?
My eyes averted from his eyes on me,
Why should I feel that this is all my fault?

Yet reach, of course, into my wallet thick
With crumpled little notes worth nothing much.
The accelerator roars. The pincered pencil stubs
Catch at the offering. We do not touch.

And all the distance to the airport, trapped
In a tight vacuum of sweat and dust,
That voice beseeches and those stubs implore.
Ignore this if you like. Or want. Or must.

272 *Calcutta: 1830*

We carried Bibles, Shakespeare, Bacon, Locke.
Temples and shrines storeyed with tangled limbs
Held things unwholesome. How to tend our flock
When Krishna cast out Matthew, and our hymns

Were drowned by prayers to Pooja? Addison
Might teach them a pure style but could not teach
Serious piety. To make comparison
Between our code and theirs was out of reach.

Untouchables in their fastidious way,
Yet sedulous in following the text:
They sat and read, but would not kneel to pray.
Something within them balked, and sulked, and vexed.

Here on the shelf, two images contend:
Francis, his face transfigured with God's love,
And Jagannath, whose eyes blaze and distend.
They stand together. But they do not move.

Our cemetery holds such images,
In Park Street, where we buried our own kind;
But who can hazard what our gardener sees,
Who, quietly chanting to himself, is blind?

273   *Tughluqabad*

These ruins did not need me to record them:
They told themselves of ruin as they rose
High on the banks that Tughluq built to hold them.
They told what he had built they would depose.

These tall slumped walls, these domes pocked deep with holes,
These slopes strewn hopelessly with shattered stone,
Were destined to be broken like the bowls
And jugs and pitchers smashed, sherds split with bone,

Their terracotta bleached white in the sun.
Only one emblem rises up and stirs
Life back into their death: vermilion,
Slashed deepest blue, a peacock screams and veers

Up from a brackish pool, its brilliant fan
Thrown out, then folded, volleys towards a tree.
The ruins crumble in the steady sun.
The peacock hides in swathes of greenery.

274   *More Indian Images*

The edicts of Ashoka cut in rock.
A rat behind the bar sniffs at a glass.
The langurs in the branches leap across
Festoons of foliage. The station clock
Is stuck at Queen Victoria's jubilee.

At Dhali in the rock-cut shrine I take
Honey and yoghurt from the offered hand.
At Puri the big waves break on the sand
Among the sewage. The village potters bake
Soft earthenware under a heap of gorse.

Mother Teresa's famous hospice stands
Against the compound plot where Shuju Roy
Recalls how things were when he was a boy.
His grandpa knew Tagore. With folded hands,
The sage in Oxford with a stiff-necked youth.

At Bhubaneshwar the majestic cart
Of Jagannath is hammered tier by tier.
The Lord's eyes blaze like fury at your fear.
This is the night halt. Next morning, you will start
Another journey, on another day.

275 The Rug

Among the red and yellow tangles
Grubs squirm, wings brush the rotten weavings,
The fabrications of a Basra market.

The old couple have not noticed. They sit
Among their trophies of Iraq and India,
Accumulations of five decades' journeys.

He was an envoy. Now he tells us how
He will write a book that proves the Maori
Voyaged from Libya, left inscriptions there.

She was a pianist, studied under Schnabel.
She thinks she remembers Schoenberg. Her legs swell,
Her tight white bandage stained with orange pus.

In the corner of their room, along a shelf,
Six Buddhas squat and praise longevity.
The rug from Basra crawls with bright decay.

276 Recreational Leave

They have come back. The next lot is in,
Landing at the port. Soon they will be here,
Some a little bit drunk, some a lot drunk,
With their money, their condoms, their loud pink faces.

They will be here soon. I tidy up the place,
Making the mattress nice, hanging the curtain
Just in the right place, bringing the water
So they can have a wash before it begins.

And afterwards too: they like to have a good wash
Before and after. I put out a tray with two cups,
Which some of them will fill with whisky or beer
And some of them will not. I want to make them happy.

Some of them are happy already, but I hope not too happy.
I don't want a lot of noise, or slapped faces,
With my baby here close by under the netting.
On a good night, I can have maybe ten of them in

With their money, their condoms, their loud pink faces,
And no trouble at all, if they are not too happy
With whisky or beer or whatever they want to do
To show they are proper men and enjoying themselves.

Nobody wants any trouble. Anyway, I don't.
If they are happy, and pay, and go away,
I shall be happy. My aunt will be happy too.
I put on my good dress, and wait for the sound

Of their funny voices banging about outside,
And try to guess what sort of a night it will be.
Baby, be quiet. I am here. I am fifteen.
This is the way I live, on the edge of the port.

277 *At the Struga Festival*
(for George Szirtes)

'There stood a man of Macedonia, and prayed him, saying, Come over into
Macedonia, and help us.'

Acts, 16:9

The Hyatt Regency in the capital,
As big as Diocletian's palace, tranquil.
Tourists eschew the smell of civil war.

Then the plane south to Struga, and four score
Poets converge to celebrate the Word,
Speaking in tongues. One local well-oiled bard
Greets us with bloodshot eyes, then falls away.

A shower of fireworks; poems; speeches. Day
Breaks brilliant on the lake as rumours run
Hither and thither, polyglot and loose.
A seminar with headphones. Can you scan
Slavic hexameters? The tree of man
Was never quiet. How define the Use
Of Poetry when the referendum looms?

Brodsky the Laureate is absent. Tombs
Carved for dead kings surround the citadel.
Bulgars and Greeks among us mutely tell
Legends of empire. On the bridge, more verse.

The situation in the North grows worse.
The airport bus. Embraces. Flying home,
We see the placid lake busied with foam.

278 *Elegy*

No haven and no shelter and no home.
A language tangled among frontiers –
Quick rivers, mountain chains, sand barriers.
Come out of nowhere, nowhere can they come
Into a place that they can call their own.
Far to the south, mud ruins' syllables
Spill across deserts, potsherd-littered tells:
Ur, Eridu, Kish, faces of stone,
Eroded Babylon, abandoned gaols
Whose brick on brick the conquerors laid low
Among the dunes, so low, so long ago,
Where now the serpent gathers up its trails
Ready to strike at enemies to come.

No haven and no shelter and no home.

279 *Freedom*

Through the vast crowded wards, thousands came round.
Limbs twitched; mouths opened, uttering strange old cries;
Wild smiles and tears, and snarls at what went on
Through decades of paralysis.
                              Bodies are found
Strewn in the corridors. A doctor lies
Battered in blood. The warders have all gone,
Savaged by patients who woke up to see
The doors were open. Healers are unmasked
As torturers; nurses crucified
When drugs, withdrawn, reveal them all to be
Captors and guards.
                    And those who this way died
Are faceless as their patients.
                                And some asked
How the great hospital would care for those
Who lie there still, free, in a deep repose.

At the International Poetry Festival
   (for Douglas Dunn)

I think I can recognise the word *freedom*
In seventeen languages. It seems to be popular.
Here is another poet at the microphone
Waving an arm here and an arm there.
And now an African who writes in English
Prays that the rivers will flow with torrents of blood,
And I want to talk to him about Enoch Powell.
But now an Italian takes over, mellifluous,
Telling us the festival means *pace* and *bella*
And of course *libertà*, and then there are several
Odes to the Leader, and the self-invited American
Prowls round the back of the stage muttering
Not in protest but because he needs a fix.
In the front row an Indian falls asleep.

One hundred and seventy-six poets are groaning with boredom
In the warm summer air as the moths interfere
With the television lights in the fragrant southern air.
The brows of the organisers are shining with sweat
And exhaustion and alcohol, but at least they know
One hundred and seventy-six poets, with subsidised travel
And supported by generous hospitality, have arrived –
Some of them famous outside their own countries,
Some notorious inside them as well.
It is good for the autonomous republic, it is good for the hotel
Where all these bards bed down after fourteen hours
Devoted to symposia, slivovitz, and hanging about in the lobby
Complaining about their hosts, their fellow-delegates, their
   digestion.
I do not know the Mongolian for *freedom*.

(1981)

The name is history.
                    The thick Miljacka flows
Under its bridges through a canyon's breadth,
Fretted with minarets and plump with domes,
Cupped in its mountains, caught on a drawn breath.

There on the pavement, absurd souvenir
Of past dramatics, Princip's spoor is set:
The exact spot, the precise grid of war,
A kerbside view of a choked and bloody street

Where, regiments in step, a world moves
Or drifts away from its moorings like a ship
Propelled down-river between crowded wharfs
And only a collision can make it stop.

The muezzin calls, the bells and pigeons float
Above Sephardic, Muslim, Catholic graves:
Provincial, dated, their low stones map out
Haphazardly the place that history chose.

                                        (1973)

282   *Sarajevo: II*

'Narrow streets, profane and sacral architecture'
Sarajevo: A Guide, Dr Smail Tihic, 1973

The sacred is profaned, profanity
Thumps its large casual lobs on narrow streets
Where people queue for bread, fill buckets, sprint
Through dereliction towards safety. See
How none are safe. See how each building greets
Each blurred escapist with a different hint
Of how each separate faith may end in grief,
And some in blood.

And twenty years ago I got it wrong –
Fit emblem for a past I never knew
But saw as ikon for a long-gone war.
It was an elegy, a plangent song
Composed out of composure: nothing new.
I saw the place, I struck a spark from flint.
There is nothing sacred, only profane belief:
Nothing understood.

(1993)

283   *Final Verdict Tours*

Having crossed the ultimate checkpoint to our friendly nation,
You have twenty minutes to see this ancient city.
There is the Black Fort and the Basalt Church,
The Basilica of Unrighteousness, the Mosque of Envy,
The Lukewarm Baths, and the successive quarters
Inhabited by the Extremish, the Waverish, the Vilipends.

Behold the monuments to antique unfortunates:
The sad exit of Hadad the Excitable
Torn to pieces in a popular rising,

The sublime martyrdom of Rashap the Vulgar
Subdued by applied arachnids under the armpits.
We are proud of our heritage among such enactments.

Observe our more recent manifestations of culture –
The picturesque garments of the tolerated minorities,
The gorgeous pictography of the eliminated tribes.
(Avoid the offered sherds, the reproductions:
You may be seduced by cunning artifices
Replicated in the bazaars and in humble courtyards.)

Here are the products of the curious contemporary,
Desirable to those with an eye for excellence:
Embroideries by hand, paintings by foot
Achieved by those whose hands have been excised
For various offences considered capital
But for the amnesty of our President and his mercies.

We allow for a rest-stop at the end of such plenitude –
A packed lunch available, the spirits extra:
Any currency is valid, though temptingly fluctuating.
Then back to the bus, please, in orderly fashion.
Tonight at Happy Hour the evening's rubric.
Tomorrow our departure for the last resort.

284   *The Rev. C.L. Dodgson*

Somewhere in Oxford, in a Christ Church quad
Or by the Cherwell's sluggish brownish flow,
You watch a nervous slender scholar go
Muttering to himself, perhaps, or God.

He talks to little girls who talk to flowers.
To them he does not stammer. His mild eyes
Gaze at what is, turn it contrariwise,
And penetrate a world that is not ours.

357

And yet it is our world, made happy-mad,
Where playing-cards and cats, chessmen and sheep,
Inhabit those asylums where we sleep
Beyond the logics that we thought we had:

Beyond sense, things at which to laugh or weep,
Where everyone is guilty, no one sad.

285   *Accumulations*

The exhaustion of museums, of libraries:
It is nothing to do with dust, or being old, or dead.
The dust is removed daily, and the ageing is also our own.
As for being dead, we can live with that.

No, it is the accumulation of so many pasts,
So many things written, things made, each so different
They cover the universe with their quiddities.
We grope hopelessly through all this stuff.

Each page, each book, each sherd, each pot, bequeaths us
A multitude of silted pasts. To read them,
To bring them back to life in whole or fragment,
Exhausts us. We look up, are blinded by them.

It will not stop. We step through endless doors
Opening and shutting, going on down avenues
And corridors, between cases and shelves, until
The doors close behind us. Even then, it will not stop.

For after that, the others follow us
And find us piecemeal in succeeding rooms,
In stacks of cabinets, ranged along drawers, in spools
Of tiny film that turns and turns and turns.

286 *Levellings*

Where people lived, where people threw their things,
Their piles of mess, their bonfires, secrets, scraps,
All end like this, these endless levellings,
Shaded and laid in contours, like old maps.

The damp mud cliff, laid open as a sore
Dripping its weight of yesterday made bare,
Unloads a cataract of petty lore
Which I pick over, delve into, and share.

From East and West these lived-with things once came,
I name them as I take them in my hand:
Some valued once, or ordinary, the same
Bits of a past I grope to understand.

And grope towards a meaning in our mess,
A sudden knowledge of this piece of past,
Whether of value or quite valueless,
Of what will fall away or what will last.

287 *Gone*

Down in the dark water
Where the quick mill-race flows,
Something hidden rises,
Something secret goes.

Rising, it flashes whitely.
Going, it sinks below.
You cannot recognise it.
You see the water flow

Quickly under the mill-race,
Race down and reach the pond.
Whatever you have seen there
Goes on and out, beyond

Your vision or your knowledge,
Untethered to one place.
It glints, and hints, and teases,
And shows you your own face

Peering below the sluice-gate,
Watching the mill-race fall
Forever and forever,
With not a word at all

Of what you saw – or fancied
You saw – rise up and sink
One moment in the water,
The next over the brink.

288   *The Dust of the World*

Proverbs, 8:26

Unseen until it settles, all around
It hovers in the crannies of itself,
So faint and soft it never makes a sound.
It gathers on the books along the shelf.

My finger strokes it from a pot-plant leaf.
The leaf would fall without it anyway.
The dumbness of the world, numbness of grief,
Settling on silence, well prepared to stay.

The world, the flesh, the devil – these old runes,
Renunciations of this trinity,
Themselves drift off, like half-forgotten tunes
Into the dustbowls of infinity.

289 *Memoir*

He writes what he remembers, innocent,
Though now he is no longer innocent:
What he remembers, what he tries to write,
Is how things were. He cannot get it right.

The words go down on paper. In between
Another sheet of paper lies between
The sheet he writes on and the page beneath.
Something is lying down there, underneath.

And it is those words, on the page below,
That somehow stick, as he goes down below
Experience to innocence, and finds
The thing he looked for is the thing he finds.

But in the morning, reading what he wrote
Last night, the only words he finds he wrote
Are on the surface. And the page below
Is blank as things he did not want to know.

290 *Nescit vox missa reverti*

The voice, or word, that goes
Far out into the world
Lies on the ear or page.
Water and metal flows,
Ice melts, steel weapons hurled
Towards another age.

What drops, and sticks, and stays
(These words that seem so frail)
Settles. It makes its stand.
Through brief and shifting days,
Fading, receding, pale,
It shows the living hand

That wrote them, transmits the voice
That spoke them. So we see
Years later what was said,
Written or spoken, choice
Not theirs to oversee,
Not theirs, who now are dead.

291   *For George MacBeth*

Wasted away –
Limbs, speech, and breath –
Such mockery, such sprightly gay
Spirits smothered, friend
Stubborn to call it death.
Make it all end.

Last words are right:
You whispered them
That last intolerable night,
Darkness itself, deep
Gathering of choked phlegm –
'How long will I sleep?'

To turn again these faded pencilled pages,
Their neatly cancelled lines, precisely dated,
Their doodles of frustration, sudden rages
Or mocking self-contempt, before the next
Refining or reduction's contemplated,
And then the immaculate and final text –

This is to hear you speak, not just to read you,
Familiar words-by-heart plumbed deep and strange
Down to the nerve of hurt, the pains that feed you
Raw as they are, a present tense, not past,
Thronged with the power to strengthen through their change,
Poised to the lines we know, and built to last.

293   *Elegy for George Barker*

And there, beneath a bull-nosed Buick
Inert in Kensington, the poet lay,
Grease smeared on cheek-bones, a fallen god
Who rose to greet me, seventeen, with Blake
And Langland in the triptych. Stay
Yet a little longer, genius of the place,
Fitting my footprints in the prints you trod,
Letting me see those lineaments, that face.

It was apotheosis. It was epiphany.
Already there were elegies at hand,
Mellifluous and celebrating
The mystery that was also poetry.
Whatever words flew up, whatever scanned,
Became that moment. St George had claimed his own.
Imago, image, creator and creating
Took root within the reliquary bone.

Years past, years gone. I have learnt since then
You were no god, for only God is that.
That was a truth I know you would endorse.
And yet some angels mingle among men,
And have some essence, pure, dark, uncreate,
Extending through subtention. This was yours.
You rose, and fell, and took your vagrant course
Among men, mandrake, and all mysteries.

The vocative takes off in memory,
Almost becomes a perfect O to bless
Your wicked simulacrum resting there,
Elbow on bar, seducing those like me
From Id and Ego with your sophistries.
Forget it. What we never shall forget
Is that brow-wrinkled, basiliskian stare
Stabbing at the cold heart. It stabs me yet.

294   *In Memory of Howard Nemerov*

Convened, if not coerced, four years ago
At an all-chattering jamboree for rampant egos
In the silver dollar state of Colorado,
You stood like a pillar of some rarer metal
Muttering asides in a sort of heightened prose
Between your poems, of which each syllable
Distinctly stood as proof that sanity
Still had something to do with poetry.

The laughs from those who heard you mostly came
In the right places, and naturally you forbore
To point out to the thin audience that your name
Was unlikely to fill a theatre like this,
In spite of all the 'honours' that you wore.
Wry smiling wilful brilliant courtesies –
I see you now, as then, a self-styled dinosaur
Magnificent on the muddy, slipping shore.

295 *September 3rd 1939: Bournemouth*

My summer ends, and term begins next week.
Why am I here in Bournemouth, with my aunt
And 'Uncle Bill', who something tells me can't
Be really my uncle? People speak
In hushed, excited tones. Down on the beach
An aeroplane comes in low over the sea
And there's a scattering as people reach
For towels and picnic gear and books, and flee
Towards the esplanade. Back at the hotel
We hear what the Prime Minister has said.
'So it's begun.' 'Yes, it was bound to.' 'Well,
Give it till Christmas.' Later, tucked in bed,
I hear the safe sea roll and wipe away
The castles I had built in sand that day.

296 *Evacuation: 1940*

Liverpool docks. The big ship looms above
Dark sheds and quays, its haughty funnels bright
With paint and sunlight, as slim sailors shove
About with chains and hawsers. Mummy's hand
Is sticky in my own, but I'm all right,
Beginning an adventure. So I stand
On a deck piled high with prams, the staterooms shrill
With mothers' mutterings and clasped babies' cries.
I squirm and tug, ten years impatient, till
Loud hootings signal something . . . The surprise
Of hugging her, feeling her face all wet:
'Mummy, you're sweating.' They were tears; not mine.
She went away. I was alone, and fine.

Pleasure, and guilt. Things you do not forget.

297 *Maturity: 1944*

A son, fourteen, home to father and mother
After four years away. The one who went
A child, this one returning as a man
Almost: his voice broken, speaking American.
He was their son, but somehow now another:
The years of absence forced them to invent
New habits for this foreigner.
                                        So then
The father, fooling about, faced up to the boy,
Put up his fists: they could behave like men
In manly parody. And the son, to join in the game,
Put his up too, pretending they were the same,
And struck. The father's nose gushed out with blood.
The son watched, appalled. And never understood
Why his father leapt, and cried, and cried with joy.

298 *At Jamestown*

By Greyhound south from Washington's white domes,
Passing low factories and supermarkets,
Along a road where no one ever walks
But touched only by hot and whining rubber,
I reach the first frail enclave of these states.

Jamestown. Its relics dredged from swamp and fever,
It lacks even the substances of ruins
But must be dug for in its lost encampments,
Each scrap and sherd and shred disjected tokens
Of failure never staunched, of pointless landfall.

Imperial peninsula! Beyond
The crammed museum the rich landscape swarms
With cemeteries of cars, the stench of waste
Fanned upward from Virginia's garbage cans,
The sewage of a whole half continent.

Magnolia comes to blossom as the cameras
Snap at these smaller, rarer sediments.
Down the brown estuary fresh water flows,
And far behind it all the prodigal
And violent issue briefly fathered here.

(1970)

299 *Old South*

Old Dominion, Old Heritage, Olde Glory Fireworks,
Olde Discount, Old Hickory, Old Grandad, Old South.

How new it all is, vacant lots, gas stations, the WALK signs
flashing abruptly and whitely,
Dad's Old Bookstore crammed with Confederate lore,
a First of *I'll Take My Stand* priced far above rubies,
the Antique Malls, the Primitive Collectibles,
all among drive-ins and thruways
and sidewalks where I am the only walker,
eccentric among odd joggers, waiting for the WALK sign.

And suddenly, at this intersection, the slope
running one way downtown in this urban wilderness,
looking at that slope down to a battered frame building
(a house maybe, once, or a store gone derelict),
my eyes take in a distant simulacrum:
Don Abrahams' farm in Fairfax County, Virginia,
in the dip of the country road that ran from my uncle's house.

It was 1940. I was new from England.
Don and I played in his yard, and he took me to shake the
    hand of
Pa Abrahams, 90, old grandad, skinny in his rocking chair,
and then to see
out back, on a peg, a small shabby grey peaked cap,
the little Confederate drummer-boy's, back in '64.

Old Mobile Estates, Grand Ole Opry, Old Hickory TV
    Appliances,
Old Timer Log Homes Marketing, Old South.

300   *Snakes (Virginia, 1940)*

Down in the creek, snakes:
Snakes in the opposite wood.
There were snakes everywhere.
This was new. This was good.

At home in England, snakes
Were pets in a glass cage.
Here they slipped free, and swam.
This was a golden age.

Most folk I knew hated snakes,
Shrank if I brought one back
And let it run over my arm
Or gathered and then lay slack.

Whipsnakes, cornsnakes, snakes
Swollen, and black, and green,
Crept through my days and nights.
This was the primal scene.

And there were other snakes,
Ones to be cautious of:
Cottonmouths, copperheads, once
A rattler I saw in a grove.

How to account for these snakes
In a boy uprooted at ten
In a war that spanned a world
He would not see again?

Eden did not have snakes:
Only one snake, it is said.
We know what that single snake
Did. Or so we have read.

I had not read it then.
All I knew was I loved the things.
Years on, I call them all back,
Sinuous rememberings.

301   *Sunday by Belmont*

The ante-bellum, gracious, columned, white,
Holds itself back in this high mansion, dead
Sure of nothing but its being right,
Its 'sense of values' others have long shed.

Tradition, that gaunt fugitive civic ghost,
Erects its shrines, its annals, its steel plaques.
The few-starred flag defiantly is tossed
Above a shopping-mall where only blacks

And a few derelicts one might call white
Wait at the bus-stop: others hurtle off
Towards vague neighborhoods, in daily flight
Down highways hacked sheer, sharp, a limestone trough

Speeding the Gadarene across the state
But not over the cliff. At least, not yet.
Among the unfavoured stationed few I wait
Here at the bus-stop. Winter breezes fret

That antique flag over bleak carpark wastes,
Defeat, defiance souring, as I board:
Downtown to Christ Episcopal. My tongue tastes
The bitter wine of some unrisen Lord.

302   *Franklin and Nashville: 1864*

These tracks of blood over these frozen ruts
Were made by unshod men,
Hood's threadbare remnant. Watch them, then,
Stumble across the scrub, as from the heights
Others are watching: in those piled redoubts
Cannon and howitzers incline
And rake the ragged line.

Retreat and stand, fire and fall back. The trees,
Armoured with ice, are bound
In iron earth. All that disputed ground,
All those encumbered bodies, freeze
Into a blizzard of cold certainties:
'Perfect example of the art
Of war', 'a model chart

Judged so instructive that academies
All the world over trace
Again and yet again each move, each place . . .':
Decisive and meticulous strategies.
Meanwhile, among the stiffly rattling trees
Two thousand stones mark out
What it was all about.

303   *Philip Larkin in New Orleans*

Suppose he had come here, two days after Mardi Gras,
The wrong time. It would be raining
In sheets up from the Delta, the banquettes awash
And the gutters running with all the festival trash:
Laughing-gas capsules, confetti, a tinsel star,
Cheap beads, purple and golden and green,
Bottle-caps, condoms, masks. Somewhere too far,
Somewhere too foreign. He would be complaining
This wasn't the dream he had had, the dream-place he'd been –
Tapping his feet in a bar in Bourbon or Basin, the moan
Of riverboats drifting through the Vieux Carré
Mingling with a familiar saxophone,
And the girls stepping out on the streets at the end of the day.

His Crescent City is much further off,
A paradise where love and trumpets play
In tune, and out of time, beyond belief
In ordinary days or usual grief,
A place in which all doubt is put away.
Tonight I caught his authentic other note,
Fixed, finite, steady in its monotone,
As I passed an old black with a graveyard cough,
An empty bottle, a funereal hat,
Who muttered something as he cleared his throat,
Trembled, and batted off the rain, and spat
Somewhere between Decatur and Wilk Row,
His hopes expelled with an enormous no.

from *Selected Poems 1956–1996* (1997)

304   *Deus Absconditus*

In every temple compound, under some tree
Exhausted by its effort to grow
Unwatered, yet festooned in faded silks,
These bits of broken holiness abound:
Stone, plaster, plastic, terracotta, wood,
Carved, moulded, fired, gaudy with crimson and gold,
The head or the feet of the Buddha, a smashed plaque,
A dancing acolyte dismembered, strewn
Together with green sherds of splintered glass,
Spirals of dog-turds, spills of litter, muck
Preserving all this shattered deity.

One in particular I coveted –
A headless ivory figurine, its arms
Spread out in blessing, each tiny fold of robe
Distinctly beautiful, and intricate,
And perfect in its three-inch skilfulness.
Discarded, not destroyed; not thrown away;
Not quite abandoned . . . No one would know, I knew,
And yet I knew I could not pocket it,
Assembled, humbled, among all that trash.
Lust for possession stunted me, a tree
Knowing there might be life there, somewhere, still.

305   *Coming Back from Kawau*

Coming back from Kawau, on the last ferry,
We passed them on the way: a smaller island
From which projected a small jetty
And on the jetty half-a-dozen, waving.

We hadn't seen them on the way there, coming
Early in the brilliant day, the sun
Glaring across the bay, our concentration
Fixed on Grey's miniature Victorian mansion –

A white colonial outpost among ferns,
Composed and elegant, the edge of empire
Preserved in its own tidiness, remains
Unpeopled among urns and furniture.

I saw its set perfection, its apartness,
Its faded photographs, proconsular
Relics of duty, its still orderliness,
Remote and separate as a distant star.

Yet coming back, those valedictory waves
Came back more strongly, strangely, as we passed
Too far to hear them, or to see them clearly,
Like an experience, somehow, we had missed.

They dipped into the distance, and were gone,
And ours, the day's last ferry, journeyed on.

306   *Changing Ties*

Changing my tie in the lavatory
From black to flowery,
In the train from the funeral
Travelling south to the wedding,
Having said farewell
To the dead and preparing a greeting
To those about to be married –

In the same dark suit appropriate to either
One or the other,
Only the fancy tie is different,
A quick metamorphosis
Scarcely planned or meant:
Leaving what was, moving towards what is,
The past, the present, the living, the dead.

307 *Snake in Autumn*

A lithe fat flash of light below the compost
Reveals his coils, flesh swollen, slowly writhing
In warm October leaves. One eye is blind.
A wound along his body weeps with pus.
I pick him up and cradle his old age,
His sightless eye, his unhealed stinking gash,
Study his proud exhaustion, his sad fear,
Then gently put him down. He slithers off
Back into barricades of compost, back
Into the winter of death, and out of sight.

308 *Trebonianus Gallus*

My father's joke – *Trebonianus Gallus* –
An obscure emperor's name, that made me shout
And jump about and go for him . . . How this
Ritual was endorsed, or how the joke began,
I do not know, I can't remember. Eight,
Perhaps I was, or even younger, when
This private bit of nonsense started. It
Must have been something shared through Roman coins,
Fingering all those scraps of well-rubbed bronze
Bought with my pocket-money: tray on tray,
And Seaby's catalogue spread out between us,
Puzzling, identifying. *Trebonianus Gallus* –

I had forgotten him, until today
The name, your impish face, our childish game,
Sixty years later broke into my head,
Hearing my grandson tease me with the same
Complicitous sharing, as I threw a name
Towards him, knowing you there, and dead.

309   *Passing On*

Simon, my grandfather, born in '72,
Told me the tale of how, as a young boy
He stood in Bradford City Hall and saw
The high-winged collar Gladstone wore wilt low.

The great man spoke for hours. The sweat poured down.
Nothing he said could Grandad quite recall.
Tonight, in '96, I pass this on
To my own grandson. But I cannot tell

Whether, a hundred years from now, his own
Grandson will tell this thing that once was said
About the sweating high-winged orator, one
Who spoke across two centuries, unheard.

310   *Object Lessons*

I

'But there's no index', I said, turning the pages.
'Ah, yes', he said. 'And you're not the first
To comment on that. But we wanted to give more space
To the stuff itself, which is what most people want'.

The stuff itself flicked under my fingers,
Lots of it, moving at speed, till it seemed
Like those fat little joke-books I had as a child:
A cartoon animated by the turning pages.

Then I got to the end, and no index. Then
I made my comment, and he responded.
It seemed the end of the conversation.
A blur of pages, with no index at the end.

II

Because it was damaged, he said, he would bring down the price.
I couldn't see any damage, but I kept quiet,
Not wanting to show I'd not noticed. With a set face
I turned it round in my hand, and thought it all right.

He brought down the price, and I bought it. And now and again
I fetch the pot down from the shelf and examine it all
In the palm of my hand, never finding the flaw or the mend
That made me buy it at the price at which he would sell.

III

I found it on a market-stall in Skopje,
Not knowing what it was: bright tapestry,
Orange and red. It was a mystery.
My mother made it into a tea-cosy.

Now, when I'm pouring out a cup of tea
From this transmogrified fragility,
I sometimes face a visitor with a query:
'What do you think this curious thing might be?'

It seems it was, at least originally,
A decoration for a trousered knee
Worn by some Macedonian. But could it really be
A relic of the sole one-legged evzone in Skopje?

311 *Elegiac Stanzas*

The famous poet's mistress, forty years ago,
Now heard five times a week on radio
Acting an ageing upper-class virago.

'The deadbeats of the Caves de France, the suicidal',
The substance of a novelist's rapt recall,
One who escaped the death from alcohol.

The ravaged visage of a copywriter
Who was an intimate of him and her,
Encountered at the funeral of another.

And at memorial services the pews
Filling with this and that long-unseen face,
This one thought dead, that one no longer news.

And, rooting among boxes in the attic,
Letters another wrote, witty, ecstatic,
Who dwindled down to paperback-roundup critic.

And in the obit. columns an old queen
Wheeled on weekly recalling the has-been
Who've died in Tokyo, Paris, Golders Green.

These are the days of death, *memento mori*:
'I knew him as an undergraduate, before he . . .'
Turned into nothingness, the old old story.

These are the daily shades, the presences
Among the shadows, pricking the five senses
As they reveal themselves as absences.

These are the scourers, enemies of promise,
Rubbing out vanity and fame like pumice,
Asking to see the evidence like Thomas.

The famous poet's mistress, forty years ago,
And boxes crammed above, pews full below.
These are the things we hear, and see, and know.

312   *Education*

It used to be learning things over and over again
In a drone round the room repeating the things that were said:
The names of the countries, the names of the famous dead,
The multiplication tables, the figures for sun and rain
On the countries, the dates of the battles won
And the battles lost, the different spellings of words
Sounding the same, and − to make it a bit more fun −
The names of the butterflies, moths, mammals, fish, birds.

And now it is making up shapes and colouring each
For something called Projects, and making up other stuff
For something called Poetry, which no one wants to teach
Because it has rules and no one knows enough
To know how the rules work, and no one can hear
Because of the noise all round and the weight of the stuff
Out there in the world, full of names, dates, figures, fear.

313   *The Property of the Executors*
(i.m. G.F.H.)

It might have been a wedding, or a wake,
Some sort of celebration, a solemnity:
Or is it just shopping for shopping's sake,
A ritual cupidity?
Arriving through the morning mist, the cars
Inclined these visitors
Towards the great dead house now stripped, the striped marquee
Smothering with canvas and plastic the long lawns
He had kept in order, until his will bent,
And he put the gun to his head, and the whole thing went
Down to this one event.

My neighbour yawns
After four hours of this, the auctioneer
Jollying along each lot by lot by lot.
Yes, I agree with her, it's much too hot,
And my other neighbour reaches below his chair
For a swig at his beer, and the objects are raised in the air
By acolytes who respond to the numbers called
By the man who calls out money-names without fear
Of interruptions because, however appalled
Some of us are at this show,
This is the way such rituals must go.

The tables, the chairs, the mirrors, the carved blackamoor,
Then the pictures ('After' whoever and all),
The big mahogany chest that stood in the hall
Along with the cracked Staffordshire, the pattern fish slice,
The wrought-iron door-stop against the front door,
Silver, and screens, and glass.
All of them have their value, most of them fetch their price.

Then the books are parcelled out. Some singles, some pairs,
Some 'Miscellaneous. Quantity'. Here
Is one signed by all of the children for Mama, then *Paradise
Lost*, red morocco, Victorian, all
Jumbled up as home used to be, some below stairs,
Some elevated like trophies, things you could call
Treasures. But the auctioneer
Hurries on to the 'General Contents', the job lots,
At the end of a long hot day.

I stay, anyway,
To Lot Seven-Eleven, 'A Collection
Of Power and Hand tools, etc.', to see who may
Make a bid for it. But when it comes, late on,
The lot is split: Seven-Eleven A
Is what I look for, now described 'As Is':
A leather gun-case, initialled on its lid;
Inside, its wooden rods, its brass accoutrements,
Its roll of cotton pull-through; but the space
In which the shotgun should have been, not hid
But glaring open, empty, like the face
Of someone who should have been there. No offence
Intended. An emptiness instead.

Lot Seven-Forty goes. That is the end.
Loud quacking county voices void the tent
Bent on returning home to Cley and Wells.
I grope through autumn twilight, smell the smells
Of furnace-wood cut by a man now dead
Whose stuff this was, who maybe never meant
To cause all this, this sale, this wake, but can't transcend
What he has brought about. Whatever he meant.

from *A Move in the Weather* (2003)

314   *In 1936*

'Sabbat-Goy: a gentile hired by Jews
To carry out the Sabbath household tasks
Which their religion forbids them to perform.'

*

It was in Leeds in 1936,
In Roman Terrace, by our red-brick house.
I stood there with a boy, who said to me:

'That house just opposite – take care
You don't walk near it on a Saturday.
They're Jews, and they might grab you, make you cook

Their dinner for them.' I didn't ask him why.
I couldn't even boil an egg. At six years old
What did I know of *Jews*, even the word?

Now, sixty-four years later, I remember
That mystery, that warning; and remember
Ariadne Rothstein, the strange

Name of my friend at school, with frizzy hair,
I hugged and kissed and (so I'm told) once bit
In an excess of friendship. It was 1936.

315   *Summer of '39*

In the barber's chair in Hathersage
I forgot who I was. The summer of '39.
Heat in the hedges among the butterflies.

Looked back on now as I move into old age,
That terror too comes back, as I sit, aged nine,
In the barber's chair and feel the heat rise

From the tangle of hedges outside, my body, my head
Buzzing and helpless under the clippers, fear
Blanking me out as I lose identity.

It was as if I was already dead,
No longer anywhere, not even here
Wherever I am, silently screaming 'Me!'

316   *Garaleska and Paragoda*

They had their mountains, frontiers, capitals,
Principal products, rivers, forests, lakes,
But most of all they had their armies, each
Regiment numbered, each with uniforms
Distinct, badges of rank, precise gazettes
Of infantry, artillery, and names
Of generals and commanders. Behind these
Were lists of cabinet-appointments, dates
Assigned to revolutions, executions,
The histories that these two countries had.

And when was this? The years before the War,
When I was eight and coming up to nine.
They were my countries, safe inside my head
But needing this enumeration, dreams
Enacted in these drawings, maps, lists, all
The imagined stuff I had to get correct.
Dreary compulsions, maybe: not to me,
Who wanted them to make sense of a world
In which I stood poised on the very edge
Of unimagined things that soon were true.

Next door was empty, and the next-door yard
Was overgrown with flowers floating high
In tangles among weeds, where wild things stirred
That were not weeds: lizard, butterfly,
Cicada, mantis, big-horned bug. At night
The firefly blinked its hot excited light.

Sub-tropical suburban paradise,
That long-baked summer set me there transfixed,
And everything was fire as sharp as ice,
The new and recognised blindingly mixed.
A scarlet cardinal bubbled and flew by,
Huge turkey-buzzards drifted in the sky.

And I was there alone, all of it mine
To linger in away from everything,
To count each mottled brilliance, each pronged spine,
Distinctions on the palette of each wing.
Day after day the next-door yard lay there
To drug me with its jungle-laden air.

It was America, and I was ten.
The place was commonplace: I did not know.
I try to bring it back as it was then,
Try to make present what was long ago.
But it won't come to me, that wilderness
Next to an empty house, an emptiness.

Dredging through all these folders, papers, files,
Meticulous accounts, the scurf of money
Long spent, my mother's reading-lists, things any
Archivist might properly sort out,
I plan to bin the lot, a bonfire's-worth of blaze.
I should have done all this a year ago,
After her death, twenty years after his,
But sifted through, uncertain.
                              Till these fragile pages came
Into my hands, a sheaf of typescripts, all
The poems that my father wrote that year
In 1941 – all the poems
He ever wrote, that year of war, while I was far away
Safe in America. Later, he said
They coincided with a TB spot
Found on his lung, and doctors blotted out:
As if, at thirty-eight, the romantic blight
Forced him to write them.
                              No, they're not much good,
Bits of Masefield, Belloc, Chesterton,
Or wistful Georgian lyricism, like the stuff
He used to quote to my embarrassment
When I was nine, and hated poetry –
Turned, in these poems of his, to simulacra,
Desperate gestures, quietly discreet,
Unlike the man I knew, my father, faint
Pastiches lingering on and out of sight.
And yet they speak to me, tell me much more
Than I can cope with in this silt of mess.
They must be saved, and handed on. The fire
Eats up the accounts, the lists, and all the rest.
These faded yearnings will evade the flames.

Down to the tiny harbour,
The western edge of the peninsula:
Five herons chevroned in a tall pine tree
Fly off and suddenly let loose the rain,
Drenching the landscape till we only see
An umbrella's distance beyond the pure stain
Of the liner lying there on the jetty's edge –
That white perfection, with its brass plate clear –
Stella Polaris.
                    The name rings to me
Across the decades, the same ship that bore
Me off to Norway, 1947.

The symmetry of ships, chaos of seventeen.

It was the same ship, built in '27,
A vessel for a millionaire, transformed
To pleasure-liner, and finally to this
Moored relic in Japan, by chance found
Here in the tiny harbour in the rain.

What happened there, fifty-four years ago,
That cynical seduction by suave 'Maurice'
(So eager to hear my adolescent lusts
Rehearsed until he took me like a fish)
Turned me to stone, to liquid, swept me back
Against the breakers to another shore.

Back to the jetty, then, my own old self,
The temple at the harbour-entrance, where
Five herons left the pine tree empty, rain
Shuddered in sheets, and where
Chrysanthemums scattered on the cypress floor.

320 *Bohemia*

Lifting a half of bitter in Fore Street
In the company of the poet and printer Guido Morris
And the painter Sven Berlin, with intimate talk
Of the absent poets Barker, Graham, Wright,
I visit for the first time those fabled shores.

I had met these luminaries in the second-hand bookshop
Run by two willowy brothers who spoke in code
Of all these exalted beings, artists who clung
To the rungs of fame with no visible support
Except that passport to my yearned-for country.

St Ives, Cornwall, is the real place.
I am eighteen, on holiday this Easter
Before the army claims me. Mother and father
Are there, and pay for it; but are not there
In the pub in Fore Street with my new-found friends.

Fifty years later, I read of Guido Morris,
Who died, unknown, as a London Underground guard;
Of Sven Berlin, who ended up in the gutter.
I went to another place, a different country.
I have never since visited Bohemia.

321 *Basic Training: September 1949*

A sack of straw suspended from a frame,
And six of us lined up with 303s
Extended with our bayonets held at ease
Until the brisk sergeant-instructor came
And told us what to do and how to do it.

Advance – in, out, in, out, twist, and pull clear –
And then advance again. The straw sack swung
This way and that, and that shrill raucous tongue
Lashed us for feebleness, for sloth, for fear:
'You *hate* the bastard – *show* him how much'. The sun

Shone down on Hampshire hills, and our platoon
Formed and re-formed and did it all again.
Ten thousand miles away, other young men
Would do the same in earnest, very soon,
Told what to do, and doing it, and dying.

322   *The Ruins of Anangke*

A place where every dune is topped with stone,
Dressed stone brought low and littered on the sand,
Where shifting winds reveal these scattered sherds
And in whose acres you must be alone.
There in the heat you stand
In a lost landscape, and are lost for words.

This is the place you know, or think you know,
From times when you were young, or thought you were.
It will not go away. It stays with you
In dreams and daydreams. And it will be so
In that far landscape where
There will be nothing left of what you knew.

323   *Archaeology*

How would it be if we remembered nothing
Except the garbage and the rubbishing,
The takeaways, the throwaways, the takeovers,
The flakes and breakups, the disjected members
Scattered across the landscape, across everything?

Nothing stands up, nothing stands clear and whole,
Everything bits and pieces, all gone stale,
All to the tip, the midden topped up high
With what we used, with what we threw away:
How would it be if this was all we could feel?

That will not be. Remembering, or feeling,
Or knowing anything of anything,
Will be the last we know of all this stuff.
It will be there for others, seekers of
Things that remain of us, who then are nothing.

324 *Bauerntanz*

They move so solidly across this space –
He curls his left arm round her willing dress
From which one breast breaks loose; and his right hand
Twiddles a sword that could be something else.

In front of them, an interrupted drunk
Spews copiously, hands held above his head,
Helpless and knock-kneed, while his wife looks back,
Her face obliterated with disgust, or age.

Uncertain, on the left – a man, maybe,
Lurching towards them: to the right, another
Arm intervenes, curtailed. Above, below,
Words run in strips, clumsy, reversed, obscure.

In stiff and fixed licentiousness, around
And yet around, though broken to a sherd
Jagged and arbitrary, all that's left
Of prancing peasantry, stamped with two big initials –

IE – Jan Emens: and a neater date –
One five seven six. The crafty potter caught
By name, in time, four centuries ago,
And more. The figures move, and dance – quick quick quick, slow.

325 *A Cabinet of Curiosities*

A Bib of Lace of the late Queen's Maid of Honour.
A little fragment of an Indian's skin.
Some Chinese engines made to ease the Ague.
Some feathers from an Angel in a Tree.
A Nun's long stockings worn for Chastity.
A mummied Rat from an Egyptian Tomb.
A gut-stone passed by a hanged Sodomite.
Another Stone formed like an ancient Worm.
A great Bird's beak, too large for a living bird.
A painted ribbon from Jerusalem
With which our Blessèd Saviour was bound
To the Temple's pillar when He was crowned and scourged.
An Instrument for measuring the wind.
A Vase of glass to hold a Roman's tears.

326 *Late*

Late in learning how to tie my tie,
To know my tables, boil a kettle, drive a car,
Now I have come this far
To face new skills I can't begin to try:
Ways to employ a mouse, or pay a visit
To websites full of dots, or drill my fingers
To log into a message-board. What is it
That makes me tardy, clumsy?
                                        What is it lingers?
Have I come all this way to know no more
Than what I learned so late and long before?

327 *One of the Planets*

Catching the train that day, there opposite
Was Imogen Holst, by chance, recognised
Quite how I don't know. Laid out between us
Sheets of music paper, all the lines and notes
Under her quick bright eye and poised pen
Held almost like a baton.
I could just make out, on the top margin, the name –
Gustav – upside down. What she was up to
I was ignorant of, dear devoted daughter
Making her stabbing, almost nervous marks.

But as we approached London
After those hours of fixed concentration,
She looked up, caught my gaze, and a great smile
Irradiated her small neat serious face;
And in my inner ear there soared that tune
Pulsing through Jupiter, the bringer of joy.

328 *Siberia*

Now it comes back, twenty-two years ago;
The name, the place, where I was asked to go –
Middle of nowhere, further off from Moscow
Than London was from Moscow, to a name
That sounded like a parody of itself:
Novosibirsk.

And 'British Week'. A flight of 'experts' (art,
Industrial design, geology,
Music – a Scottish bagpiper'd been hired
By Caledonian Airways – fashion, science)
Flew, and I with them: 'British Poetry'.

What stays, then, what comes back?
                              A concrete wedge,
The Union Hall of some official sludge,
In which this Cultural Festival took place.
Endless reshufflings of the rubric planned –
I made unwise remarks on censorship
Before the censor intervened: a band
Of mufti secret-police stood, with each face
Bewilderingly the same. And then came on
A gorgeous troupe of local models, clad
In all the latest London rag-trade stuff,
And Solzhenitsyn was forgotten.

                              Britten
Was briskly done by some well-skilled quartet;
And so to dinner, vodka-toasts before
Numbered on the fingers of two hands.
Companion on my left, an Irish violin
Who slumped into his soup; and on my right
A fluent speaker of American
I took to be our minder, KGB.
Emboldened with potato-spirits, I
Took up my set of freedom-cudgels, leant
Towards this smoothy, and spelt out my spiel –
Why did this vast and powerful panoply
Bother about a few stray 'dissidents'?
He inclined towards me, gazed into the air,
And told me this: 'Ah, Mr Thwaite, you err
In your imagined notion of our strength.
We are not strong: our East and South are full
Of Muslimites who breed unheedingly
Like rabbits, and they know their time will come,
When they will overthrow us. We must keep
Vigilance, always, against these Asian hordes,
Though they pretend they're Soviets, like the rest.
Let one speak out, the others will join in,
Our whole great enterprise collapse and die.'

Next morning, an unscheduled trip downtown:
One stop, a bookshop, with another hood
In charge of us – until he had to go
On some more urgent business. At once
Customers moved towards us, whispering,
Asking us questions suddenly and fast,
Telling us things we almost dared not hear.
It did not last long. We were whisked away,
On to another numb 'exchange of views'.

And then the model schools, Akademgorodok,
Where some of us were drafted in to judge
The language-skills – and plausibility –
Of white-bloused boys and girls arranged in rows
To speak their English to us for a prize.
Each question brought a prim and ready answer,
Mouthed prettily, and clearly learned by heart,
And recitations, Shakespeare, Byron, Scott –
'My heart's in the Highlands, my heart is not here' –
Until that twelve-year-old who faced us down
With hesitances that seemed all his own,
A boy who knew his mind in that charade:
'I think that Byron was not true with women'.
We gave the prize to him. He went away,
But never took it up – the foreign trip
Our rules insisted. He returned to school
And did not come to England: 'Security'
Forbade it.

Then we flew back. Moscow Airport,
Some bother over forms not signed on entry,
Some bureaucratic blunder – tired with this,
I pressed ahead beyond the barrier,
To be met by some grey-clad tough with a grey gun:
I gently pushed him to one side, and went
Onto the tarmac. Later, I realised
The folly and the danger. But we flew
Out of Great Russia, far from Novosibirsk,
Safely to London; middle of nowhere, never
Ever again the same. Siberia.

329   *Throes*

Being with her now is a kind of boredom,
A dullness in which guilt and pain both ache,
When all my childish anguish after freedom
Has long since vanished. Now I wait to take

Her back to her own loneliness, where she
Can follow boredom of a different kind,
Routine quite unresented, and set free
From all required constraints. She is resigned,

Stoic and still, to what is left to come:
First blindness, then a sequence no one knows –
Choked lungs, paralysis, delirium?
Each one may follow where the other goes.

We act out cheerfulness to one another,
Exchanging memories, recalling names:
Son in his sixties, ninety-year-old mother,
Playing our boring, life-sustaining games.

330 *Watching*

Old mothers, their time running out, when time doesn't matter,
Keep on consulting their watches, as if puzzled how time
Runs on, even when
Meals arrive on time, and each day a different carer
Arrives and takes over:
Even then
They look at their watches again and again and again.

Again and again and again they look at their watches,
As if puzzled how time runs on and on and on
Even when meals arrive
On time, and each day a different one
Arrives and is eaten:
Still alive,
Old mothers, when time doesn't matter, time running out.

331 *Worst Words*

The worst words, the words that hurt,
Are the words you don't use.
You are afraid to use them, because they hurt
And you know they will hurt.

So you go on using another sort of words.
They are the words that please, or at least get by.
They make life easier, they grease the wheels,
And no one notices them as they go by.

Until there comes a moment when the worst words
Are the ones you need, the words to do the trick,
The worst trick, to tell the terrible truth.
But it is too late. You have lost the trick of those words.

332   *The Message*

I keep it in my pocket, take it out,
Read it again, then put it back, this scrap
Of envelope with those scratched and blurred
And urgent words I found stuffed in your bag –
A cry of rage, of misery, of mad
Incomprehension, just
Enough like your familiar hand to stun
The one you wrote it to: your son.

Now I have read the words so many times
I know them all by heart; but can't repeat
Or spell them out in my own writing. Grief
Blanks out their meaning, as your stroke blanked out
Whatever happened, and whatever followed.
I take the paper out and follow it
Again, once more, its deadened, endless shout:
Why have you done this to me? Take me out.

333   *The Cry*

Not dead, not dead yet –
Like a cry curtailed
The words come back to me, and in her voice.
And it is terror that I feel at this
Impossible coming-back, the future filled
With that unstoppable presence night by night.

And yet I know she's dead, and wanted it
As I too wanted it. Why should she cry
Like this, persistent ghost
Asking to be missed
So strongly, plaintively, and nightly?
Not dead, not dead yet.

334 *A Crack of Air*

'Would you let a crack of air in' – as I tucked
Your small frail body into bed
That early night, a week before you died,
You spoke those words I hear and recollect
Again and yet again.
They seemed like hope renewed, as if pain
Might still be turned away
By letting freshness in, till a new day
Brought light through opened windows, and the sun
Rose in its old way.

But that was habit speaking. You were old
And tired and far beyond a crack of air,
Or light, or anything to hold
The darkness back in bed as you lay there.

335 *Stroke*

'I always seem to cry', he said, and tears
Stood in his eyes as if confirming this
Admission of whatever had gone wrong:
A switch thrown back; a failure in the brain;
Close-down of numbers, names; a cave of fears
Echoing mixed unspeakable menaces,
And the same thing said again and again and again.

He lay there with the others in the ward –
Others plugged in to this and that device
Constructed for emergencies not his.
They were all silent. He at least could speak.
But words were useless tokens of regard,
Shapes he could make with lips, but not entice
Sense from the cave with tears, dumb, fearful, weak.

336   *For Edwin Brock: 1927–1997*

A voice I'd never try to emulate –
Now there's a word you'd never ever use,
Edwin, south London sniffing out the false:
'Emulate' – academic Latinate,
A vocable you'd smile at, and say 'crap'.

And yet you waded through long years of crap,
Agency-talk which you turned into gold,
Campaigns and slogans and the selling phrase
Your colleagues envied. If it was a trap
You slipped out of the cage, always ran free.

You ran into the arms of someone free
To share those thirty years you had ahead:
After the mess of childhood, blue tattoos
That marked you out in some lost atrophy,
You sailed into the meadows of content.

I think of you smiling, benign, content,
And now I see you – as I often do –
Pushing a wheelbarrow, trimming a tree,
Putting a not-quite-finished poem through
Our letterbox: one I could never emulate.

337   *i. m. Lorna Sage, 1943–2001*

Out of that mess of relatives you came,
A breathless blonde, a giggling saboteur,
Silly, subversive, resolute, and clever.
You mocked, and flirted, and you had no shame.

I felt uneasy with you, always did:
You puffed out put-downs with your nicotine.
You made me think of what I might have been.
And then you made this last intricate bid –

A book on breaking-out, on making-out,
Through all those years of stress and mess, 'bad blood'
Fed through your veins, until you gasped and stood
Triumphant there, there on the last redoubt.

338   *Relict*
(Monica Jones: d. 2001)

Propped up among pillows and ruins of pillows,
Chin jutting out from an eiderdown furrowed by books,
The bedside table littered with bottles and glasses,
Confronting the world with one of your famous looks,
Your enormous spectacles bright under grease-plaited hair,
And the bedroom shrunk to that drunk, spectacular stare.

He had brought you here, in a terror of love and despair,
Both selfish, knowing you sick. He tried to be fair.
Both of you nibbled at snacks, and drank, looking at books,
While the days and the months went by. And now it passes –
Forty years and more, together, with him dead, and your looks
Lurk among heaped-up pillows and ruins of pillows.

339 *St Mary's, Wimbledon*
(for Ian Hamilton)

Your few remains,
Tight-reined, tight-lipped,
Remain. My parodies
(Those hands, that hair,
Those brief intensities)
You grimly smiled at, knowing
What I was getting at: the stripped
And naked things no one but you could do
And others only copied.
Now there is nothing here
In the packed church you'd not have visited
Unless in this sealed lid,
Except old thickened friends,
White-haired, with slowing pulse,
Our ageing hands
Handing you on to somewhere, somewhere else.

340 *Doing Business*

Have you noticed,
Approaching the cashpoint machine, your card at the ready,
Another standing there at his quiet business
And behind that person another?
The one who stands behind averts his attention
From the one who does business.
And you, the third in transaction, hold back a little
Behind your forerunner, as he behind this one who frowns
Over the aperture in front of him.

How silent it all is,
Much like the orderly manner of men who wait
In the urinal on a different business:
The reluctance to speak as the indifferent machines
Perform at a slight distance, extracting, discharging.

341   *How to Behave*

Alex is almost four, and knows ways to behave.
'Being silly' is not one of them.
He knows his Grandpa shouldn't be like this.

Kicking my feet up, pulling a face,
Putting on funny voices – this is 'being silly',
And Alex hates it, wants to tell me so.

So he takes his Grann off, and says to her:
'Please let me talk to Grandpa by myself'.
He tells me what he has to say. I promise.

And so I am not silly. I know how to behave,
At least in front of Alex. How to behave
Elsewhere is something I have still to learn.

342   *The Hall of Holy Relics*

Here is the Hall of Holy Relics
to which the Faithful make their Pilgrimages
now that the Public is allowed to see them.

Here is the Saucepan of Prophet Ibrahim,
the Baton of Prophet Moses, the Sword of Prophet David,
the Cap of Prophet Yusuf.

Here is the Description of Prophet Mohamed on a Copper Plate,
the Tooth, broken, of Prophet Mohamed,
three Footprints in Marble of Prophet Mohamed
all different in size, each a Miracle.

Here is the Famous Cloak bestowed by Prophet Mohamed
on a Poet who submitted to the Will of Allah,
and here is the Letter sent by Prophet Mohamed
with an Embassy to the Copts of Egypt
threatening the worst if they did not submit to the Will of Allah.

Here is the Dust brought from the Tomb of Holy Prophet
   Mohamed,
and here the Photo of the Document citing the Dust
brought from the Tomb of Holy Prophet Mohamed.

*

In the Chambers where helwa and various syrups were made
various glasswares are now displayed.

*

This is a Blasphemous Poem by a Christian dog
who thinks he can sneer because he has a different God.
*

He is mistaken. Wrath will descend on him.
The Hall of Holy Relics will extinguish him.

343   *Names*
(for Ortwin de Graef)

The Buenos Aires telephone directory:
Benito Takahashi, Ricardo Jones,
Moelwyn Rodrigues, Hanan Fricasee.
They hide behind their hidden telephones.

Japanese-Tuscan, Cymric-Lebanese,
Polyglot fore- and surnames on each page,
Do they spell out profuse misceganies
Or just the casual mixings of the age?

To ask this is a dubious business, true.
Septimius Severus, with his Punic burr,
Escaped such censure by being someone who
Adopted names which would avoid the slur

Of acting Emperor under alien guise:
He took protective colouring, and shed
African origins. And this proved wise.
When he lay sick in York, and then was dead,

He handed on the imperial sobriquet.
It is not thus with those who still bear here
Misnomers of a more plebeian day.
Their names may carry stigma, and they fear

Questions upon the road: 'Seamus?', 'Othman?'
Somewhere in Kosovo, or Lebanon,
These are presented. In victory or defeat,
At Belfast checkpoints, in a Bosnian street,

Your mother's name, or patronymic, blur
Into a confrontation, insult, threat.
You answer to your name. And some infer
It smells of ancient, hostile matters yet.

344   *On High Down*

The gorse pods explode under the sun
Strewn on the chalk hump of the down
Where at another time there stalked tall Tennyson,

Muttering into his cloak, with his hat pulled down,
Looking daggers at anyone or no one,
Breathing his sixpenny pints of air under the sun.

And now there is no one there, or anyone,
Just his tall memorial Celtic cross on top of the down
As the gorse pods explode like the mutters of Tennyson.

345   *Speaking Personally*

My poor old tired eyes –
I catch a headline, and it says
ANTHONY THWAITE:
My paranoia surfaces, and then
I see, though dimly, the true phrase –
ANTHRAX THREAT. Since when
The world seems safer, at least to my eyes.

346   *At the Millennium*

It was a dead time. Ice on the river,
Snow on the banks, snow on the far field,
Sky white to the top, trees bare.

And nothing moved. Stiffly, the landscape held
Steady as rock, steadier than ice. The wind
Had dropped into a wide unmoving stare.

Till something moved: a thing with wings came down
Looking for something there, whatever it was.
There on the snow a brilliant patch, a stain

Concentrated, and still. And there it lies,
One spot of colour, gathered, focused, where
Whatever happened happened. What it was

Disturbs the landscape, hides itself away.
It is as if some angel in the air
Came to its aim on the appointed day

And touched the other's tongue with a cinder of dead fire.

347   *Short Circuits*

Yesterday, half a Saxon glass bead
In a field at Shotesham.
Today, a pound in the gutter in Long Stratton.

Waiting all day for six o'clock:
My first cigarette.
Such will-power. Such weakness.

Hearing a grandchild's voice
In the night: is it my child
From forty years ago?

Reading these old cuttings
Does nothing but tell me how
Somehow I wrote them once.

Deciding not to write
An obituary of my friend
Even before he dies.

Today, I put off again
Something which yesterday
Was all I had to do.

Trying to put into words
My objection to four words:
'And also with you'.

'Vain repetitions' – a phrase,
However archaic,
Both solemn and exact.

'Never again', she said
Over and over again.
Thus remarked, again and again.

The cloud of unknowing
Never far away
From the fog of ignorance.

348   *The Sumerian Anthology*
          (for John Mole)

First we must put in Ur
Because he began everything:
Everyone knows that.

Then decent representation
Of Enki, Enlil, Nannar –
Try to include some less obvious pieces.

The early stuff of Uruk, that elegy
By Eridu, at least something
By Lagash before he dried up.

So far, easy. But approach the present –
What about Kul, Dhrondro, Salugi,
Nobut, Luth . . . ? Difficult to sort out:

They look a bit arbitrary. Well,
Pick one by each of them. Make sure
The headnotes balance respect with limiting judgements.

It will all be the same in five thousand years.

349   *The Art of Poetry:*
      Two Lessons

I

Write in short sentences. Avoid
Unnecessary breaks. Strictly control
(Or totally eliminate) the adverb.
Eschew such words as 'myriad'. Adopt
Current demotic, yet be wary of
Brand-names, and proper-names
Limited by time. The Latinate
Is out, except for satire.
Ease yourself into the vernacular.
If you are male, try to forget the fact:
If female, use the fact as document –
It will allow you entry as yourself.

These are beginnings: when you have begun,
Forget the lot, and try to swim alone.

Travel. Hot countries. Half an anecdote,
The other half left to imagined things.
Of these you will not speak. Strew here and there
Stray relatives – your people people poems.
In the alembic, scatter something rough,
Not easily digested. Let the mix
Come to the boil, cool off.
Hint urgency, but not in too much a hurry.

All these are precepts, and not recipes.
Whoever lays down laws lays down his head
On reputation's stiff, objecting block.

The aspirant asks, 'Why, if these things are so,
Have you not done them?' And I reply,
'The very fact you ask will tell you why'.

350 *Untitled*

Sometimes you want to tell everything –
Not all in a rush, but plain and full and true,
And all in good time: everything you knew
And all you have always known, telling
All, without qualification,
Without explanation.

What holds you back, then, from this great recital,
This major melody, this noble strain?
Ah, that is what you never can explain:
You know how it goes, you even know the title,
But the act of making
Is an act of breaking.

351 *Tune*

Humming and ha-ing to a tune in the head
Not knowing whatever it is that lies up ahead
But going on strumming away at whatever it may be
It sits deep inside like an egg or a baby.

Don't try to push it too hard or it may drop away
Like a dinosaur's coprolite fossilised in the clay,
Or a light that is quenched, or a drink that has sunk too far,
Or a star out of sight, or a shape beyond reach of radar.

Nothing will tell you when the right time has come
Tapping and titupping on its hesitant drum.
You will know when it happens. You may know what it means.
But nothing shows clear on the murk of the blurred screens,

Till the word trips up, and the trap trips over, and then
The sounds rebound and the voice begins again,
Dictating the straight sense you know you knew
And the humming and ha-ing tune in to the new, the true.

352 *Major Poem*

This is the big one for the end of time
Which will survive the end of time:
Not yet written but as good as written
If I can get it right.

This is what I am about to write,
Something that will never be forgotten
Even when there is no idea of time
Or very little time.

353   *So Easy, So Hard*

So much is so easy, a current that flows as it goes
Over its long smooth bed, between reeds that bend
Unhindering anything, under a wind
That blows in the way things go, on to the end
Where rivers descend to the easy beckoning seas.

So much is so hard, a push up a bend that sticks
With a clutter of mud meshed hard against banks that jut
Congested with logs that lash together and get
Plaited with clay and stick like a stuffed gut
That rids itself of nothing, can never relax.

354   *For Kettle*

Poor old creature, friend for eighteen years,
Your spine and ribs too sharp, your cry so quiet,
You lie disconsolate, and bring to mind
The lion of St Jerome in that altar-piece,
The saint's companion in this passing world,
Who now lies miserably curled
At the side of the bed which has just become a bier:
As if in dumb reaction to the grief
Others more piously indicate above
With praying hands, letting a devout tear
Drop in the margin of this Pietà,
You and that big cat behave
With weary instinct, imitate with grace
Something we want somehow to mark as love.

355   *Wilderness*

First it was wilderness. Then it was cut down,
Tamed and settled. Now wilderness again.
Here and there, distant, a small town
But thickening forests between.

There they are now, in the heat of late afternoon,
Dense screens of green, with the creek and the pond between
Grumbling with bullfrogs, and three deer suddenly seen
On the edge of a meadow which almost becomes a lawn.

Beyond that clearing, rank upon rank of trees
Slip into solid blurs, as dense as night.
The heat unravels in the evening breeze
Gathering far shudders of smudged light.

So from the porch, the past moves under my eyes
Without a meaning, and without a cause,
And the mist from the tall hills and down in the valleys
Hovers over it all. So it is, and was.

356   *Saint's Day, Cardoso*

They bicker in the square in celebration
Of the saint whose day it is, as voices rise
And butt against the bells, as candles run
Across and pour in each piazza, as the day's
End flows down the mountain in its floods
Of heat and mist and silence through their words.

And we are silent here who hear such things
Late in the late afternoon, come drowsy back
From a long lunch across the bridge. Hot wings
Bear up flown creamy clouds, blown thick
With sun and saturation, clefts and trees,
The river's drought, rocks spilling down the valleys.

The saint's one day evaporates in ritual:
He is carried here and there in delicate balance,
And the swifts fall and rise, rise and fall,
Above these annual urgings towards reverence,
Then glide away towards the sky's dark edge
Where there are no words; no piazza; mountain; bridge.

357   *To the Waterfall*
   (for Ronald Ewart)

Walking again the track to the waterfall
Twenty years after, same heat, same smell,
Blown from late summer, and still

The sullen shade that shakes down from the trees:
Remembering this walk is not what it says
Now. It has become its memories:

Dogs scampering ahead, and children's voices,
And sudden laughter in high picnic places,
All shaken into far too many pieces.

But that is not it, either. All that air,
All those sounds and stones and leaves, nowhere
Except where they gather here –

417

Particular, different, not to be expressed
Distinctly, vague as the mist
Down in the valley below, a vast

Diffusion of each step we chose to take
Time and again, as those leaves unshook
Year after year, walking along that track.

358   *Syria*

At every intersection, in each square,
Stone superman, bronze bust, or smiling father
Ride above traffic-fret gigantically.

They promise force, and fear, and permanence,
They warn and chasten, clenched in one strong man.
They stand unshaken and invincibly.

*

South of Aleppo blow the plastic bags:
Tatters of polythene in thornbushes,
The desert wind shredding them fitfully.

These stunted leafless junipers, festooned
With such parodic fluttering foliage,
Quiver and jerk and twitch continually.

All other rubbish rusts, rots, vanishes
Along the dunes among the dusty trees.
Only these remnants last perpetually.

359   *The Adoration of the Magi*

There in the background are the soldiers,
Helmeted, pikes held ready,
One looking on intently
At the stooped offerings presented,
The big black chieftain standing to the side.
Someone is muttering in Joseph's ear.

Those unimportant onlookers Bruegel put there
Are Spanish. They are the occupying power,
Distrusted, loathed, alien.
And they are there because the message is
Even the enemy must come to this
Moment when God arrived to save all men.

360   *Epiphany*

'Perched like an eagle' (in the guide-book phrase),
Five thousand feet up, pocked with caves and graves
Packed into scoured-out rock, where the defile
Slices its course through channels long run dry
Except this trickle turning dust to mud,
The mountain gives way to this orifice.

Inside the chapel, an oval granite womb,
Sounds from outside are muffled, or distorted,
Or shrunk to nothing. We shed our shoes, go soft
On long-rubbed stone. The light reflects bright ikons
Littered along the rock-face, kaleidoscope
Of gaudy golds and crimsons, saints and halos.

All this exotica, in this tourist-trap,
Plucks at me fitfully, almost resented –
A pointless pilgrimage. Till suddenly
A girl's pure voice utters alien words,
Those Aramaic cadences that begin
'Abba', flow on, as if known, to 'Amen'.

In this dry place my eyelids fill with tears.

Maalula, Syria

361   *Psalmodics*

These old arcane contritions, ancient sounds
Compounded of such alien traditions –
Shinto, Judaic, Syriac, Hindu – thread
Beseeching wails with solemn ululations
Over the holy places, over the buried dead.
Canticle, veda, sutra, chant their still
Archaic keening among the killing grounds,
The darkness into which their pure sounds spill.

Something to do with love, with grief, with death,
All share this common melody, ascend
And fall and rise again, repeat again
Cadences that return, that never end
Until the melisma of extended pain
Shudders and drops in wordless stubborn stress
With resignation, with exhausted breath,
Over the risen hope, over the hopelessness.

362 Movements

As ice keeps the shape of the bowl
after the bowl is broken,
and the pad in the mud is sure of the bird's sign,
and the bruise on the skin is taken
as a mark of the blood underneath troubled and shaken,
so is the shape of the invisible soul.

As the current wavers and suddenly changes,
plucked by the wind, which no one has ever seen,
and leaves shaken above turn again and again
from white, then to grey, to black, to green,
and their branches fret above from now to then,
so the door between *then* and *now* shifts on its hinges.

As the mist in the headlights lifts and comes down again,
marking a move in the weather we did not know,
and the river rises with only a flurry of snow
melting under a warmth we could not see,
nothing is sure, nothing can ever stay,
so much is the one thing sure, as sure now as then.

363 *Summer of 2003*

Hearing Jack's saxophone and Will's guitar
This June evening, almost the longest day
So that up there a single star
Dissolves in distant sunlight, there's delay –
If only for an instant – of the end
I must reach. In this music, they suspend
My life, and lift it up, and hold
Whatever has grown old,
And rinse it clean, and make it new and clear.

And yet their music is as far away,
Almost, as that midsummer star to me,
However well they play
This long light evening, spilling out their free
Syllables of skill and being young.
Some dull thing weighs me down, my tired tongue
Limps in its utterance, goes dumb
Where all the others come
Singing and dancing, growing, separately.

364   *Not for Translation*

Weird the day-people, the hydro-follicles,
Invading the island daily, in doubles and triples
Spilling into the food-places, the drink-receptacles,
Speaking barbarian in the cineraria,
Dropping excreta in the sanctuary,
Making free-licence in the blocked cloaca.

It was not thus in the former epochs
Before the tribes from the peninsula
Dismembered their cadavers in urn-chambers,
Before the horn-shaped handles turned to muzzles,
Before the lingots of crude mangled bronzes
Replaced obsidian and diminished us.

Showing their passports to soporific warders,
Texting their messages in the votive precincts,
Among glazed sherds in desultory stupor
They wander listless as the campanile
At noon throws down its fractured metal tablets
Dictating punctuation to the package people.

Where we are now is in a cusp of periods
Speaking transitional dialects, to be translated
Into a multiglossia by aliens
Daily disembarking in the harbour,
Polluting the pools and inlets along the shore-line,
Discarding their plastic tumblers in the crevices.

New Poems

365   *Lines Lost in Antwerp*

How slow the days go by when you're alone –
Translating 'esurient' as 'taking the piss',
Putting on habit like a swart glove
That fits too tight. So, has it come to this
Repetition, something over as soon as it's done?
Nothing much gives way, as *push* meets *shove*.

A blot from the blue, a shogun wedding, and then
Joining up the dolts – these use the time left.
It was the irregularity, the punctuation
Ebbing away, that made me feel bereft –
That, and the realisation when
I smelt the embers of Extreme Unction.

So it was time to go: I might have guessed it,
Like coins dropped from pockets pocked with holes.
In a room where a table stands with a hoop of paper
Untorn till now, a man runs up and bowls
And though from the start everyone knows he's missed it
The whole slow day lifts off in a puff of vapour.

366   *Scarecrows*

As a child, I hated them: hunched in allotments
Wind-tossed and crucified, or flickering by
On train-journeys, their menacing presence
Visited later in dreams, grimly
Revealing skull-faces,
Tattered grimaces,
Skeletons dancing to distant and terrible tunes.

Now, in my seventies, I enjoy puzzling out their runes –
The perfunctory ones, the elaborate, and the sly –
And none intrude as they did, when their shrouded stains
Covered me over forever. Preparing to die,
I greet the bird-scarers,
The solicitous carers,
Who when it comes to it will see me off, inevitably.

367 *Demented*

Virginia Woolf thought they were talking Greek
But the mad blackbird who pecks at our windows
Persists in his battering monosyllables
With an utterly avian beak
And, though tongueless of course, in his own tongue.
He will not speak,
Yet the wild gleam in his eye shows
A spirit built to use something other than song
As he drills and drills.

He isn't Narcissus, in love with his own face,
Nor is he courting some image of a mate.
What he thinks he is after is his enemy,
A rival on the other side of the glass,
A foe to be put down or put away.
This is our impasse,
That we have nothing to do but wait
Till he begins the very next day
Drilling away.

Day after day this demented creature comes
Not only to one window but seven by turn,
Soiling them all, waking us up at dawn
With his stuttering roll of drums.
We have pasted up hawks' images, pulled down the blind.
He will not learn.
And as the lights go off and the curtains are drawn,
Whatever we turn to, in the end we find
He has not gone.

368 *Spring*

I have spent a lifetime picking away at remains.
Never a day goes by without testing the past,
Turning over what lasts and what remains
Of whatever has come into view or whatever has passed.

I have heard a note strike that doesn't sound right.
As the logs smoulder away in the steep ash
The hot bricks speak against the iron grate.
This is beyond the pull and the drift and the wish.

All this in spring, when the world wakes and renews,
When each dawn should seem fresh and surprising.
Out there I can almost hear, as I hear the News,
The steady stealth of the river, and the fish rising.

369 *Statement*

There may be more in this type of thing:
Turning up a note on that stolen bag's a release
Setting off a tiny bang. It warms the grease
Controlling the wheels. So it goes, giving away nothing.

The face of the man stepping into the lift
Through the door marked EXIT – what a picture!
The date in my diary didn't mark a fixture.
Nil-Nil was the score. What a gift!

Irony gets you nowhere. Something you need,
Tuning up before the tune begins,
Is the straight route through to where the organs bleed
Cadenzas so wonderful that all sins

Dissolve into unspeakable bliss, or have never happened.
Go on then – go for it! Not a hair of the head
Was harmed, as the door of the tomb opened.
No one can stop you talking to the dead.

370   *Pity*
      (for E, aged three)

I picked a beetle up and let it go,
And that was pity;
But not the pity that you could not go
Today, as you'd been promised, to the Zoo
Because you were too sick.
So 'What a pity' were the words I spoke,
And then you asked your question: 'What is pity?'

I've searched and searched, but can't find out the trick
To tell you what it is. My glib words choke
Attempting to spell out the different sense
Of rescuing the beetle, and why you
Did not go with us to the promised Zoo.
What is the difference? How can I say
That pity is a debt I cannot pay?

371 *Sententia*

Somewhere above the Norwegian Sea
At thirty-thousand feet or thereabouts,
The outside air unimaginably cold,
A woman sits and knits with needles poised
Above a cup of water, and it sways.

What this suggests is strange. Our restless days
Are put in order, regulated, praised
When even some small skill can grip and hold
The chaos and the danger and the doubts
That float above, below, continually.

372 *The Smell*

I hate the smell of myself as I grow old.
No longer a comfort in secret,
It drags with it all the scurf, all the old stuff,
Hanging about in the ruins of myself.

Nothing can stop it for long, as I brush my teeth,
My hair, and shave, and dab a pathetic spot
Of aftershave afterwards on the bits under my chin.
It comes back again with a glum persistence.

But today it came back with a different turn,
Breathing its evil odour, its reek of decay,
As I sat here in my ruins, and smelt myself,
And settled into it, as into a mattress

Sinking down with a sigh at the end of a long day,
Bits of me splayed this way and that, held tight
By the rigid arrangements all round, till sleep
Began to come over me, breathed deeply and slowly

Into lungs that were waiting to take me
Down to the depths, the deepest bed of the sea,
Drowned, till the smell melted away
And the tide turned slowly over the empty shore.

373　*Snake, swimming*

Slim, not a whisper through liquid but still
Silently moving, elegant as silk and slender,
That yellow neck-ring poised above the water –
You move alongside, yet distant, vulnerable,

So that we too try simply to stay still,
To watch you watching us, there in the river
As if this moment might go on for ever
Until you find those reeds, hospitable

Sheltering substance, close-packed, over the still
Moving and menacing tracks that cover
Where you might go, your sole endeavour
To sound out any agent that might kill.

You are with me now, unappeased, still
Fixed in my being, giving a shiver
Along the spine and spreading all over,
Magnificent, and lost, and beautiful.

374　*I Swear*

'There's no need to swear', you say.

　　　　　　　　　　I swear there isn't.
Yet even mild folk sometimes are unpleasant:
'Dash it all', 'Drat it', 'Oh sugar', or 'Oh shoot' –
Euphemistic, but showing they're in a state.

I blame mine on the Army, each pale noun
Enriched with an adjective to put you down,
Full of ferocious fricatives, fierce and curt,
And flung down in frustration, and to hurt.

You shouldn't suffer, or feel sore. Those four stark letters
Aren't anything much at all. Whatever matters
Is in the attitude, not in the words:
They fly away like tiny frightened birds.

375 *Form*

Applicants should be aware that the interface
Makes no allowance for the matter of interfaith.
They must look out for cries of 'in your face',
Which may well lead to intifada.

Whatever there is in this type of thing,
The main point is to give away nothing.
We accept that this may seem merely soothing,
But those of the faith must hold to the true thing.

Accept that, and all else follows.
Set your hand to the plough, and the plough's felloes,
Set as they are, lay out the fields' furrows.
The nipples are there for the laid-out farrows.

376 *Missing*

It went off somewhere, and did not come back.
It spent itself in some place out of sight,
And what it might have been I do not know,
Or whether it was true, or good, or right.
All that I know is: it did not come back.

What was it, anyway, that made me miss it?
What was it when I noticed it at first?
What did I recognise as I first spoke?
And how much permanent, or on a visit?
A small thin drizzle, or a violent burst?

Question on question, and then no replies.
Night after night the nagging absence sits
Close to my elbow as I sit and think
Of how it came with what may have been lies,
Or truths exploded into little bits.

377   *Faith*

Uttering nothing, going through the motions,
Bent in obeisance, or obedience, or nothing
But the spent ritual of inheritance –

Suddenly in the ruined gaps between
To see with such gladness the contortions
Light makes as it spreads over everything,

Creating this blinding moment of sense
In a rift of the clouds and the sun's beneficence,
If only for this moment, this clear evidence.

378   *Flotation*

Sifting exactly all the voided seeds
After two and a half millennia,
She separates and gives a certain name
To each sieved particle. And so she reads
The menu when the customers have gone
Into the dark, and paid their final bill.

This process – mechanical, meticulous –
Do not despise it: it counts out the stuff
That made them what they were, and gave to us
(Greedy for every scrap) a catalogue
Of how they harvested, and fed, and left
Immortal messages of feasts and fasts.

379   *On the Island*

Having left the Nostalgia Hotel
I reached the Forbidden Zone
But was not allowed to approach

The House of a Hundred and One Rooms
In which, it is said, he who enters
The 101st room is in paradise.

Unable to go back through the door
I attempted the Martyrs' Gate
Facing the five-fingered mountain.

There the courteous Dragoman
Showed me the British Council
Where I signed my name in the book.

I asked for the Library
But a double-tongued damsel told me
It had gone: 'nobody wanted it'.

Haystacks of barbed wire
Towered between bastions
As I sought the Northern Gate.

'Dual – the Lucky Plant –
I Need Only Water and Air'
Announced in the Buffer Zone,

And the Princes of Tyre and Antioch,
The Counts of Jaffa, the Kings
Of Cyprus and Jerusalem,

Looked down from ward and portcullis
Silently. Till a minaret
Spelt out metallic orisons

Over the sound of a bell
Distant under my pillow
In the Nostalgia Hotel.

380 *The Space Between*

Tonight I heard again the rat in the roof,
Fidgeting stuff about with a dry scuff,
Pausing in silence, then scratching away
Above my head, above the ceiling's thin
Skin that separates his life from mine.

So shall I let him be, roaming so narrowly
In a few finger-widths of carpentry?

The evening passes by. I sit and write
And hear him skittering here and there, in flight
From nothing. Maybe he hears
My scratching pen, my intermittent cough,
Below the frail thin lath that keeps me off

From harming him, as it too keeps him there,
Heard but unseen in narrow strips of air.

Bibliography

Poetry

Fantasy Poets no. 17, Fantasy Press, 1953
Home Truths, Marvell Press, 1957
The Owl in the Tree, Oxford University Press, 1963
The Stones of Emptiness, OUP, 1967
Penguin Modern Poets 18 (with A. Alvarez and Roy Fuller), 1970
Inscriptions, OUP, 1973
New Confessions, OUP, 1974
A Portion for Foxes, OUP, 1977
Victorian Voices, OUP, 1980
Poems 1953-1983, Secker & Warburg, 1984
Letter from Tokyo, Hutchinson, 1987
Poems 1953-1988, Hutchinson, 1989
The Dust of the World, Sinclair-Stevenson, 1994
Selected Poems 1956-1996, Enitharmon Press, 1997
A Different Country, Enitharmon Press, 2000
A Move in the Weather, Enitharmon Press, 2003, repr. 2004

Criticism

Essays on Contemporary English Poetry: Hopkins to the Present Day, Kenkyusha, Tokyo, 1957; revised edition as *Contemporary English Poetry: An Introduction*, Heinemann, 1959
Poetry Today 1960-1973, Longman for British Council, 1973
Twentieth-Century English Poetry, Heinemann, 1978
Poetry Today: A Critical Guide to British Poetry 1960-84, Longman for British Council, 1984
Six Centuries of Verse, Thames Methuen, 1984
Poetry Today: 1960-1995, Longman, 1996

For Children

Beyond the Inhabited World: Roman Britain, Deutsch, 1976

Travel and Topography

Japan (with Roloff Beny), Thames & Hudson, 1968

The Deserts of Hesperides: An Experience of Libya, Secker & Warburg, 1969

In Italy (with Roloff Beny and Peter Porter), Thames & Hudson, 1974

Odyssey: Mirror of the Mediterranean (with Roloff Beny), Thames & Hudson, 1981

As Editor

Oxford Poetry 1954 (with Jonathan Price), Fantasy Press, 1954

New Poems 1961 (with Hilary Corke and William Plomer), Michael Joseph, 1962

Penguin Book of Japanese Verse (with Geoffrey Bownas), 1964, rev. 1998

The English Poets (with Peter Porter), Secker & Warburg, 1974

Poems for Shakespeare 3, Globe Playhouse, 1974

New Poetry 4 (with Fleur Adcock), Hutchinson for Arts Council, 1978

Larkin at Sixty, Faber, 1982

The Gregory Awards Anthology 1981-1982 (with Howard Sergeant), Carcanet, 1982

Poetry 1945 to 1980 (with John Mole), Longman, 1983

Philip Larkin, *Collected Poems*, Marvell Press and Faber, 1989

Selected Letters of Philip Larkin, Faber, 1992

Longfellow, *Selected Poems*, Dent Everyman, 1993

R. S. Thomas, *Selected Poems*, Dent Everyman, 1996

Philip Larkin, *Further Requirements*, Faber, 2001

George MacBeth, *Selected Poems*, Enitharmon Press, 2002

The Ruins of Time: Antiquarian and Archaeological Poems, Eland, 2006

Recording

Anthony Thwaite reading from his poems, The Poetry Archive, 2005

Critical Studies

Hans Osterwalder, *British Poetry between the Movement and Modernism: Anthony Thwaite and Philip Larkin*, Carl Winter. Universitatsverlag, Heidelberg, 1991

Anthony Thwaite in Conversation with Peter Dale and Ian Hamilton, Between the Lines, 1999

Biographical note

Anthony Thwaite was born in Chester in 1930. He spent his early childhood in Yorkshire but was evacuated to the United States (1940–44). After national service in Libya he read English at Christ Church, Oxford. He worked as a producer for BBC radio, was literary editor of the *Listener*, assistant professor of English at the University of Libya, literary editor of the *New Statesman*, Henfield Writing Fellow at the University of East Anglia, and co-editor of *Encounter* (1973–85). In 1986 he was chairman of the judges for the Booker Prize. Together with Andrew Motion, he is literary executor of the estate of Philip Larkin and he has edited Larkin's *Collected Poems*, *Selected Letters* and *Further Requirements*.

Thwaite is a former director of the London publishers André Deutsch and was Poet in Residence at Vanderbilt University, Nashville, in 1992. He has lectured and read for the British Council and in many universities all over the world. He holds honorary doctorates from the Universities of East Anglia and Hull and was awarded the OBE in 1990. His many collections of poetry stretch from a Fantasy Poets pamphlet in 1953 to *A Move in the Weather* in 2003.

An interest in archaeology has influenced much of his work and he curated an exhibition at the Sainsbury Centre, Norwich, entitled *A Poet's Pots* in 1998. He was elected a Fellow of the Society of Antiquaries in 2000, and has been a Fellow of the Royal Society of Literature since 1978. He was visiting lecturer in English Literature at Tokyo University (1955-7), and co-edited the *Penguin Book of Japanese Verse* (1964, revised 1998). He returned to Japan in 1985 as Japan Foundation Fellow for a year.

He lives in Norfolk with his wife, Ann Thwaite, the biographer and children's book writer. They have four daughters and ten grandchildren.

List of Subscribers

Dannie Abse
Anna Adams
Fleur Adcock
Manuel Borrás Arana
Tom & Eleanor Arie
Paul Assey
Chris Athey
Brian Ayers
Ann Baer
Dr William Baker
Joseph Bailey
Michael Baldwin
Robert & Janet Balfour of
  Burleigh
Richard & Helen Barber
Pat Barr
Nina Bawden
Martin & Judy Bax
Peter Beck
Paul Bennett
Bernard Bergonzi
Oliver Bernard
J. S. Bingham
Robert Binyon
David L. Bisset
Thelma Black
Margery & Gary Blackman
Piers & Sally Blaikie
James Booth
The Bradbury Family
Melvyn Bragg

Piers & Vyvyen Brendon
Simon Brett
Derek Brewer
Alan Brownjohn
Denise Buckley
David Burnett
Dr Neil M. Cheshire
G. E. Church
Lee Colegrove
Alan B. Cook
Wendy Cope
The Revd. Wendy A. Cranidge
Siba K. Das
Thomas Davidson
Gerald Dawe
Winifred Dawson
Dennis Detweiler
Tom Deveson
Colin Dexter
Hugh Dickson
Martin Dodsworth
Lord (Bernard) Donoughue
Margaret Drabble & Michael
  Holroyd
Ian Duhig
Katherine Duncan-Jones
Jane Duran
Alistair & Barbara Elliot
Tim Ellis
Tony Ellis, Kings Lynn Poetry
  Festival

Dr Barbara Everett
Ronald Ewart
U. A. Fanthorpe & Dr R. V.
  Bailey
David Farrow
James Fenton & Darryl Pinckney
Kieran Finnegan
Michael F. Flint
Marc Florent
Pablo Foster
Gill Frayn
Michael Frayn
John Fuller
Richard Furniss
Andrew Geary
Robert Gomme
Alice Goodman & Geoffrey
  Hill
Sylvia & John Gordon
Dr F. John Gregory
Paul Groom
John Gross
J. C. Hall
Alan Hancock
Janet Hanna
David & Margaret Harrop
Jean Hartley
Anne Harvey
Ronald Harwood
John Hegley
Basil Highton
Brian Hinton
Richard Holmes & Rose
  Tremain
Eric & Judy Homberger
Jeremy Hooker
David Hopkins

Alan Howarth
Liam Keaveney
Patricia Kennedy
Rosalind Kent
John & Noeleen Kerry
Tetsuo Kishi
Elizabeth Laird
John Lie
Penelope Lively
David Lodge
Herbert Lomas
Michael & Edna Longley
John Loveday
Betty Mackereth
Gregory Maguire
Marion Maitlis
John Mallet
Rohinten Mazda
J. W. McCormick
Peter Meares
Brian Meldrum
Michael Meredith
Stanley Middleton
David J. Miles
Michael Millgate
John & Mary Mole
Mora Morley-Pegge
Christina & Derek Morris
Blake Morrison
Beatrice Musgrave
Jenny Nelson
Paddy Nolan
Sir Ron & Lady Jo Norman
Northern Illinois University
  Library
Bernard O'Donoghue
Masa Ohtake

Michael O'Sullivan
Bernard Palmer & Tim
    Woodward
Dr Richard Palmer
Graham Parry
Jill Paton Walsh & John Rowe
    Townsend
Stephen Payton
Stephen & Rosslie Platten
Piers Plowright
Peter Porter
Neil Powell
Anthony Pugh-Thomas
Gerry Rawcliffe
Mary Rayner & Adrian
    Hawksley
Michael J. Reynolds
The Rialto
Llewelyn & Judith Richards
Christopher Ricks
Michael Ridpath
Mary Rimmer & Adrian
    Tronson
Irfon Roberts
Barnaby Rogerson
Tom Rosenthal
Lawrence Sail
Dale Salwak
Myra Schneider
Cecilia Scurfield

John & Hilary Spurling
Jon Stallworthy
G. G. T. Stanton
C. K. Stead
Enid & Chris Stephenson
Leonard Sweet
Yasunari & Michi Takahashi
David & Rachel Taylor
Felicity & Len Taylor
Howard Temperley
Pauline Tennant
Charles & Jessica Thomas
Alice Thwaite
Emily Thwaite & Bill
    Sanderson
Lucy Thwaite & Matthew
    Dodd-Noble
Trevor Tolley
Dick & Hilary Tulloch
John Tydeman
Peter & Monica Unwin
Robin & Penny Wade
Leslie Webster
Susan Wheeler
David Whiting
G. B. H. Wightman
Andrew Wilson
David Worthington
Kit Wright
Mr P. Wybrew

and other subscribers who wish to remain anonymous